The Fiction of Autobiography

The Fiction of Autobiography

Reading and Writing Identity

Micaela Maftei

B L O O M S B U R Y
NEW YORK • LONDON • NEW DELHI • SYDNEY

Bloomsbury Academic
An imprint of Bloomsbury Publishing Plc

1385 Broadway   50 Bedford Square
New York   London
NY 10018   WC1B 3DP
USA   UK

www.bloomsbury.com

First published 2013

© Micaela Maftei, 2013

ISBN: HB: 978-1-6235-6902-0
PB: 978-1-6235-6801-6
ePub: 978-1-6235-6175-8
ePDF: 978-1-6235-6181-9

Library of Congress Cataloging-in-Publication Data
Maftei, Micaela.
The fiction of autobiography : reading and writing identity / by Micaela Maftei.
pages cm
Includes bibliographical references and index.
ISBN 978-1-62356-902-0 (hardcover : alk. paper) – ISBN 978-1-62356-801-6
(pbk. : alk. paper) 1. Autobiography. I. Title.
CT25.M24 2013
809'.93592–dc23
2012050834

Typeset by Fakenham Prepress Solutions, Fakenham, Norfolk NR21 8NN
Printed and bound in the United States of America

Contents

Introduction

This book is concerned with issues of multiplicity and truthfulness at the heart of autobiographical writing. It maps and represents a search for an understanding of autobiographical writing that embraces multiplicity in terms of narrative voice and understanding of past events, sees uncertainty as seductive rather than irresponsible, and shies away from the notion that the definition or purpose of autobiography is to give voice to a single, true story. Its roots, going several years back, lie in a loose collection of short stories written about my family. These stories were written without a clear audience in mind, and without a specific intention beyond simply writing them. They represented something of a break from the many other kinds of writing, for several different audiences, that I was focusing on at the time. However, they quickly captured my attention because they prompted a series of almost bafflingly simplistic questions about their (possible) genre. Who had written these stories? Who was the subject? Who were the characters? And what kinds of relationships had emerged between writer and characters, and between characters? These questions drew my attention towards research on autobiographical writing and urged me to read more widely within the field. As I did so, I continued to write more short stories.

I was searching for a critical framework within which to understand autobiography – a framework that included speculation and perhaps also the inclusion of unresearchable or unverifiable, even unremembered, elements. During this search, I was engaged in writing autobiographically, in a format that privileged what I intuitively called my 'version' of events. This approach included writing events that I later learned had not happened as I had remembered and recorded them, or writing elements of a story based not on any secure first-hand knowledge but, again, on an intuitive sense of what had happened, in accordance with my knowledge and understanding of the people in question.

While this writing process felt strong and confident, I was generally uneasy about relying on intuition and emotion in order to critically understand the writing I was doing, and was particularly unwilling to do so in an academic context. I wanted to find a way in which to understand and contextualize autobiography that was honest and responsible but did not insist on the 'backing up' of the claims and stories in it, what Toni Morrison refers to as the 'this is where he or she got it from' school of autobiographical writing (Morrison 1987, 193).

I was primarily worried about what I thought of as the issue of truth. Not surprisingly, insistence on using this multifaceted and unstable word complicated my view of the stories and my research. At first seeming to be a straightforward element of the writing, the idea of truth split into many strands when I began questioning it – a fragmentation I recognized in the many secondary sources I was reading and analyzing alongside my own writing. What did it mean to write the truth when writing autobiographically? Did it mean only including material that could be externally verified? What did *that* mean? Only including events and descriptions that could be corroborated by other individuals involved? Or information that had been verified by some independent source? That was wholly impractical, and limiting. Did it mean refusing to include any reported speech that had not been recorded, as there was no way to ensure the accuracy of such quoted words? Did it mean refusing to write about anyone but myself, since I could not ensure I was representing anyone but myself accurately (if even that is possible)? That was unfeasible: the story of a family is inextricably bound up in the story of a self, and vice versa. Also, the way one represents oneself can ring false upon later self-reflection, quite often making us poor self-judges.

This instability was eventually freeing. I became more confident in thinking of truth as something that could be expressed in different and not always co-existing ways. I could be true to my memories; I could be true to research that provided me with corroboration of what I was writing; I could be true to the wishes of others; I could be true to the feel of a piece of writing (a kind of assessment that itself is not always stable). Each possibility was potentially valid, even while some could be mutually exclusive. Thus, writing truthfully would take a different shape depending on my intentions and beliefs, and the writing would be received differently depending on each reader's intentions and beliefs. This understanding shifted the pressure away from the writing as finished product, and onto the writing process. Truth slowly became a (flexible, changeable) state of mind rather than a measurable outcome.

We tell ourselves stories in order to live, says Joan Didion (2006, 185); we tell our lives as a story, says Paul John Eakin. Both are referring to a crucial link between writing and living, though Eakin struggles to conceive of life without narrative, whereas Didion sees narrative as a means of

[Handwritten annotations: "ARE WE THE SAME PERSON AS IN THE PAST?" (top left), "NARRATIVE OTHERS SELF" (top right)]

understanding one's (already existing) life, as well as the lives of others. My actions lay somewhere between the two conceptions. Writing the stories fit very naturally into the life I was leading at the time: one that was focused on, almost entirely founded on, using written language to advance academically, to express myself emotionally, to maintain connections with many people great distances away and to stay afloat in the constantly multiplying professional and personal tasks I was facing. In other words, it was a life that required using written language in order to live it. I was already narrating myself through each day, using writing as a way of creating and understanding the world around me. This particular project became another aspect of the main narrative drive: I was adding these autobiographical stories to all of my other writing, which was (hopefully) propelling me into my future. These short pieces were a means of writing the story of myself: 'myself' understood in quite an extended way, including, as I did, written versions of events that happened before my birth, which I had only ever known through the spoken recollections of others.

'There is just no way to cleanly tell a story of anything that happened in my life without the context of other people', says Vivian Gornick (Botton 2010), articulating a position that appeared clearly and often in the writing and reading I was doing. Not only did this seem obvious in my own autobiographical writing, but the memoirs and autobiographies I was reading clearly showed how no person's life can exist neatly separated from the lives of others; therefore, neither can their stories. Constructing these stories, then, meant constructing part of my life. This view seemed at once impossibly grandiose and totally obvious.

Autobiographical writing seemed a natural way in which to write my 'real life' into existence; once prodded, however, this idea fell apart. This style of writing is often understood as a way of understanding, or simply leaving a trace of, one's already existing self, an idea that stands at odds with that of creating a self through writing. This is the same distinction drawn between Didion's and Eakin's views above. If one narrates oneself into being, any writing about the past is a re-writing of an already completed process. We can perform this re-writing, and it can be one of the stories we use 'to live', but it will always be a second (or third or fourth) layer overtop the first narrative that represents our lived past. And each layer, as I will discuss at length in the final chapter of this book, is related to its former versions, but is a new and independent narrative.

I also wanted to reject the idea that one shared complete identity with the protagonist of the written work, implying unity of author and subject. This was a potentially inaccurate identification, especially as more and more time elapsed between the lived experience and the time of writing. The relationship between writing oneself into existence and identifying oneself as the subject of an autobiographical work was problematic. Did later writings negate earlier identifications? The constant changes an author (any human being) experiences throughout life trouble an unambiguous connection between writer and central character.

The suggestion of unity between the two selves – that of writer and that of protagonist – appeared presumptuous at worst and incomplete at best. In the autobiographical writing I was reading, years had typically passed between event and writing. A too-strong insistence on unity discounts the very real emotional, intellectual and psychological changes human beings undergo over time. These changes can be caused or affected by new information and experiences that shift one's understanding of the world around them, and their place in it. Subsequently gained knowledge can gravely alter the meaning of an experience, its force and effect in an individual's life, and its interpretation. Additionally, crisis, loss, trauma, or any kind of profound change (not necessarily negative) has a serious effect on an individual, and can often be said to mark them permanently, making their life before and after the event distinct. The self-narration one performed at one point in time would change over subsequent years – not the same writing, not the same self.

I looked for writers whose memoirs and autobiographies enacted and discussed these notions – that writing was a (the?) means of making yourself and your life exist, without suggesting that there was any permanence about the life you were writing, or any unity between the product of such an undertaking at one point in a life compared with a later point. Virginia Woolf expresses this precise notion in 'A Sketch of the Past'. Describing her decision to reference the present moment in her writing about the past, she argues that the present informs such writing, and is important in understanding it: '… this past is much affected by the present moment. What I write today I should not write in a year's time' (Woolf 1976, 75). I deliberately chose to focus on authors who have written autobiography and also written *about* writing autobiographically. I made this choice in order to examine how the authors describe and understand some decisions (for example, structural or stylistic), in combination with textual analysis of their work.

I found Natalia Ginzburg's memoir of her family's life in Italy during the rise of fascism and World War II a fascinating example of showing how later-learned knowledge can drastically change the significance of certain events, with enough force to mute or disfigure aspects of character forever. Her authorial choice to deny the reader subsequently learned knowledge by refusing to admit the full extent of how much the past is 'affected by the present moment' (and vice versa) is powerful; the absence of the present in her account of the past makes her memoir more complex and multilayered. Joan

Didion's memoir of the year following her husband's death and her daughter's *Didion*
life-threatening illness also illustrates the way profound changes can render a
former identity or self almost incomprehensible; throughout the book Didion
notes how her present self colours and complicates her view of the past.

This division of identity into a multiplicity of selves rather than a
permanent selfhood is suited to a genre that requires flexibility in terms of
handling time. This flexibility makes itself apparent most obviously when
we consider the writing process of autobiography as one of stepping outside
a story, writing a narrative about the past from a present time which itself
must become past almost immediately. I found Gertrude Stein's handling of *Stein*
authorial division, regarding both time and identity, in *The Autobiography
of Alice B. Toklas* refreshing because of the frank joy she seems to take in
exploring these complex issues, and the tightly crafted, playful techniques she
employs. Vladimir Nabokov's approach to time, in particular his rejection of *Nabokov*
linear narrative and a unidirectional concept of time in *Speak, Memory*, was
also a useful example of the pleasure an author can take in constructing a
life story that exhibits its preoccupation with the passage of time yet does
not rely on temporal linearity in its structure. These two books also showed
me much about the enjoyment to be found in the deliberate construction
of a text, in deciding how exactly one wishes to build a narrative, and how
enjoyable working within, and challenging, these boundaries can be.

Roland Barthes's autobiographical writing was illuminating in terms of
its contrasts – comparing his posthumously released *Incidents* with his 'anti- *Barthes*
autobiography' (Eakin 2008, 65) *Roland Barthes by Roland Barthes* provided
fertile ground for exploring different ways of 'telling the truth', and how an
author can choose to frustrate a reader's tendency or desire to unify protagonist and writer. It also highlighted the differences in voice that often emerge
between writing intended for publication and private writing, showing how an
anticipated audience is often implicated in stylistic and structural decisions.

Numerous critical and theoretical works clarified the links I was drawing
between texts, and provided lenses through which to examine them. In
particular, Vivian Gornick's *The Situation and the Story* outlines her notion *Eakin*
of persona, and much of Paul John Eakin's writing describes and expands
on his view of constructing a narrative as tantamount to constructing a
self-identity. I also discovered much theoretical writing that brought deep
comfort about the very nature of this project and the joining of fact and
fiction that I had approached with some trepidation. I was uneasy, at first,
about including speculation, imagination and invention into these stories,
and I valued the multiplicity of views on what it means to be truthful that
I found.

Shoshana Felman's feminist perspective of autobiographical writing as an act of testifying helped distance these stories from the idea that autobiography tells a single truth. Her critical approach emphasizes the telling of an individual version of events in contribution to understanding, or at least articulating, a wider narrative that is too complex to be told by a single voice. John Sturrock's view of autobiographical writing as an original construction – work which converts history into a written account through language, rather than simply attaching a written account to past events – enabled me to see the writing as a new entity, not simply an extension or even complete expression of the past. As such a new, creative and created thing, it became easier to see autobiography as subject to different, and perhaps less rigid, notions of honesty than simply adherence to documenting fact. John Barbour's work on the ethics of autobiography and different kinds of truth and truthfulness were also helpful to me in this matter.

I drew much confidence and momentum from the way many of these authors employed events that had occurred in their personal lives as legitimate starting points for critical exploration, and did not shy away from using such events as an integral part of structuring a theoretical argument. Understanding the personal and individual as supremely relevant to building a critical stance and performing textual analysis of other work showed me how a rigorous piece of critical/academic writing need not pretend its author exists outside the text, and that openly incorporating one's own life into written work need not be relegated to 'creative writing'.

D. A. Miller's *Bringing Out Roland Barthes* is structured as an 'album of moments' that are his 'responses to a handful of names, phrases, images, themes' drawn from Barthes's work (Miller 1992, 17). On several occasions he describes the book as an 'encounter' or shared experience between them, and repeatedly uses references to his own personal life in developing his argument that 'To refuse to bring Barthes out consents to a homophobic reception of his work' (Miller 1992, 17). Miller places himself firmly in the text, and shows how he uses himself as a starting point for study, including references to his personal life which are as important to the development of his theoretical views as any academic project: 'I was preparing my first trip to Japan … I couldn't help taking Barthes's *Empire of Signs* as a point of departure (by no means the only one, or nearly so important as, for instance, my relation with Ben or Robert)' (Miller 1992, 4).

In his introduction to a chapter 'assessing life writing as a form of moral argument', Paul Lauritzen describes his experience writing an article about his struggle to father a child. He talks about his readers' response when, after outlining the numerous methods of infertility treatment which had failed, his wife gave birth to their first child around the time his article came into print (Lauritzen 2004, 19). The ensuing distrust and anger he

PERSONAL → CRITICAL

felt from readers is his entrance into a discussion of how and why we see personal experience as a direct means of reaching 'moral bedrock', and why it is so 'threatening' when such experience emerges as less trustworthy than previously thought (Lauritzen 2004, 20). He uses a very personal story and experience as a clear and convincing point of entry to his chapter on the work of Rigoberta Menchú, whom I will discuss in the following chapters.

Shoshana Felman introduces her feminist readings of Balzac and Freud, among other authors, with similar references to how her personal life has guided the development of her professional life and academic writing. She notes how

> the practical readings that compose this book encompass and unwittingly reveal the implicit story – and the autobiographical itinerary – of how one becomes a feminist … my current feminist positions were not a given … I arrived at them through reading, acquired them through writing. (Felman 1993, 12–13)

She acknowledges how her approach to her critical work has been motivated and directed by events that occurred external to it, or perhaps, events which she thought were external to it until later reflection: 'I realize today – but did not know at the time of writing – that my work on Balzac's "Adieu" … was itself reliving … the violent significance in my own life of a separation from a man I loved' (Felman 1993, 17). She articulates how her personal life has been in some ways an illustration of the theory of autobiographical writing as testimony she later writes about. For Felman, the practice of providing an individual story or response to a larger event is integral to what it means to be a feminist; as such, it cannot help but colour all aspects of her life: 'Feminism, I will thus suggest, is indeed for women, among other things, reading literature and theory with their own life' (Felman 1993, 13). Thus, 'reading' her own life happens alongside other forms of reading, as when she draws links between Balzac's 'The Girl With The Golden Eyes' and her own life – again, in retrospect: 'It is only today, only with hindsight … that I realize how my own life, at the time of writing, involved a similar complexity (of languages, of cultures, of relations)' (Felman 1993, 18). I valued her tendency to look back into her past and trace the patterns she finds there, academic and personal ones intertwined and occasionally indistinguishable from each other.

The refusal of these and other writers to absent themselves from their theoretical work encouraged my efforts to integrate the (personal) writing and thinking I was doing into wider reading and writing. I became more confident about using personal experiences as starting points for critical work; indeed, this reading enabled me to understand my own stories as entrances into more complex theoretical grounds, confident in seeing my own life as a worthy element of understanding broader themes. I drew on Felman's example of welcoming intuition as a guide for further work, trusting that the process will be valuable, and reflecting on her direction of travel during that process. In her introduction to *What Does A Woman Want?*, she explains 'I did not know ... at the outset ... that such a methodology was to become the focus of my attempt; I practiced it intuitively ... I discovered it in process' (Felman 1993, 9).

She too describes finding a precedent for these decisions and conclusions and the individualized point of entry, and the value of the writing process as well as the final product. Felman cites Simone de Beauvoir's description of her own process of understanding the motivation for, and aftermath of, writing *The Second Sex*:

> When I started writing—it wasn't exactly memoirs, but an essay on myself—I realized that I needed first of all to situate myself as a woman ... it was not yet a feminist commitment as I've been involved with in recent years ... I became a feminist especially after the book was read, and started to exist for other women. (De Beauvoir 1982, quoted in Felman 1993, 11)

The book's existence 'for other women' is crucial. It suggests an element of reciprocity in writing, and establishes a relationship between author and audience that enables both to learn about themselves, and each other, as well as develop their ideas. De Beauvoir notes that it is 'especially' after this relationship formed that her own understanding of herself as a feminist grew. Felman articulates the way the relationship between de Beauvoir and her readers, what she calls the 'bond of reading' (Felman 1993, 12), is integral to the becoming process – both that of de Beauvoir the individual becoming a feminist, and the book becoming a touchstone for many women as a larger movement grew. The wider audience's 'becoming' is integral to de Beauvoir's 'becoming'.

Rich

Felman also quotes Adrienne Rich's combining of research and personal experience, an approach Rich says was 'both praised and attacked for what was sometimes seen as ... odd-fangled' because it was 'personal testimony mingled with research, and theory which derived from both' (Rich 1976, quoted in Felman 1993, 135). This fusion of personal and critical 'never seemed odd' to Rich; instead, 'What still seems odd is the absentee author, the writer who lays down speculations, theories, facts, and fantasies without any personal grounding' (Rich 1976, quoted in Felman 1993, 135). Here, Rich normalizes writing that is simultaneously personal and critical, and can even be seen to query the validity of writing which deliberately avoids 'grounding' itself in the life of its author.

Felman extends this idea to discuss the collaborative reading around her own, present text, where her writing process combined with the actions of her readers, who were 'discussing [her works] in conferences and assigning them in classrooms, and [sending her] letters', showed her, though only 'much later', 'that these readings and this writing ... were also coping inadvertently – although with no awareness on my part – with the reading and writing of my own life' (Felman 1993, 13). Her ability to measure individual growth though critical writing seems to give her confidence, and the way the two streams of writing and thinking are tightly bound up influenced my own approach to this project. These sentiments also accurately represent my thoughts on this text as a whole – only now that the entire book is complete (a process which involved much writing, sharing with readers and considering their responses) do I see how far my ideas have come.

Felman's emphasis on joint reading and writing speaks to this collaborative approach: 'people tell their stories ... through others' stories' (Felman 1993, 18). She is speaking of a profound connection to other writings, and other writers, in one's understanding of one's own life. Her critical writing was influenced by her personal narratives, in a way she only recognized in retrospect; while engaged in writing the academic 'story', she was also engaged, without realizing it, in writing her personal 'story'. Reading Felman's writing enabled me to see more clearly the process I had been following, without clearly seeing the tracks I was making at the time. I was exemplifying the element of self-discovery that Felman describes as implicit in reading 'others' stories'.

This book is the story of the stories. Using primarily late twentieth and early twenty-first century texts, I will explore the development of a way of thinking about and around autobiography and memoir that has three primary focuses. One is the dismissal of unity between the subject writing and the subject of the text, an assumed unity that underlies many contemporary and classic works of autobiography. Another is seeing the possibility of autobiographical writing representing an honest version of events without understanding this honesty to imply a belief in a single true version, either the author's or anyone else's. The third is an understanding of autobiographical writing as a new, creative construction; albeit one that has a strong link to past events. Rather than a reforming or reconfiguring of event into language, the writing is connected to the past and influenced by it, but not bound by it.

Although main themes commingle and resurface throughout this book, each of the four chapters focuses on exploring one of the following questions: What does it mean to write autobiographically truthfully, and who determines success or failure in this arena? How do we understand the author as a split identity, both in terms of the temporal distance between events and writing, and as a figure who features in the story as well as writes it? What are the possible effects of seeing memory as a tool authors can choose to use in order to access past events, and how is this complicated by the way the brain experiences the act of remembering? Can we divorce autobiographical writing from traditional fiction/nonfiction categorization by understanding it as a totally new creation that relies on the past but is not bound by it?

More specifically, the chapters are structured as follows. Chapter One opens my discussion of memoir and autobiography by probing the idea of truth, and how and when (and by whom) the genre can be considered truthful. I make a distinction between truth and truthfulness, drawing largely on John Barbour's work. I then explore a closely related idea, that of a somewhat special relationship between writers and readers of autobiography, which is based on a desire to believe in the authenticity of the author's writing. This relationship, articulated by some as a pact, contract or agreement, is often seen as closely linked to the idea of truthfulness, the pact being an agreement to 'tell the truth'. Of course, seeing truth as a complex and multifaceted concept highlights why such a pact might be problematic. I discuss how and why this idea has been central to understanding autobiography, most notably by drawing on critic Philippe Lejeune's writing. I discuss some contemporary cases where this pact was shown to be very problematic, and suggest that such an agreement, in addition to being unreasonable when autobiography is considered in any context but a moral one, comes more from a strong desire on the part of readers to access the inner thoughts of another person than from any real agreement between two parties for mutually desirable ends.

Chapter Two considers the dismissal of unity (both temporal and in terms of identity) that I believe can be read, and is occasionally explicit, in much memoir and autobiography. This rejection exemplifies the way our lives can be said to consist of a series of successive selves, often overlapping, rather than a single, constant self. I will suggest that part of the appeal of autobiographical writing lies in our desire and belief that we can use such writing to access some indissoluble self of the author, expressed through their writing; I also suggest that this desire will always be frustrated and unmet because of the separation between writer and audience, and the unreliability of assessing authorial intention.

Chapter Three discusses memory in greater depth. It explores how particular authors draw attention to flaws or gaps in memory, and the way they describe and understand the extraordinary vividness and suddenness of some memories. I discuss ways in which memory can be incomplete or deceptive, and argue that what we understand as memory is always tempered by our present self, so that memory is in fact profoundly influenced and shaped by our present. Rather than a stored and then retrieved image or narrative, memory is a newly constructed thought, a product of the present moment. I discuss different examples of authors 'using' memory, through their descriptions of it as a device or tool that can be called up, exercised or put into use. I also explore instances of memory refusing to be summoned or obedient; for instance, highlighting the ways in which it can lead us astray or resist our best efforts to recapture the past, or the way it can suggest alternate meanings of past events that we may not appreciate until long after those events have passed.

Finally, building on arguments made in the first three chapters, Chapter Four considers autobiography as a new product rather than a representation of recalled events. I suggest that, because memory is always newly constructed and because the authorial self is constantly changing, autobiographical writing is influenced by an author's past but should not be read as a completely accurate representation of that past. This chapter draws on John Sturrock's notion of memoir and autobiography as products of a conversion process rather than an adhesion process, implying that the transformation of a memory into a written account fundamentally changes the memory rather than simply updating or relaying it.

This book also includes an appendix of original autobiographical writing, a sequence of short stories. These stories represent the launch pad for the research and critical writing. They were written first, and writing them encouraged the above questions, and subsequent reading and research, to develop. They are therefore profoundly connected to the project but are also a body of work distinct from it. They act something like scaffolding in the way that they enabled the critical reading and writing to develop, but are no longer essential in structuring or approaching the rest of the book.

The stories provided the starting point for much of the reading and writing behind this project. However, as I became engrossed in research and critical writing, my focus turned away from the stories. And the more critical work I did, the more I questioned my initial assumptions and decisions. This made it impossible to continue writing the short stories from the same position. In this way, my autobiographical writing provided the main motivation for pursuing this project, but did not progress alongside it. Indeed, it is accurate to say that, after leading me towards a fertile field of study, my autobiographical writing halted. Therefore, while I understand this writing as a motivator, I do not discuss it very much within these pages; I draw on my own stories only briefly.

I have chosen to nevertheless include them because of the way they illustrate the genesis of the entire project, and in the way they contain hints of the themes and questions discussed here. In fact, I so value them *specifically as a starting point* that they have not been edited, apart from very minor stylistic changes, since the time when they were written. They exist as a record more than anything else. They enabled a working through, an emergence, of ideas – a means of forming questions and directing thoughts and additional reading. Beyond this, I of course hope they may appeal to readers, but it is important to clarify that they are included in an appendix to emphasize their simultaneous connection and disconnection from the rest of the book. The chapters that follow certainly would not exist if it were not for these stories. But now, they play no central role to the main body of this work, and can safely be disregarded by readers who are (often rightly) wary of appendices.

I refer to a number of texts repeatedly throughout this book. Above, I have discussed how its chapters are divided according to questions or main themes. Several of the books I focus on have much to say on most or all of the above themes, and so they appear throughout the entire work. These texts thus require a brief, formal introduction here in order that I may refer to them in various contexts throughout the text.

Stein

Gertrude Stein's *The Autobiography of Alice B. Toklas* was first published in 1933. Although Stein's authorship is acknowledged on the final page, the book was initially released without a stated author on the cover, and with Toklas's implied authorship in the title. This decision is one of the many playfully challenging ones made by Stein in this text; it is a joyful read because of the humour running through it, the feeling of access and proximity to some of the most interesting artists of the twentieth century and the conversational tone, a voice quite different from that used in some of her other works (this difference in style prompted her to claim that the 'extraordinary welcome' she received in America did 'not come from the books of [hers] that they do understand like the *Autobiography* but the books of [hers] that they did not understand' [Stein 1937, 6]).

I examine *The Autobiography of Alice B. Toklas* most closely in my discussion of unity in autobiographical fiction – unity between both author-as-character and author-as-writer, as well as unity between the time of writing and the occurrence of the events. Stein makes deliberate and provocative decisions concerning both these topics. I should note that, despite the discrepancy between author and title, I consider this book to be autobiographical; Stein is the dominant figure in the text, placing herself in a central role from the first few pages. This is another provocative authorial choice, and I will later suggest that it is partially meant as a comment on the division (or lack thereof) between a life lived by Toklas and one lived by

Stein. The book can be seen to question such a division not only because of Stein and Toklas's very long and very close relationship, but also for the same reason that Gornick refers to above, that any story of one's life must implicate the story of other people's lives. Stein's book also can be read as an example of Gornick's theory of the persona in personal narrative being a created voice used solely for the purposes of narrating a specific story, a voice which does not correspond in all points to the human writer.

The Things We Used To Say by Natalia Ginzburg (1963) is, according to the author, the story of a family rather than that of an individual. Her account focuses on her family's life during the rise of fascism in, and the occupation of, Italy before and during the Second World War. In this text, Ginzburg makes very intriguing choices regarding the truthfulness of her account, specifically in relation to choosing not to disclose certain kinds of information on particular topics, or refusing to elaborate on incidents that, while central to her story, are very painful to her. I will be looking at these omissions within the context of the book as a whole, and examining ways in which past selves encroach upon subsequent selves, complicating the identity writing, as well as how one measures the truthfulness of a story.

Her overall approach is also of particular interest because of her intention to separate the two 'kinds' of stories that I have introduced above as being indivisible – the story of an individual and that of a family. Ginzburg intended to write the story of a family, of a group, and specifically did not want to produce an individualized account of one person's life. This already sets her apart through her rejection of one of the main criteria commonly understood to be part of writing autobiographically, the criterion of narrating an account of one's life. (We can see an interesting echo of this intention in Janice Galloway's 2008 memoir *This Is Not About Me*.) This decision also influences Ginzburg's writing style and her structural decisions.

I primarily use the 1997 translation by Judith Woolf (published by Carcanet Press) but also refer to a 1967 revised translation by D. M. Low (published by The Hogarth Press). A translator herself, Ginzburg surely appreciated the immense difficulty in translating a text so personal and one so focused on the power and effects of language. I will later compare these two editions in a discussion of how the presence of a translator complicates the construction of any text, and can affect a reader's reception of what they see as an author's intended meaning.

The Year of Magical Thinking by Joan Didion was published in 2005, and written over almost exactly one calendar year. Begun nine months after her husband of forty years, John Gregory Dunne, died suddenly at the dinner table, the book is a memoir of Didion's journey through shock, grief and mourning. It also tells the story of her only child, daughter Quintana, who was gravely ill at the time of Dunne's death; Quintana passed away shortly after the manuscript was finished, though before the book came out in print. Didion's book is one of such yearning and desperation that it is almost difficult to read. The raw, wounded writing seeks to staunch the pain and understand it and its sources, but ultimately does not find comfort.

An important figure in the New Journalism movement, Didion has spent her career applying her incisive prose and cool, almost clinical style to some of the most important events of her time, involving herself in the story but always holding something back. 'Writers are always selling somebody out', she claims, aware that, as a journalist, she works to her advantage the fact that 'people tend to forget that [her] presence runs counter to their best interests' (Didion 2006, 7). Spending most of her working life in such an atmosphere perhaps imbues her prose with the sensation that, despite her merciless eye and pen, she plays her own cards close to her chest. She is the 'cool customer' (Didion 2005, 15) who moves numbly and methodically through the immediate aftermath of her husband's fatal heart attack, asking herself, 'I wondered what an uncool customer would be allowed to do. Break down? Require sedation? Scream?' (Didion 2005, 16). In this book the steely resolve occasionally falls away, and we get glimpses of her flinging the cards away in grief, but a sense of restraint and a certain kind of distancing is present throughout most of the text.

I will be using *The Year of Magical Thinking*, occasionally in comparison with some of Didion's earlier work, to illustrate a number of main themes. These include the way Didion views her past selves and former life, and her almost obsessive search through her memory to try and make sense of her husband's final moments, days, weeks. I will analyze the way she writes about her preoccupation with trying to recapture the past, as well as her responses to past incidents which she suspects are particularly important, even while recognizing that her memories of them are unreliable. I will also briefly mention a text which has very clear and strong links to Didion's. Joyce Carol Oates's *A Widow's Story* (2011) was released six years after Didion's, but the two women's experiences were remarkably similar, and their resulting memoirs feature very close parallels. Indeed, Oates directly mentions Didion and her memoir several times in her book. I will only occasionally refer to Oates's memoir, but it is worthwhile to introduce it here as almost a companion text, and one that engages with many of the same ideas and themes found in Didion's. 'There is much melancholy wisdom here', Oates says about *The Year of Magical Thinking* in an email to a friend (Oates 2011, 154). Oates is thanking this friend for a gift of Didion's memoir, which she has already read but will 'happily reread' (Oates 2011, 154).

Vladimir Nabokov's *Speak, Memory* is subtitled 'An Autobiography Revisited', and is described by the author as a 're-Englishing of a Russian re-version of what had been an English re-telling of Russian memories' (not surprisingly, Nabokov called these revision processes 'a diabolical task') (Nabokov 2000, 10). The chapters were written in English (except one, originally written in French) and published in a variety of magazines and other collections in the 1940s and 1950s. In 1953, the collected chapters (except one) were translated into Russian, with some changes made; this version was then retranslated into English, with the 'introduc[tion] of basic changes and copious additions' as well as the addition of 'the corrections … made while turning it into Russian' (Nabokov 2000, 9). I refer to the latest version, the 2000 Penguin edition, although much of the material was written decades before this publication date.

Nabokov's text has thus undergone numerous changes and appeared in many guises. This is particularly appropriate for a book so concerned with how to (re)arrange memories in such a way as to emphasize their relationship to each other. Although he claims that the 'possessor and victim' of a memory 'should never have tried to become an autobiographer' (Nabokov 2000, xii), throughout *Speak, Memory* Nabokov makes authorial decisions that highlight memory, and the ability to search through it or call upon it, as a frustrating but ultimately glorious gift. The difficulties he describes in writing the book often have to do with his reported difficulty in remembering accurately, rather than with the notion that a memory can itself be inaccurate. When he does remember something, it is with triumph and confidence. I will discuss his use of and writing on memory at length in Chapter Three.

Readers will note that these books are all from the twentieth and twenty-first centuries. Apart from brief mentions of other works, Stein's is the earliest text used, and Didion's the most recent. The wealth of autobiographies and memoirs in print today is quite clearly of an immensity that demands rather strict boundaries in order to perform any in-depth analysis and discussion, and I have chosen not to consider autobiographies written before the twentieth century. This criterion immediately eliminates two autobiographies of great importance to the genre, Jean-Jacques Rousseau's *Confessions* (1782) and the *Confessions* of St Augustine (c. 392). Although these accounts are important to the field of autobiography studies, they have been given ample treatment by generations of scholars, and I prefer not to add my voice to that particular body of work. I believe that the analysis and writing I do here can confidently stand alone while remaining within the boundaries of this century and the last, without drawing in these two important early examples of autobiography.

I have also privileged/chosen authors who have written both fiction and nonfiction, and specifically authors who wrote not only autobiographically but also wrote critically about that process, as noted above. This was important to me because of the fusion of fiction and memoir present in the short stories, and because I wanted to consider writers who had commented in some way about the decisions made during their autobiographical writing. Readers will inevitably be able to think of books that could have found their way into this writing, but the urge to include everything one finds interesting in a particular work must be carefully monitored; limits must be carefully set and then respected. Certain boundaries must be put into place for reasons of space and time, but also in order to strike a balance between the breadth of sources consulted and discussed, and the specificity and detail drawn out through this discussion and analysis. I am confident the sources used here represent a wide range of writers and ideas, and I believe the analysis performed is adequate to discuss these in sufficient depth while also including as many interesting connections as possible.

A final introductory note: this book uses the terms memoir and autobiography fairly interchangeably. This is done because my main concern is with choices made by the authors of such texts, and the ways in which readers can understand and read them. For clarification, I understand the two terms to describe very similar writing, with the difference lying primarily in cut-off points: autobiography tends to encompass longer periods of time, approaching a whole life, whereas memoir is concerned with the time around a particular event or series of events, or during a particularly intense time period, e.g. adolescence, wartime, etc. For this reason, memoirs might be seen to usually or often focus on times of crisis or difficulty. (It is noteworthy that such times of stress might make recollection even more complicated and prone to error, and indeed may activate certain kinds of memory specific to frightening or traumatic events, as will be discussed further in Chapter Three.)

Some authors and critics also consider memoir as a kind of writing that is more permissive of invention or distortion, but I do not believe this is a universally, or even widely, held view. In any case, autobiographies will also feature times of difficulty or crisis, and the authorial choices made in both subgenres are equally relevant here. The two terms can be understood to indicate slightly different forms of writing (though the categories are by no means clear and rigid) but, for our purposes here, can be considered analogous. In all cases I am interested in choices made about the writing of past events, whether such writing appears in a book which limits its focus to a particular time period, or one that encompasses most of a lifetime.

1

Truth and Trust

It is appropriate to begin with a chapter on truth and truthfulness. Memoir and autobiography are commonly held to be 'true' writing; they are understood to be based on events that occurred in reality. Shelved and sorted with other nonfiction titles, they are usually defined as accounts of experiences that actually happened to their authors. Moving no further than such an understanding, however, is simplistic. The most basic, everyday interactions, in which we find ourselves misunderstood, surprised or confused by the perceptions or actions of others, begin to confuse the notion of a singular, verifiable truth that all parties involved agree upon, and deny a straight-forward mode of perceiving events. Most interactions feature multiple viewpoints and interpretations. We understand our fundamental inability to see the world through the eyes of anyone but ourselves; this inability brings with it a fixed gaze that can never be sure of the veracity of another's interpretation. In this way, an author can describe an experience that 'really' happened to her, and find that someone else who was present disputes or even rejects the description.

As well, there are many understandings of what it means to write the truth. Expectations of the author and the writing fragment according to each reader's particular understanding of the term: do we expect the author to rely on external documentation to support all their claims? Do we expect their story to be corroborated by other individuals? Or are we satisfied with a claim that this is their memory, without any form of support?

There are multiple truths bound up in most events and interactions. I believe this is self-evident. Critic and memoirist William Zinsser illustrates the point when he recalls his experience writing and publishing recollections of his deceased grandmother in the memoir collection *Five Boyhoods* (1962). After reading his account, Zinsser and his own mother realize they have conflicting ideas about the grandmother, because they each have different memories of her: 'Grandma wasn't really like that', is his own mother's response to Zinsser's account, suggesting a single 'way' that she 'was', a way that Zinsser failed to reproduce (Zinsser 1998, 11). Of course, by providing her own interpretation of events and judging the grandmother accordingly (as well as judging Zinsser's account), Zinsser's mother is simply offering her own truth. But Zinsser trusts his memories and his construction of the memoir, and he stands by his version.

The crafting of memoir, he says, is the phase during which memories take shape and are turned into autobiographical writing. Constructing narrative from the 'jumble' of memory requires what he calls a 'feat of manipulation' (Zinsser 1998, 6). This feat eventually leads a memoirist to 'arrive at a truth that is theirs alone, not quite like that of anybody else who was present at the same events' (Zinsser 1998, 6). This phrasing is potentially very useful to writers working on an autobiographical piece. Rather than emphasizing a backwards-looking approach, in which the author must endeavour to return to the past in their current work, Zinsser's words encourage dexterity, 'manipulation', sorting through the 'jumble'. These are actions that are very much in the present, and working through them will hopefully bring the writer to a new, desired place. The piece will be 'arrive[d]' at, rather than

 returned to. Such phrasing can be influential in how we approach a piece of writing, as readers and/or as writers. Emphasizing the individuality of the account helps discourage anxiety about how an event or memory appears in the work, particularly in relation to others' recollections or beliefs, and instead validates unique, even disputed, accounts and forms of expression.

Zinsser's statement suggests numerous truths, and their more or less peaceful co-existence – if not in the same text, at least in the world. Zinsser does not suggest that conflict and dispute are inherent to this manipulation/writing process. If we understand memoir and autobiography as representative of a unique, individual and subjective truth belonging to an author, then it is up to the individual to define. This includes both readers and writers. Nevertheless, we can find many contemporary cases of angry reactions from readers who discover that a book they thought was true (in the sense that it adhered to whatever their definition of truth is) was not. This calls into question exactly how readers can be, or feel, betrayed, if their understanding and categorization of a book is final. James Frey's *A Million Little Pieces*, a book I will later discuss at greater length, is possibly the most famous recent example, but there are many. These conflicts illustrate the relationship between author and reader which is often integral to an understanding of what autobiography 'is', and what rules some readers expect it to follow.

Zinsser complicates his position of multiple truths when he expands on the clash between his and his mother's memories. 'The truth lay somewhere between my mother's version and mine', he says, 'But [his grandmother] was

Truth → Mum's version →
My understanding

Write multiple [...]
on same event
from diff. pov.

like that to *me* – and that's the only truth a memoir writer can work with'
(Zinsser 1998, 12). It seems probable that both his version and his mother's
version of events were true in the sense that their overall (and lasting) image
of the grandmother was closely aligned with events or experiences they
shared with her, from which they compiled a particular idea of the 'way she
was'. It is possible that his grandmother was strict and unyielding at times, or
with particular people, as he describes her in his writing, and also 'unhappy
and really quite shy' at other times, as his mother recalls her (Zinsser 1998,
12). The memoirist *can* 'work with' alternate truths, alternate versions of
events, or at least allow them into the scope of the work. Indeed, establishing
one's own story out of the stories of all other implicated individuals seems
to necessarily involve carving one's account from all possible accounts/
constructions, thus involving 'work[ing] with' multiple truths. Ultimately,
one can only be sure of one's individual truth, the way a particular experience
or event happened to them, but this does not mean that this is the only truth
they can 'work with'.

In the example above, I see the triangle of Zinsser's version, his mother's
version and the truth he sees as lying 'somewhere between' them as
problematic because, although I suspect he is telling this story in support of
his own actions, and as an example of the multiplicity bound up in telling
stories of the past, by suggesting that the truth lies elsewhere than in their
words, he is implying their words' untruth. I see this triangle as featuring
truthfulness in two, and possibly all three, points. He describes his version
and his mother's version in ways that suggest they are both relating stories of
the past without wilfully distorting or misrepresenting them, and I believe it
is wholly possible that a third or fourth or tenth account of the same woman
could be told with the same honesty of approach and still describe different
aspects of her character. This illustrates the way truthfulness can be found in
the storyteller's actions and motivation, rather than in the resulting stories,
an idea I will revisit in greater detail later in this chapter.

Although I think authors of memoir and autobiography do work with
multiple truths while cultivating their own, Zinsser's view quoted above is
useful in that it suggests choice, action, shaping. While the craft aspect of
autobiographical writing clearly influences the text (and its reception), this
idea of 'work[ing] with' the truth implies excavation, discovery, decision,
interpretation, revelation. This phrasing suggests that, as I will later discuss
with reference to memory, truth is not a static entity or characteristic that
is either adhered to or ignored, discovered or betrayed. It is more complex,
more nuanced, more pliable. Regarding reportage (another form of personal
narrative whose readers often insist on 'the truth'), journalist Bill Buford

QUOTE

argues: '[Reporting] is meant to relay and record the truth of things, as if truth were out there, hanging around, waiting for the reporter to show up' (Buford 1990, 180). Truth, even if one believes that it is singular and fixed, can still be worked with, slowly discovered, seen from different angles and viewpoints.

KARR

Mary Karr, whose 1995 memoir *The Liars' Club* is seen by some as one of the earliest texts of the late 1990s memoir boom (particularly the 'misery memoir' subgenre), openly approaches this issue of establishing her own truth during her recollection and writing process. *The Liars' Club* is the story of Karr's childhood; much of it is told from her perspective at seven years of age. On numerous occasions within the text she refers to how the book would read differently if written by her sister, or explicitly mentions that her sister claims, and remembers, events happening differently from how Karr describes them. (This is a practice which continues into her second and third memoirs.) She describes her writing process in interviews. After writing a first draft alone, without doing research, in order to access her own memories without external influence, she 'may visit places and check stuff out, to clarify details' (Karr 2009). She also mentions describing events to her family members, to gauge their reactions to her truth, and to verify what she has written (Karr 2009). Although she takes this sort of verification of factual details more seriously than some authors, and relies on 'so many drafts' in which she can 'poke and prod and question', she still reverts to a basic, individually determined definition of truth: 'I know better than anybody else how I felt at fifteen or at forty. You might remember something I did that I don't remember, but I know how I felt' (Karr 2009). It is worth noting that information about Karr's writing process (like many authors') is often found in interviews, another forum in which she is able to speak according only to her version of truth. This mode of expression, as well as her outspokenness about her commitment to honouring her own memories, may help create the image that, for instance, Stephen King got from her first memoir: 'she is a woman who remembers *everything* about her early years' and presents it 'in an almost unbroken panorama' (King 2000, 3).

Karr expresses distaste for the increasing acceptance of stretching the boundaries of factual accuracy in autobiographical writing ('It pissed me off when I saw James Frey on Larry King … if it didn't happen, it's fiction. If it did happen, it's nonfiction' [Karr 2009]). Although in her acknowledgments to *The Liars' Club* she credits her older sister Lecia, who is a large presence in the book, with 'confirm[ing] the veracity of what [is] written', the memoir features many interjections where Karr suggests that Lecia would/does claim that an event happened in another way, acknowledging an alternate truth. In her third memoir, *Lit*, she does something quite similar with her ex-husband's imagined version of the truth: 'Were Warren laboring over this story, I'd no doubt appear drunkenly shrieking; spending every cent I could get my mitts on … none of this entirely untrue' (Karr 2010, 87).

These interjections and admissions of other truths complicate her seemingly straightforward distinction between fiction and nonfiction, even if the events in question appear minor or trivial. For example: 'I didn't remember my mother's paramour … being particularly goodlooking. Lecia said, Oh yes, he had steely white hair, blue eyes, and he was muscular' (Karr 2009). Incidents like this suggest that, in principle, the truth is not 'out there, hanging around, waiting for' her to show up, but rather recalled differently, debated, sometimes never resolved, or even impossible to resolve. Little details can soon give way to larger issues. In *The Liars' Club*, Karr experiences a car crash while her mother is driving. The text suggests that her mother may have deliberately caused the crash. Had Karr recalled that event differently, believing her mother to have definitely intentionally crashed the car, perhaps she would define that version as the truth, because she knows 'better than anybody else' what her impressions were of that experience. But if a later police report, for instance, found Karr's mother guilty, or innocent, but this completely conflicted with Karr's memory, which she knows 'better than anybody else', on which side would the truth lie?

Autobiographical writing necessarily involves the intersections between one's own ideas of what is true and the ideas of others. Even while only being able to hold fast to one's own version of events, the memoirist must incorporate the truths of others, even indirectly, acknowledging that they may deviate from one's own, and may indeed contradict them outright. This handling, or negotiation, of multiple versions of an event is inherent to autobiographical writing. For Karr, acknowledging conflicting views and allowing them into her text is her way of providing the maximum amount of relevant information and highlighting the ambiguity or uncertainty of some experiences, while still arguing for, and defending, her own version of events.

Determining the truthfulness of a piece of autobiographical writing often reverts to a discussion of authorial intention, a problematic approach to discussing almost any kind of writing. Leading on from my reading of Zinsser's view, which implies that truth is something requiring action, reaction and particular approaches in order to 'work with', I turn to John Barbour, whose distinction between truth and truthfulness was particularly illuminating and freeing in my consideration of how I (or anyone) could attach labels of honesty or truth to my (or any autobiographical) writing, and indeed how I could understand and approach the autobiographical writing I was reading. 'It is easier to show specific achievements or failures of truthfulness in particular autobiographies than it is to define the nature of truthfulness', Barbour claims (Barbour 1992, 26). This echoes the famous statement by US Supreme Court Judge Potter Stewart, regarding an obscenity charge: 'I know it when I see it' (*Jacobellis v. Ohio* 1964). Stewart's statement has become almost shorthand for phenomena which are simultaneously extremely difficult to define and instantly recognizable. Yet they are only instantly recognizable on an individual level – obviously if obscenity was recognized by everybody in the same way, there would have been no need for Judge Stewart to consider it in a professional capacity. That he did, and that his ruling is both opaque and understandable, speaks to the subject's simultaneous familiarity and uncertainty.

Barbour continues:

> Truthfulness must be distinguished from truth. Truth is usually thought of as a kind of correspondence between human thought and reality, or as a matter of coherence among different ideas and propositions. Truthfulness, in contrast, is a process or quality of a person, a virtue we ascribe to certain individuals and not others … the autobiographer may err; he is as fallible as any human being in interpreting reality. The autobiographer may, however, demonstrate truthfulness, which is an active search for the most exact and insightful understanding of past experience. (Barbour 1992, 26)

These words are closely aligned with the notion of truth requiring excavation or 'work' by the author in order to shape it and help it emerge. Here, Barbour associates truthfulness with a quality, or approach, a way of handling one's role as a writer. Writing autobiographically is an act at which one can fail, or 'err', while still maintaining the mantle of truthfulness if one remains committed to 'interpreting reality' in the most 'exact and insightful' way. These words do not suggest that truth is static, waiting to be accessed and written about by someone who can do it justice. These words show an understanding of the complexity of writing truthfully, and place a burden on the writer *not* to ensure 'correspondence between thought and reality', but rather to interpret the material they have according to certain principles. Once more the intention and behaviour of the author are drawn into discussions of the veracity of the writing.

The views quoted above are, I believe, satisfactory in establishing an important distinction: truthfulness describes an action or kind of behaviour, whereas truth is a state of affairs (of course, an unstable and not universally acknowledged state of affairs). It is impossible for a reader to be sure of an author's intentions, but for writers, this framework bolsters the desire to allow the writing to stretch beyond the borders of the known in the name of truthful (and engaging) storytelling. Barbour describes the way this approach allows for more efficient handling of parts of an author's life when considered as potential ingredients in the writing:

> truthtelling in autobiography is not only a matter of honesty in commu-
> nication with others, for it concerns also honesty with oneself ... just
> as not every fact about an autobiographer's life qualifies as significant
> truth, so not every omission, exaggeration, or inconsistency counts as
> self-deception. (Barbour 1992, 19)

William Zinsser's description of writing recollections of his grandmother comes from his introduction to a collection of essays by writers of personal narrative. *Inventing the Truth: The Art and Craft of Memoir* is a provocative title that, from the outset, complicates the categories of invention and truth by binding them – and making both relate directly to writing memoir. The collection features a number of memoirists discussing choices made in their autobiographical writing, and the varied voices illustrate the multiplicity of understandings of what it means to write truthfully. Toni Morrison contributes a chapter to the collection, and she introduces it with the note that what appears to be a 'misalliance', that of a novelist being included in a collection of memoirists, is 'not completely out of place' (Morrison 1998, 185). She makes a convincing case for why much of the writing she does, though fictional, can be considered alongside memoirs and autobiographies, and she does so by drawing on similar issues of authorial intention as those discussed above.

Morrison speaks of her commitment to particular ideals that inform her work, citing a 'deadly serious[ness]' about being true to 'the milieu out of which I write and from which my ancestors actually lived' (Morrison 1998, 192). She is speaking specifically about American slave narratives, primarily from the nineteenth century (among her many examples are Harriet Jacob's and Frederick Douglass's accounts), and her own novels focusing on individuals living in that time period. The 'milieu' is 'the absence of the interior life, the deliberate excising of it from the records that the slaves themselves told' (Morrison 1998, 192). This is the space where she situates some of her fiction, trying to give voice to the silenced and repop- ulate these narratives with experiences which would have been deliberately shielded from the books' intended audience. She seeks to expose the interior lives of the writers, to tell the stories which found no place in their own published and recounted narratives, to 'rip that veil drawn over "proceedings too terrible to relate"' (Morrison 1998, 191). (Her phrasing here is inter- esting, and can be easily linked to James Weldon Johnson's preface to *The Autobiography of an Ex-Coloured Man* [1912], which claims that 'In these pages it is as though a veil had been drawn aside: the reader is given a view of the inner life of the Negro in America' [Johnson 1912, xii]). Because Morrison wants to tell stories that have deliberately remained untold and also been erased from history, 'Only the act of imagination can help [her]' (Morrison 1998, 192).

The examples of her writing that Morrison references here do not relate to her own life experiences, of course, and so are not strictly personal narrative. However, her ancestry links her to this 'milieu', and she maintains a connection to these events that is valid without relying on personal experience. Morrison draws on memory and research, both her 'own recollections' and 'the recollections of others' (Morrison 1998, 191). This is a process that extends far back in time, and in discussing it she quotes Zora Neale Hurston: 'Like the dead-seeming cold rocks, I have memories within that came out of the material that went to make me' (Morrison 1998, 192). Although Morrison is inventing the material with which she works, it is authentic to her, and this authenticity is extremely important to honour. It can also be seen as linked to her through her history, through the 'material that went to make [her]', even if not from direct experience. Her inventions would be truthful, even if they are not the truth, because she is 'active[ly] search[ing] for the most exact and insightful understanding of past experience', even when she did not live through that experience. This understanding of truthfulness as a process, approach or intention is evident in Morrison's words, as is the distinction between truth and truthfulness.

This is an intriguing example, but one that does little to satisfy the inherent uneasiness in relying on authorial intention for any sort of guarantee of the accuracy of autobiographical writing. Often we cannot access evidence of such intention, and even if we can, we cannot be sure of it. In their classic essay on authorial intention, W. K. Wimsatt and Monroe Beardsley concisely argue 'that the design or intention of the author is neither available nor desirable as a standard for judging the success of a work of literary art' (Wimsatt and Beardsley 1954). Here I believe we can safely remove the idea of success or failure, without altering the main argument. 'Judging' a work of art is not benefitted by what we may think is 'the design or intention of the author'. Even if we understand or define autobiographical writing as writing which is premised upon an author intending to truthfully recount events in their lives, we can be no surer of their 'design or intention' than with any other writing. Perhaps from this uncertainty comes the strong desire many readers have to believe in such writing; perhaps because we know that it is so easy to lie, autobiography takes on moral overtones.

According to many critics and readers, once an author begins working in the genre of memoir and autobiography, she is no longer simply making artistic decisions but also moral ones. This is also true among peers – when

MORALS   AUTHOR INTENTION

Karr expresses anger at James Frey's conflating of fiction and nonfiction, she is making an implicit moral judgment, and she is doing so in part as one writer speaking of another. Paul John Eakin states: 'When life writers fail to tell the truth ... they do more than violate a literary convention governing nonfiction as a genre; they disobey a moral imperative' (Eakin 2004, 2–3). This comment suggests that the genre only exists as a genre in accordance with an understanding (sometimes unspoken) between writer and reader, which outlines one's responsibility to the other. If we agree with this statement, we cannot consider the genre without considering the author's intentions. Incorporating authorial intention into literary analysis is not inherently invalid. However, I believe that a mode of understanding writing which hinges on a supposed agreement between writer and reader is very problematic. We cannot know the author's intentions, much as we may like to. Such intentions may be unclear to the author himself. Therefore, to use authorial intention as a foundation for a way of understanding writing is highly unreliable, and thus, in my opinion, not useful. Eakin's view of a 'literary convention' involves complex relationships. It relies on two parties operating according to similar terms: the author agrees to be truthful, and the reader agrees to accept autobiographical writing as truthful.

The 'moral imperative' Eakin speaks of is a somewhat separate matter. Similar to our concepts of truth, a moral code is a very individual thing, and is often developed over the course of a life, depending on the lessons one learns from various experiences. As we understand truth differently, so too do we understand morality differently, and so cannot accept a universal moral imperative, recognizable to all readers and writers. This literary 'moral imperative' also makes itself apparent almost exclusively in discussions of the genre of autobiography and memoir. If a book released and marketed as a comedy fails to make us laugh, we do not feel betrayed; if a thriller does not thrill us, we are similarly not angered. This is primarily because we understand these reactions to be deeply personal; one reader's sense of humour will not necessarily match another reader's. But in autobiography, the treatment and understanding of truth that comes through the text – an understanding that might be entirely at odds with a reader's – makes such texts' genre identification more potentially problematic. This is perhaps precisely why some authors whose writing contains clearly autobiographical elements prefer to release their work under the label of fiction, rejecting the associations and implications that come with the classification of autobiography – we can see evidence of this in the works of Natalia Ginzburg and Roland Barthes considered in later chapters.

It is very interesting, however, to consider how John Barbour combines Eakin's view of such a 'moral imperative' and also extends Eakin's view of living narratively. In *The Conscience of The Autobiographer*, Barbour defines conscience as 'moral self-assessment', and argues that part of the role of this process or practice is to 'protect the integrity of the self, and to maintain the self's continuity and identity' (Barbour 1992, 9). In *Living Autobiographically*, Eakin indicates that his 'basic proposition here is that narrative is not merely something we tell, listen to, read, or invent; it is an essential part of our sense of who were are ... I believe that our life stories are not merely *about* us but in an inescapable and profound way *are* us' (Eakin 2008, ix, x). Barbour thus extends this life-giving power of narrative: an active conscience works to 'maintain' this construction of identity through narrative, and is integral to this sense of self's 'continuity'.

Autobiography as testimony, writing as survival

Pursuing my intention to write truthfully while navigating the plurality of the histories I was considering in these stories (and very aware that other members of my family were only too ready to vocalize alternate versions), I found Shoshana Felman's articulation of autobiographical writing as testimony very apt. Felman's 1992 *Testimony*, co-written with Lori Daub, offered a new way of seeing artistic responses to crisis. In this text they consider artistic works created after the Holocaust, which the authors consider to be 'the watershed of our times' and, importantly, an event which is 'not over, a history whose repercussions are not simply omnipresent ... but whose traumatic consequences are still actively *evolving*' (Felman and Daub 1992, xiv). Felman and Daub claim their book is 'about how art inscribes (artistically bears witness to) what we do not yet know of our lived historical relation to events of our time' (Felman and Daub 1992, xx). I did not see myself as responding to crisis but could relate to their description of artistic response to events of great significance, unfinished events made up of memories and stories.

In their view, 'art' (the writing) 'bears witness to' the past, which is imperfectly understood, but can be clarified through our 'inscrib[ing]'. We can discover and/or better understand our relation to events in our lives through artistic expression, as well as using it to express our growing understanding. Arguably, each person's life is made up of periods of great significance involving events which are not yet completed. Writing about these events as testimony thus becomes a method of attempting to understand, or expressing a search for understanding, as well a means of adding our own voice, 'inscrib[ing]' our story as part of a larger collection of narratives.

Writing as testimony becomes an expression of a process rather than evidence of a completed event. If we use the past to understand the present, the above quote perfectly describes autobiography, in that we 'do not yet know' our relation to our own history, and can use writing as a means of approaching an understanding of it. Our writing in the present can thus enable greater awareness and understanding of the past, but can also make these events more complex and multifaceted.

One of the key ideas here is the suggested sense of the contribution one's writing makes to a larger whole. One testifies by giving an account which represents one voice, or perhaps segment, of a larger whole, or narrative. Thus, writing as testimony permits writing about the past in a way that explores and informs, but does not act as a single account, or an account of the 'whole' story. Joyce Carol Oates sees this as a 'seductive' aspect of memoir specifically, which is 'the most seductive of literary genres' (this seductive power also makes memoir, in her opinion, 'the most dangerous of genres') (Oates 2011, 300). The seduction lies in the fact that the memoir is 'a repository of truths … but the memoir can't be the repository of Truth which is the very breath of the sky, too vast to be perceived by a single gaze' (Oates 2011, 300). A greater, singular truth, which she here differentiates stylistically through capitalizing it, cannot be found within a single memoir, within a single text. What can be found, however, in this 'seductive' and 'dangerous' kind of writing, are multiple truths, co-existing in the text and linking to other voices, other texts, other truths.

I found a faint echo of this articulation in Sarah Wilson's study of modernist writing which formally expresses the 'melting-pot' thinking that developed in response to the rapid and exponential rise in immigration in the United States around the start of the twentieth century (Wilson 2010, 7). This huge influx of people caused notions of identity, nationality and belonging in America to fragment bewilderingly. In a discussion of scenes of chaos and overwhelming human crowdedness and movement in New York that appear in Henry James's *The American Scene*, Wilson lingers on his description of a particular moment as 'phantasmagoric' (Wilson 2010, 68). Wilson writes that this word of 'unclear origin' (Wilson 2010, 214) here represents 'that which exceeds the individual perspective: that which can be grasped, imagined, approached only through a multiplicity of positionings' (Wilson 2010, 68). Her language is helpful in describing something so large, so difficult to fathom or contain, that it cannot be grasped as a whole but must be seen (and described) in pieces. This segmentation not only encourages artistic expression as a collection of voices and accounts but, by doing so, also encourages a sense of process, as more and more voices make themselves heard and a greater narrative gradually establishes.

TRAUMA + WOMEN

Not sure
about this

In her 1993 book *What Does a Woman Want?*, Felman continues to explore how autobiography can be written and read as testimony. She argues that women's writing is unable to be autobiographical in the same way as men's because women have been 'Trained to see [them]selves as objects and to be positioned as the Other' (Felman 1993, 14). This reliance means, for Felman, that a woman's writing of her own life cannot exist in the same way as it might for a man, who would have a developed (existing) sense of self as an individual. Thus, a man can 'write autobiographies from memory … by the self-conscious effort of a voluntary recall' (Felman 1993, 15). Women, on the other hand, can write 'what the memory cannot contain – or hold together as a whole' (Felman 1993, 15). This lack of an identity leads Felman to then suggest that women's lives are centered around, fundamentally built upon, 'explicitly or in implicit ways, the story of a trauma' (Felman 1993, 16). This trauma as a condition of femaleness suggests to Felman that women's autobiographical writing, by existing in response to trauma, makes it a testimony of their survival in the face of this trauma, and 'survival is, profoundly, a form of autobiography' (Felman 1993, 13).

In developing this theory, she encourages a new understanding and definition of trauma, drawing on the work of clinical psychologist Laura S. Brown. Brown argues that the definition used by the American Psychiatric Association indicates that trauma is that which lies 'outside the range of human experience' (Brown 1991, 120). This definition, argues Brown, eliminates instances of repeated rape, abuse or other violence that 'are not unusual statistically', that 'are well within the "range of human experience"' and that 'are experiences that could happen in the life of any girl or woman in North America today' (Brown 1991, 120). The definition of trauma above thus normalizes some instances of violence (spousal rape, for example) and not others (a war injury, for example). In this understanding, trauma can be an everyday occurrence for many individuals, but is not acknowledged as such.[1] This leads Felman to suggest that it is a condition of many women's lives, making their writing a response to trauma, and a record of survival in the face of trauma.

Moving so swiftly from autobiography to survival may seem sudden and rather extreme, but if we understand living as a process by which we create a narrative identity, then narration generally, and writing specifically, become bound up with notions of survival, and a response to death as a threat to that

---

[1] It is useful to note that the definition Brown refers to has changed over time, including significant changes to understandings and descriptions of trauma and stressor-related disorders, which will appear in the most recent version of the *Diagnostic and Statistical Manual of Mental Disorders*, published by the American Psychiatric Association, scheduled to appear in May 2013.

survival. Here I mean that writing can function as a means for the author to live beyond their own death, through the permanence of text compared to the human body (though of course books are burned, manuscripts are lost), or that writing can be a means of forestalling death itself through extending a narrative (as happens with Scheherazade's ongoing story in *A Thousand and One Nights*).

There are many examples of this theme of writing as evidence of survival and a response to death. Margaret Atwood discusses at length her 'hypothesis ... that ... *all* writing of the narrative kind, and perhaps all writing, is motivated, deep down, by a fear of and a fascination with mortality' (Atwood 2002, 156). We have just seen this intention above, in Toni Morrison's desire to recreate the 'interior life' (Morrison 1998, 192) of her characters, to preserve their full lives beyond their literal death, including aspects which were obscured or eliminated in their own narratives. This act is closely bound up with mortality, both in terms of refusing to let the previously blurred interior lives die by restoring them to life in a text, and in Morrison's own awareness that this is her heritage, and she is writing about people whose lives could have been those of her ancestors. Understanding one's place in a sequence of lives is inextricably related to one's own mortality.

Autobiography is survival for obvious reasons – because only a living person can write, and in autobiography one writes of past experiences, i.e. those one has lived through. Writing also leaves a physical trace after a life ends, thus satisfying a very powerful human drive. Autobiography is evidence of a self, of a life. Critic Philippe Lejeune states: 'Au fond le véritable problème de l'autobiographie n'est pas de représenter de manière fidèle le temps d'une vie, mais de maîtriser ce temps immaîtrisable et de lutter contre la mort'[2] (Lejeune 1987, quoted in Bainbridge 2005, 23). Here he identifies control or mastery over death as a fundamental aim of autobiographical writing. In *Speak, Memory*, Vladimir Nabokov recalls his uncle's rediscovery of some books he had read as a child (another manifestation of text having the ability to recall, or keep, the past). Nabokov then describes finding the books again later in his own adult life. The crash of memories – his uncle's memory of his childhood, Nabokov's childhood memory of his uncle, and the 'present' memory of those layers of memory – all combine to give him 'a sense of security, of well-being', where 'nothing will ever change, nobody will ever die' (Nabokov 2000, 62). In this passage, writing is given the ability to move the writer, and reader, back in time, but also functions as a way of forestalling death, a means of living beyond the decay of the bodily self.

---

[2] Ultimately, the real issue/goal of autobiography is not faithfully representing the story of a life, but of conquering unconquerable time and fighting against death (my translation).

Susan Bainbridge's *Writing Against Death* has a specific focus on Simone de Beauvoir's writing as a response to death, a preoccupation she traces in de Beauvoir's various autobiographical texts; in particular, the 'further "adieux"' of *La Cérémonie des Adieux* coming after *Toute Compte Fait* possibly suggesting 'a certain resistance to closure' (Bainbridge 2005, 26, 27). Bainbridge also draws on Elaine Marks's examination of the sheer size of de Beauvoir's oeuvre as a way of 'evad[ing] confrontation with her own mortality' and, within the texts, a 'refusal to cut or trim words, sentences and experiences can be explained by the obsession with death ... Simone writes to ... ward off the future' (Marks 1973, quoted in Bainbridge 2005, 19). In *The Year of Magical Thinking*, Didion reflects on her writing process (of another piece of work) as she nears the end of the first year after her husband's death: 'I have never written pieces fluently but this one seemed to be taking even longer than usual: I realized at some point that I was unwilling to finish it, because there was no one to read it', thus equating a delayed finished product with a delay in acknowledging the finality of death (Didion 2005, 214). Of the memoir itself she states, very near the end, 'I realize as I write this that I do not want to finish this account. Nor did I want to finish the year' (Didion 2005, 224–5). Although the death has occurred, her irrational attempts to hold on to Dunne (for example, resisting giving away his shoes, because he would need them when he returned) relate to her writing process. Both are closely tied to a resistance towards fully acknowledging, and thus moving on from, death. Joyce Carol Oates writes that 'All memoirs are journeys, investigations' and some are 'pilgrimages' (Oates 2011, 368). This invokes the sense of process and recording that I think is emphasized by seeing writing as testimony, but Oates also notes the completion of the process, of the journey: 'You begin at X, and you will end at Z. You *will end* – in some way' (Oates 2011, 368). In this articulation, there is no possible evasion of the end, whether by writing more slowly, or by writing almost endlessly, as in Marks's understanding of de Beauvoir's huge output. The end is not negotiable for Oates and, while writing can be a form of survival, an end to the project must still exist.

Mary Karr also identifies the relationship between writing and death as a particular reason for the attraction to autobiography: 'it's a kind of survival testimony. The fact that the person lives past the book, that the character goes on, is a kind of hopeful thing, a priori' (Sterling 2003). What is 'hopeful' here is the notion that authors do not die completely if they exist in print, as well as the notion that, whatever the events described in the writing (and in many memoirs they are particularly stressful, dangerous or difficult), the writer has evidently emerged alive, or is still emerging. Memoirist Dani Shapiro speaks to a similar quality of narrating the past. She describes attending Alcoholics Anonymous meetings where 'The stories were often harsh and painful, but there was redemption in the very fact that the teller had lived to tell the tale. It was never too late to begin again' (Shapiro 2010, 92). Although she is describing a process of verbal self-narration, the stories do eventually find their way into print, in Shapiro's own book, and the message is the same – that words can provide evidence of pain, fear and trauma, as well as the passing or easing of such experiences. The 'eloquence rising out of despair' that she describes alerts us to the despair as much as it does to the movement or passage suggested by 'rising', the way the narration moves away from the event and offers a degree of hope (Shapiro 2010, 92).

I do not see such a fundamental difference between the lives of men and women as Felman does, and, while I find Felman's discussion of how trauma is defined and how this definition often runs counter to the reality of many women's lives intriguing, I do not agree that all women's lives are built around (often repeated) instances of trauma. My focus here is instead to examine the way she sees women's writing as a response to such trauma:

> Because trauma cannot be simply remembered, it cannot simply be "confessed": it must be testified to, in a struggle shared between a speaker and a listener to recover something the speaker is not – and cannot be – in possession of. (Felman 1993, 16)

This sentence succinctly and intriguingly encapsulates some of the main themes I am engaging with in my short stories.

In particular, I appreciate the distinction she draws between memory of an event and participation in a form of reconstruction. Denying women's autobiographical writing the ability to be a 'confession', she immediately distances it from, most obviously and significantly, St Augustine's and Rousseau's *Confessions*, two major early autobiographical texts, but also from all autobiographies that adopt the idea of a unified voice confessing a story they are in full possession and awareness of.

I welcome her suggestion of a kind of writing that is almost collaborative in its shared effort towards discovery. For Felman, the bond between reader and writer is absolutely essential. In discussing Felman's approach, critic Linda Anderson suggests that 'Testimony is called for in a situation where the truth is not clear' and 'implies a relationship to events as evidence of truth' (Anderson 2001, 127). This understanding of autobiographical writing as testimony speaks to the multiplicity of stories making up an experience, a history, a life. Also, I submit that 'a situation where the truth is not clear' can describe the majority of human interactions.

This approach lifts the onus of establishing and stating the truth from the writing – the narrative becomes a voicing of a particular version, rather than a site in which a single truth is located. To write (and read) autobiography as testimony allows one to voice a memory, position or story without making any claim as to that story's exclusivity. The notion of a relationship to truth implies a fundamental division between 'the truth' and 'the story': if they can have a relationship, they cannot be the same thing. Such an understanding of autobiographical writing creates space for multiple, even conflicting, stories, which together can form a more complete (and complex) picture. Providing testimony, or offering one version as a contribution to a larger narrative, enables the complex web of entwined stories which make up any historical or individual event.

Testimonio as a subgenre

Testimonio as a genre or subgenre emerged mainly out of narratives of Latin American social injustice. This kind of writing is inextricably bound up with issues of multiplicity, collaborative reading and writing, and unfixed notions of truth, making it important to mention here. According to John Beverley, who has written extensively on testimonio, the closest English equivalent for this 'narrative form' is 'testimonial narrative' (Beverley 2004, ix). Beverley points out that although

> testimonio-like texts have existed for a long time at the margin of liter-
> ature … we can say that testimonio coalesced as a new narrative genre
> in the 1960s and further developed in close relation to the movements
> for national liberation and the generalized cultural radicalism of that
> decade. (Beverley 2004, 31)

He defines the form as:

> a novel or novella-length narrative in book or pamphlet (that is, printed
> as opposed to acoustic) form, told in the first person by a narrator who
> is also the real protagonist or witness of the events he or she recounts,
> and whose unit of narration is usually a "life" or a significant life
> experience. (Beverley 2004, 30–31)

Testimonio is a form of literary witnessing – it comes from a sense of, or situations of, 'catastrophe, unjustified massacre, irremediable loss, displacement, trauma, incomplete or inadequate mourning, and anger' (Beverley 2004, 24) and, using Felman and Daub's terminology, it can be read as a way to 'bear witness to … what we do not yet know of our lived historical relation to events of our time' (Felman and Daub 1992, xx). The above definition shows how testimonio binds the personal and the sociopolitical. It is a way of integrating an individual's story into a larger narrative of social injustice or violence; situating the self within a greater narrative is characteristic of testimonio. It is the voice of one telling the story of many: 'It speaks to us as an "I" that nevertheless stands for a multitude' (Beverley 2004, 27). Because so many testimonios tell the story of oppression and violence in a particular geographical area, the narrative uses an individualized voice to express to an often foreign reader a wider sense of the social and cultural atmosphere from which this voice speaks, thus 'facilitating an emotional identification with a distant other' (Lauritzen 2004, 24). In this way, testimonio is a tool or platform in addition to a personal narrative.

A particularly intriguing example is *I, Rigoberta Menchú* (1984). Nobel Peace Prize-winner Rigoberta Menchú's book consists of sections of an interview (transcribed and edited by Elisabeth Burgos-Debray) in which she recounts her life and that of her family 'during one of the most brutally repressive periods in [Guatemala's] history' (Lauritzen 2004, 22). In her account, Menchú describes the 'kidnapping, torture, and murder of her mother and another brother' (Lauritzen 2004, 22), and her witnessing of other events that are startling and very unsettling in their gruesomeness and violence. Subsequent research, most notably by David Stoll in his book *Rigoberta Menchú and the Story of all Poor Guatemalans* (1999), claimed that some events described in Menchú's text had not in fact been witnessed by her, primarily the death of her brother, and therefore pointed to the invention or fabrication of parts of her text. Stoll's claims were based on interviews he conducted in the area the killing of Menchú's brother was said to have occurred, and his conclusion that Menchú could not have been present led him to ask, 'What if much of Rigoberta's story is not true?' (Stoll 2008, xviii).

Support for Menchú and her text used the book's genre to defend the author's actions. This support suggested that, as a testimonio, the book speaks as a record and witness of many events in many lives, and testimonio is usually a political act in that it attempts to give voice to a previously silenced or oppressed group. With this goal, the testimonio speaks for more than one life: 'the first-person narrator almost always is emblematic of the larger group. She typically seeks to give voice to collective experience through narrating personal experience' (Lauritzen 2004, 26). As a testimonio, Menchú's text therefore would incorporate the lives of many in the combined story of the group. In agreement with the subgenre's specifications, Menchú's account could have included events which had actually happened to other individuals; as a spokesperson or collective voice, her words could include the stories of people who are not her; however, her account of her brother's death, if she was not present at that time, might complicate Beverley's definition noted above, if she was 'the real protagonist' but perhaps not a 'witness of the events he or she recounts'.

Another argument in support of Menchú's work was that of a 'bigger picture'. Because *I, Rigoberta Menchú*'s primary aim is to tell the story of an oppressed and violated group, it ultimately does not matter if Menchú was physically present at particular events, or if sequences of events occurred in precisely the way she describes. The point of the document is to use the voice of an individual to tell the story of a group, and bear witness to a collective experience. To break down events into researchable segments and research each strand of the story is to fundamentally misunderstand or ignore the subgenre and its greater purpose:

> The substantial truth is that the Guatemalan military did systemati-
> cally kidnap, torture, and kill Mayan Indians; the truth is that land is
> concentrated in the hands of a few and that landowners force workers
> to labor in unsafe and oppressive conditions; the truth is that Mayan
> Indians were forcibly relocated by the government. These truths are
> not in doubt ... so whatever details Menchú got wrong, they pale in
> comparison to the larger truth to which *I, Rigoberta Menchú* calls our
> attention. (Lauritzen 2004, 28–9)

Paul Lauritzen's choice of words above is interesting; I suspect that his support for the book extends to the 'details' that Menchú incorporated into the text while knowing that they had not happened to her, as well as the 'details' that she 'got wrong'. His support is also interesting considering his earlier-quoted understanding of testimonio as writing that seeks 'to give voice to collective experience through narrating personal experience' (Lauritzen 2004, 26). He seems to support the inclusion of others' stories in Menchú's account, but this definition seems to suggest that such inclusion should only happen if the narrator can share those stories through having had the same 'personal experience'.

The definition of testimonio is crucial to these interpretations of the text. If Menchú describes an event which later research shows she did not witness, the genre argument suggests that this is irrelevant – if the story functions to further awareness of these greater truths, or what Lauritzen calls 'the substantial truth' (Lauritzen 2004, 28), and if the story can be assumed to have plausibly happened to one of the group her testimony is representing, her invention is still truthful. Another individual would have witnessed this event, another victim would have been held captive or tortured, another sister would have seen the murder of her brother. Menchú's identification as speaker of this testimonio should not suggest that hers is the only important or relevant experience.

What did Menchú herself say? It is worth returning to the text itself, to consider her opening:

> My name is Rigoberta Menchú. I am twenty-three years old. This is my testimony. I didn't learn it from a book and I didn't learn it alone. I'd like to stress that it's not only *my* life, it's also the testimony of my people. It's hard for me to remember everything that's happened to me in my life … the important thing is that what has happened to me has happened to many other people too: My story is the story of all poor Guatemalans. My personal experience is the reality of a whole people. (Burgos-Debray 1984, 1)

The notion of learning testimony (and indeed learning it collaboratively) complicates thinking of it as a highly personal and individualized truth or report, and suggests that it can be learned or passed on. This is echoed in her claim that she can speak the testimony of others. This narrator admits the weakness of memory and therefore admits that certain events may be misremembered. She also posits her own voice as encompassing those of many other individuals, which undercuts debate over her authority to narrate events at which she was not physically present. John Beverley notes that the genre of testimonio is such that 'each individual testimonio evokes an absent polyphony of other voices, other possible lives and experiences' (Beverley 2004, 34). This statement can be seen to support Menchú's introduction, but I think actually advances it: if the words of the narrator of testimonio can speak for 'other possible lives and experiences', this opens up the writing to include a bewildering array of 'possible' stories and individuals, and further removes it from an account of actual happenings.

A comparison of essays by John Beverley, who has written widely on the Menchú case, opens up the discussion further. In his 1996 essay 'The Real Thing', Beverley outlines Stoll's claims, and states that Menchú 'categorically denied' Stoll's suggestion that she did not see her brother die (Beverley 2004, 71). However, in his 2001 essay 'What Happens When the Subaltern Speaks?', Beverley notes that, in response to Stoll's claim that she was not an eyewitness to things she claims to have been, Menchú

> has publicly conceded that she grafted elements of other people's experiences and stories onto her own. In particular, she has admitted that she was not herself present at the massacre of her brother … and that the account of the event … came instead from her mother, who (she claims) was in fact there. She says that these interpolations were a way of making her story a collective account, rather than an autobiography. (Beverley 2004, 81)

It is curious that Menchú would shift from categorically denying something to conceding it, especially considering how clearly her position is expressed in the text itself. For instance, her introduction seems to indicate that what follows is not an autobiography. Was there a need for other means of reinforcing this statement? David Stoll also speculates on why Menchú made the choices she did, and he thinks it was for a slightly more specific reason than 'making her story a collective account'. Stoll claims that Menchú 'drastically revised the prewar experience of her village to suit the needs of the revolutionary organization she had joined' (Stoll 2008, xx). In this description, collectivism becomes ambiguous because Stoll sets up 'her village' and 'the revolutionary organization' as distinct groups without wholly common interests.

Much of the debate between Stoll and Beverley (and others) reverts to a debate over testimonio generally, and what the genre permits. Indeed, David Stoll has recently reflected that it may be 'time to liberate *I, Rigoberta Menchú* from the category of testimonio' because her unreliability as an eyewitness has been established (Stoll 2001, 406). According to Beverley, in testimonio, 'the metonymic function of the narrative voice', i.e. the narrator's voice standing for the voice of many, is part of the 'narrative convention' of testimonio, 'even in those cases when the narrator is, for example, a drug addict or a criminal' (Beverley 2004, 34).

At this point it seems particularly appropriate to discuss James Frey's *A Million Little Pieces* (2003). The case is a famous one, but I will briefly introduce it here. Frey published the book as an account of his experience in an alcohol and drug rehabilitation institute. In the book he is twenty-three and close to death as a result of his abuse of alcohol and drugs over a period of years. He describes his recovery and, briefly, some significant events from before he entered the institution; the book ends with strong suggestions that he has fully recovered. The book was wildly popular and quickly garnered many fans, notably Oprah Winfrey, who was partially responsible for pushing Frey into superstardom through her effusive praise of both book and author. However, in 2006 *The Smoking Gun* website published a scathing and excruciatingly researched article outlining where and how Frey had invented his past. Although he initially insisted there were no fabrications, Frey eventually admitted these were present in his memoir. Public outcry followed. Many readers felt betrayed, especially because the book had resonated so strongly with them. His writing about addiction and recovery was seen as unreliable because the experiences on which the book was founded were now in question. His publisher indicated that all subsequent editions of the book would contain an author's note in which Frey explained his actions, and offered refunds to all customers who felt they had been deceived.

The book might have been received differently had James Frey claimed it as a testimonio, thus allowing it to speak of a collective experience of overcoming drug abuse. However, he claimed the opposite, that it was his own story. In this light, it was perhaps his insistence that this was a personal story that provoked much of the violent public reaction he faced. Whereas fabrications in Menchú's book may be understood as simply an element of the testimonio genre, fabrications in Frey's book were looked upon very differently. Frey's writing contains events which could plausibly be expected to have featured in the lives of many individuals addicted to drugs; as a story of overcoming substance abuse, it could be said to speak for many. Frey did not claim his book was a testimonio, although he touches on such an interpretation by arguing, in his author's note, that his book tells a story of recovery: 'I wanted to write a book that would detail the fight addicts and alcoholics experience in their minds and in their bodies, and detail why that fight is difficult to win' (Frey 2003, v).

In this comparison, setting aside the fact that Frey mainly suffered as a result of his own actions and decisions rather than being systematically oppressed by a government, his account can be said to be the voices of many told by the words of one, without being any less believable than Menchú's. Such collectivism opens up the narrative to include numerous voices, including some that are invented or hypothetical: 'If these things are not literally true about her own life', argues Paul Lauritzen about Menchú, 'they are certainly true of many in Guatemala … what happened to hundreds of Guatemalans could have happened to Rigoberta Menchú' (Lauritzen 2004, 27). Of course such events *could* have happened to Menchú. A claim like this stretches to include writing that is simply speculative, and can be said to lose the authenticity that initially gave it added weight and significance. In fact, it leads straight back to Lauritzen's introduction to his article, where he details the response he faced after describing his infertility and then the birth of his child. In the introduction he suggests that

> Experience is understood to be largely unmediated, a sort of brute fact on which one can build an argument. So the appeal to experience functions as an effort to reach moral bedrock. This is why the possibility that the experience is not factual is so threatening. If the experience is fictional, there is no foundation on which the arguments finally rest. (Lauritzen 2004, 20)

This quotation helps to unpack the interesting comparison between the two texts. Both include fictionalized elements. These fictional elements could very plausibly have happened to other individuals within the greater 'groups' that Menchú and Frey belonged to, but they still did not happen to Frey and Menchú. Narrating events that probably happened to someone is not quite the same as narrating events to which one was a witness or participant. And yet there is a very palpable difference between Laurtizen's (and others') defence of Menchú's text, and the public scourging Frey received after *The Smoking Gun* broke its story.

David Stoll recounts the atmosphere during a conference when John Beverley 'swooped down ... and dropped the bomb' about Stoll's 'doubts' regarding Menchú's text:

> Gasps and "no's" escaped from some of the audience. Meanwhile, who should be holding forth in an auditorium but the cult figure herself [Menchú], who was often an honored guest at these occasions. (Stoll, quoted in Beverley 2001, xiv-xv)

The suggestion of Menchú's unreliability is received with horror. Compare this with Karr's criticism of Frey, noted above, and Frey's own account of his experience: 'On more than one occasion, I was walking down the street and somebody walked up and served me with legal papers ... I got sued for a lot of stuff by a lot of people' (*The Oprah Winfrey Show* 2006). This quotation comes from Frey's appearance on *The Oprah Winfrey Show*, a platform which reaches millions. This was the venue where the person who had played a large part in his success swooped down and dropped her own bomb: 'it is difficult for me to talk to you because I feel really duped. But more importantly, I feel that you betrayed millions of readers ... Why did you lie?' (*The Oprah Winfrey Show* 2006). These two controversies played out in very different realms, but I think a comparison is nonetheless illuminating and useful. Do both these books build their 'arguments' on an equally solid 'foundation'? Is one fictional experience more 'threatening' than another?

For *A Million Little Pieces* and *I, Rigoberta Menchú*, both texts rooted in personal experience and both featuring inconsistencies and fabrications, to receive such different receptions encourages us to compare them more closely. It is unsatisfactory to simply say that Menchú's text deserves more respect and consideration because she is talking about human rights abuses and violence against innocent victims, whereas Frey can be the receptacle of public vitriol because his book is about a remarkably self-destructive wealthy young man who makes a series of ill-judged decisions. It is equally unsatisfactory, in this context, to claim that Frey's book is worse than Menchú's, that one author's piece is better crafted and thus more worthy of praise. I am not interested in literary merit here; I am interested in how readers react to texts in which they 'discover' false elements, and the fact that these two texts are similarly featured and yet almost diametrically opposed in terms of author reception is an intriguing entrance into thinking about how we define and react to exposed untruths.

We may be angry at Frey for profiting financially from deliberately stating that things had occurred to him which had not actually occurred to him, and disapprove of his choice to release his book as memoir rather than a novel. Likewise, we may accept that Menchú's choice to include fabrications in her account resulted from her choice to work within the testimonio genre, and from a (more valid?) desire to transmit the atmosphere of systematic violence and abuse against 'her people'. To believe either possibility relies on considering authorial intention, making both possibilities frustrating and ultimately unknowable. Even if both scenarios are true, both authors' actions are still technically the same.

A final point on Frey's text refers to what I above call his choice to release his book as a memoir. In actual fact, this was not exclusively his choice at all. The environment into which books are released is highly relevant to their reception, and it should be noted that Frey did originally try to sell his manuscript as a novel. He was repeatedly unsuccessful in this attempt, and it was eventually released as a memoir. This decision was very likely motivated by issues of branding, of marketability, and above all of profitability.

When Frey's book came out, it was well-placed to benefit from a readership hungry for memoir, specifically stories of great personal difficulty. His book served a fascination with witnessing personal anguish, and for this reason, his readership was probably much higher than it would have been had he published the work as a novel. His publishers would have suspected this, and the decision to release the manuscript as a memoir had much to do with projected income. As we have discussed, autobiographical writing, or writing that claims to be autobiographical, has the ability to connect with readers, or the ability to encourage readers to try to connect with it, in a particularly intimate way. It allows many readers to feel 'spoken to' and invited into an author's internal life, in a way that other writing does not. This is because so many people value truthfulness and transparency, and value the difficulty that often comes with releasing personal narratives. For this reason, Frey's book would likely have been judged to carry more of an impact, and thus sell more, if it could be considered by readers as autobiographical. The decision to market it as a memoir had much to do with the higher sales that would hopefully ensue (and in this estimation the publishers were entirely correct), and perhaps this specific context and set of circumstances is behind much of the fury and disgust Frey met with. The clear suggestion that Frey was entirely willing to deceive his entire readership for financial gain, and that he was supported in these actions by his publishers, who also stood to benefit financially, drastically affected the way readers considered his actions and the appearance of fabricated elements in his account. He and Menchú differ not so much in their actions, but more in the context into which their books were released, the subject matter with which they dealt and the sheer scale of reader response.

The approach to writing testimony, and the reading of texts as testimonies, as illustrated in this chapter, removes the burden of absolute truth from telling a story about one's life, and introduces an aspect of shared effort, or joint work, towards understanding a greater narrative. Personal histories are multiple, and the complexity of human experience, as well as the nuance of individual perceptions, means that an account with depth, validity and accuracy will necessarily include multiplicity, in terms of tellers, in terms of viewpoints, in terms of response. This multiplicity need not take away from the truthfulness of the writing; it should be understood that readers can and will bring their own interpretations and views to a text, helping shape their response to it.

Paul John Eakin discusses the multiplicity of truth in a reading of Mary Karr's *The Liars' Club*. Eakin identifies how Karr 'wants to get it right' (Eakin 2008, 64), shown by her efforts to verify (or at least find support for) her memories through consulting photographs and asking other family members to confirm them. But 'get[ting] it right' can mean different things; in Eakin's reading of Karr's book, 'what seems to count most for her is her memory's report of what she once thought and felt; *this* is the past she seeks to reconstruct' (Eakin 2008, 64). And indeed, this echoes Karr's own words quoted earlier: 'I know better than anybody else how I felt at fifteen or at forty. You might remember something I did that I don't remember, but I know how I felt' (Karr 2009). If Karr's 'allegiance to truth ... is less an allegiance to a factual record that biographers and historians could check than an allegiance to remembered consciousness' (Eakin 2008, 64), the contents of the book are rooted in memory rather than otherwise recorded events. This allegiance has the potential to colour all authorial decisions, and Eakin's differentiation between the two allegiances becomes fascinating when he introduces evidence of the fiction of memory; that is, that the brain perceives memory as an invention rather than a reconstruction or mental retrieval of past events (I will explore this topic in greater detail in Chapters Three and Four).

Eakin's identification of multiple 'allegiance[s]' punctures the borders between fact and fiction, allowing truth/untruth and truthfulness/untruthfulness to intermingle, all complicated by the distance between lived experience and writing process. Does this distance create the ambiguity? In other words, do untruthful elements begin emerging when one re-works life events, shapes them into a narrative, orders and chooses which ones to present? I do not think so. The ambiguity exists from the start – ambiguity over how things took place can occur in the absence (or presence) of any written account. Human perspective and perception are so diverse that, especially if, like historian and memoirist Jill Ker Conway, we understand there to be 'no meta-narrative ... no fixed history, no history that is true', the very nature of transforming experience into language requires the choosing of one transformative sequence, authoring one version, at the cost of all others (Conway 1995, 57).

This inherent rejection of other versions in establishing our own version extends to all writings. Conway provides an example: 'if you want to tell the history of the world in 1492, we Westerners talk about Columbus, but if you're from the Arab world a very different series of events is important' (Conway 1995, 57). By its nature and processes, autobiographical writing cannot reflect a whole truth, not because we cannot produce truthful writing, but because the lack of any single truth renders attempts to verbalize it impossible. We can write *a* truth rather than *the* truth, and our writing can be truthful without being researchable.

Toni Morrison describes her strict relationship to her material, and her responsibility to it, when she says that her 'single gravest responsibility ... is not to lie' (Morrison 1987, 193). She explains how she can write fiction while honouring this responsibility by seeing her work as a filling-in process. She describes her combination of invention and fact as 'a kind of literary archaeology: On the basis of some information and a little bit of guesswork you journey to a site to see what remains were left behind and to reconstruct the world that these remains imply' (Morrison 1987, 192). This practice is made fiction 'by the nature of the imaginative act', but still 'yield[s] up a kind of truth' (Morrison 1987, 192).

This kind of truth resurfaces in Virginia Woolf's *A Room of One's Own*, where she suggests that 'when a subject is highly controversial', 'one cannot hope to tell the truth' (Woolf 1929, 4). Instead, one can only 'give one's audience the chance of drawing their own conclusions as they observe the limitations, the prejudices, the idiosyncrasies of the speaker. *Fiction here is likely to contain more truth than fact*' (Woolf 1929, 4–5, my emphasis). Here she echoes Morrison's truth born of fiction, but she also refers to the act of writing as testimony, where the addition of one's voice, complete with its 'limitations ... prejudices ... [and] idiosyncrasies' can contribute to the formation of a truthful narrative.

· Haruki Murakami's *The Wind-Up Bird Chronicle* (1998) plays with these questions of what is real (and really happening), and how we can ever determine this. This is a novel, rather than an autobiography, but it has much to say about how we can access truthfulness through storytelling, and how we approach writing as a means of learning about ourselves. The protagonist,

Toru Okada, slowly becomes drawn into a world where hallucination and real experience seem indistinguishable, and identity is easily shifting. He encounters a man named Cinnamon, who does not speak but leaves messages for Okada through a computer programmed to allow him to read a sequence of sixteen stories that Okada learns are based on real events. This arrangement clearly posits the sixteen stories as a substitute for conversation with Cinnamon, or any other form of verbal language exchange through which Okada might learn the answers to his questions about Cinnamon's life and past. This is also a good example of living narratively – Cinnamon never speaks, which frustrates attempts to get to know him, but has found another way to narrate his life into being, and share such narration with others. By reading these stories, Okaka is getting to know Cinnamon, and discovers that:

> He was engaged in a search for the meaning of his own existence. And he was hoping to find it by looking into the events that had preceded his birth.
>
> To do that, Cinnamon had to fill in those blank spots in the past that he could not reach with his own hands. By using those hands to make a story, he was trying to supply the missing links. From those stories he had heard over and over again from his mother, he derived further stories in an attempt to re-create the enigmatic figure of his grandfather in a new setting. He inherited from his mother's stories that fundamental style that he used, unaltered, in his own stories: namely, the assumption that *fact may not be truth, and truth may not be factual.* The question of which parts of a story were factual and which were not was not a very important one for Cinnamon. The important question was not what his grandfather did but what his grandfather *might have done.* He learned the answer to this question as soon as he succeeded in telling a story. (Murakami 1998, 525)

This passage is worth quoting at length because it so perfectly encapsulates my intention in my own stories, and a fundamental argument in this book. The fact that a novel, a work of fiction, so aptly explains and describes the intentions of this project, which is deeply rooted in lived history, is an irony I take pleasure in. Okada realizes that this ambiguity between truth and fiction is central to Cinnamon's project, and indeed it is crucial to mine. The line between truth and fiction is not clear, or maybe there is no line, or maybe sometimes you can see the line and sometimes you cannot. It does not matter, because sometimes *'fact may not be truth, and truth may not be factual'*, so spending time sorting stories into categories may defeat the purpose of having written them. Much the same way many of the texts I have discussed approach truth and fiction as though they are not two distinct and mutually exclusive entities, my own stories move between invention and fact, and indeed occasionally confuse one for the other.

A good example is the story of my brother's narrow escape from a cumbersome forename of illustrious origin ('Isambard'; see Appendix). This story was repeated endlessly in my childhood. I only discovered how I have misremembered it when the most superficial research revealed a factual error in my version of the story. Thus the story is not strictly true, but I include it as one of a series of truthful stories about my childhood – this was the source of my brother's name to me, for years.

The story is now rooted in the 'fact' of my childhood rather than the 'fact' of my parents' experience naming my brother. The story of my memory of their experience has become fused to the initial story of their actual experience, despite the two happening years apart. This fragmenting and layering is also alluded to in another passage from Murakami's novel, a passage that highlights the organic process of storytelling, the way it develops and grows, sometimes independently of the teller(s). In this passage Cinnamon's mother describes the way that

> Cinnamon asked me to tell him the story again and again. I must have told it to him a hundred, two-hundred, five-hundred times, but not just repeating the same thing every time. Whenever I told it to him, Cinnamon would ask me to tell him some other little story contained in the main story. (Murakami 1998, 444)

This is how stories operate, of course. There is never really a 'main story'. Rather, 'Everything [is] intertwined, with the complexity of a three-dimensional puzzle – a puzzle in which truth [is] not necessarily fact, and fact not necessarily truth' (Murakami 1998, 527). Instead, these categories are so blended that they become distorted, and then detract from the point, the articulation of memory. The story, in its telling, changes the memory. Instead of the memory that I took as truth, what I now have is the articulation, the verbal description, of an error, a mistake that I believed in for a long time, which can still represent a kind of truth, and which I can still be truthful about.

The creation of persona

Memoirist and critic Vivian Gornick's views on authorial honesty and truth also relate to an understanding of the narrative voice as a structure, or

PERSONA/VOICE

device. This tool permits deviations from fact in the service of better story-telling. According to Gornick, the autobiographical author must establish who exactly they 'are' in the writing process, and in the work itself. She names this establishment process the creation of persona, claiming it is integral to successful personal narrative. The persona is not synonymous with the author, and is specific to the work. The persona is an essential tool in memoir and autobiography, as it fixes the person writing in their relation to the story; it is 'the instrument of illumination' (Gornick 2001, 7). The persona is indivisible from the story; indeed, it is the method of telling. This created voice is the means through which honest, truthful autobiographical writing emerges. It is the way that an author relates 'the most exact and insightful understanding of past experience' (Barbour 1992, 26).

The persona is fashioned 'out of the raw material of a writer's own undis-guised being' and becomes 'integral' (Gornick 2001, 6) to the telling of the tale: the persona is linked inextricably to the telling, and is distinct from the multitude of other elements present in the author's character that have no bearing on the story. The image is one of a particular self being constructed from parts of a person's other selves. This constructed voice is distinguished by existing solely to tell this particular story. In explaining the origin of this theory, Gornick describes watching a woman eulogizing her former mentor: 'The speaker never lost sight of why she was speaking – or perhaps more important, of *who* was speaking' (Gornick 2001, 6). Here she echoes Virginia Woolf, who finds that 'so many [memoirs] are failures' because they describe occurrences, but neglect to 'say what the person was like to whom it happened' (Woolf 1967, 65). For Woolf, the 'whom' is essential: 'the events mean very little unless we know first to whom they happened' (Woolf 1967, 65). Of course, defining or even fully describing this 'whom' does not come easily, but here Woolf indicates that, for a reader at least, meaning only arrives once identity is somehow understood/expressed. Gornick continues with her example of the eulogist:

> Of the various selves at her disposal (she was, after all, many people – a daughter, a lover, a bird-watcher, a New Yorker), she knew … the only proper self to invoke was the one that had been apprenticed. That was the self in whom this story resided. (Gornick 2001, 6)

This process of creation, then, involves identifying, understanding, selecting, isolating and using a particular voice, refusing to allow other selves to intrude upon this instrument of storytelling. In writing *Pilgrim at Tinker Creek* Annie Dillard faced another manifestation of this problem: what to put in and what to leave out – in other words, what was the story really about? She decided to 'leave out many things that were important to my life but of no concern for the present book ... I see no reason to drag everybody off to Wyoming just because I want to tell them about my summer vacation' (Dillard 1987, 154). The summer vacation in Wyoming may have been a critical time in Dillard's life; or maybe it wasn't. We don't know because Dillard has decided we don't need to know. Even if it was critical to her life, it is not critical to telling the story of *Pilgrim at Tinker Creek*, and the narrative persona that Dillard has constructed to tell this story is not connected to that experience, and so it stays out.

The persona is therefore simultaneously the author and not the author. It cannot be divided from the story, and, in memoir and autobiography, the story is usually that of an individual. Yet it is fashioned, constructed in a conscious manner, *by* the individual, and exists at a distance from the material at hand. Erica Jong describes the four primary characters in her novel *Inventing Memory* by saying: 'Each had a distinctive voice and way of looking at the world ... each was me and not-me' (Jong 1997, 68). Even in her fictional characters, Jong finds this process of simultaneous linkage and division between her identity and her characters, but, she notes, 'a memoir is tethered to one's own experience in a particularly limiting way: The observing consciousness of the book is rooted in a real person' (Jong 1997, 68). If we understand 'observing consciousness' as another way of saying 'persona', Jong is articulating the same process as Gornick, though Jong seems to find it a more limiting process than novel-writing. This observing consciousness, this crafted, fashioned, narratorial voice, is both self and not-self; tied to a real being, but developed by that being into a functional identity – its function limited to its use in the story it relates.

The persona, or narrative voice, once established, has itself a double relationship with the events in the book. The persona is both bound up in those events and stands aside and apart from them. As the subject matter largely concerns the individual who has fashioned the persona, and indeed dictates the fashioning process, the story itself serves to highlight the author. Autobiographical writing is a means of singling oneself out, stepping into the light, broadcasting yourself to the world. 'Autobiography begins in dissociation', according to critic John Sturrock; it is 'the writer stepping out front on his own in order to impose himself on us' (Sturrock 1993, 12). Personal narrative remains a genre in which the author is taken as a subject, usually *the* subject. Paradoxically, to do so requires an element of distance, of remove. For the author to construct a narrative overlying a framework of lived experience and past events, it is necessary to stand apart from them, even while constantly figuring as the subject matter.

The creation of persona was the most complex aspect of my own project, but something I gave little thought to before reading more extensively about the process. Questioning how these stories were about me only took place after many of them were written. Many early stories were built closely along the lines of stories I had heard as a child, over and over again. I did not question that these stories were about me, since they played such a pivotal role in my developing understanding of who I was and where I was from; it almost did not occur to me that they might not be about me. I understood, of course, that some concerned events that had happened in places I have never been to, during a time when I was not alive, to people I had never met, but on a deeper level they were such a part of the fabric of the way I saw myself, that it seemed they *were* me, and therefore about me. I read my assumption as an example of Gornick's view that telling 'a story of anything that happened' in one's life 'without the context of other people' (Botton 2010) is impossible, and Felman's belief that 'people tell their stories ... through others' stories' (Felman 1993, 18).

However, in a more literal way, these short pieces were not about me at all; many had occurred long before I was born. As I wrote more, my understanding of my role in them changed, as did my understanding of my status as the storyteller. Because they covered such a large period of time, my relationship to them needed to be flexible. This flexibility enabled me to simultaneously describe events that had happened to my parents long before I was born, as well as comment on experiences that happened to me as a young adult, or assign intention and action to family members I had never known.

This multiplicity was fascinating to me, and its relativism was something to take comfort in. If my understanding of autobiographical writing was that it simply represented one version of events, my understanding and telling of my own stories was valid. The stories included in this book are ones that directly entered my life through being told or through actually happening in my lifetime; one of my goals was to break down the initially significant difference I saw between those two methods of experiencing, or 'receiving', a story. Hearing a story is an experience of a narrative; featuring in a story is another kind of experience. If I was true to my own experiences, be they of lived events or heard stories, I could claim that I was being truthful to my version of events; like Mary Karr, I knew best how I remembered something. Didn't I? My stories exist according to a fundamental wish to express my truth of particular events in my family's life. The writing persona, then, was one fashioned out of my 'undisguised' self, one privileging my actions as a writer. I was most interested in exploring these memories through stories that gave me space to test the boundaries of authorship.

Gornick explains how, upon re-reading some favourite authors (Joan Didion among them), she saw that in each case the writer was possessed of an insight that organized the writing, and in each case a persona had been created to serve the insight … it wasn't their confessing voices I was responding to, it was their truth-speaking personae. By which I mean that organic wholeness of being in a narrator that the reader experiences as reliable; the one we can trust will take us on a journey. (Gornick 2001, 23–4)

In this quotation, the personae are identifiable to her. I read this description as suggesting that the persona, because active in the storytelling, is developing as the story is, rather than initially being developed and then commencing the story. Although I can find in her words the suggestion that the creation of persona should take place before the writing process (if the persona influences the writing and indeed is the method of telling, it follows that the persona must precede storytelling), I see this creation as a process that can intertwine with the writing process.

I am intrigued by her belief that an identifiable and trustworthy persona is key to writing that a reader can connect to and believe in. More specifically, in my stories I wanted readers to 'trust' that I would 'take [them] on a journey', but attaining 'organic wholeness of being' as a narrator seemed too subjective. No matter how recognizable these personae are to Gornick, they remain her projections onto other individuals (the actual writers). I felt unable to be the judge, or even witness, of how others saw my narratorial wholeness. A discussion of this potential trusting relationship between author and reader, and the deep desire many readers feel for this kind of trust, will conclude this chapter.

At its root, Gornick's theory suggests that to write memoir that others will believe, an author must have clear knowledge of where the narratorial voice is coming from. She finds this to be true in her own autobiographical writing, as well as in that of others, as we can see from her comments above regarding the 'truth-speaking personae'. As a result of this persona comes trust on the part of the reader, trust that the author is well-placed to transport the reader to a new world, through the writing. We can understand this desire to believe in a story in different ways. Across genres, we can understand it as synonymous with strong, well-crafted writing, believable characters, engrossing plot, etc. This is why fiction can draw us in so powerfully and convince us of its world. This is also why we often turn to fiction to understand (our) reality, because the storyworld can be a useful tool to understand the world outside the story.

But in memoir and autobiography, this desire is often complicated by the desire to believe not only in the storyworld, but also in the fact that the events we are reading about happened in the real world. Readers often want to not only become engrossed in the narrative, but also to know that what is being described happened, and not just in the pages of the book. If we believe that it did happen, we do not have to agree to, or even accept, the illusory elements of a sustained narrative, because this sustained narrative does not rely on or employ invention/illusion.

Coleridge coined his famous phrase at the beginning of the nineteenth century, arguing that poets who could 'transfer from [their] inward nature a human interest and a semblance of truth' could engage their audience into a 'willing suspension of disbelief', i.e. if an audience could find a way to relate to the artist, and had a willingness to believe in the art, they would be prepared to receive a work of art as though it was true (Coleridge 1817, 6). The idea that the audience is 'willing[ly]' suspending disbelief speaks to this idea of desiring to believe in a piece of art, a desire that I think is accentuated when engaging with a form that allows us, even encourages us, to think that this form does not provide a 'semblance of truth', but rather the real thing.

This 'willing[ly]' is important. It indicates agency of both audience and artist. The artist produces the work, but the audience does not simply receive it passively. They are active during the performance, or reading, and Coleridge's 'willing[ly]' suggests the way that an audience comes to a piece of art with their own desires and expectations – desires and expectations which can only be assumed by the artist.

Suspension of disbelief is now more loosely used, referring generally to an audience's willingness to engage with a piece of art on the terms it presents. This suggests a conscious submersion into the world of the art, which is desirable in all writing, I believe, but has a different initial motivation in terms of autobiographical writing. However much we note our own distance from the author/subject, we are inclined to proceed from the knowledge that this did happen to someone. In a way, I believe there is a strong desire to reject suspension of disbelief when reading autobiographical writing – we want to believe, rather than agree to our own unbelieving. We are attracted to the idea that a particular piece of writing *can* be believed, will not provoke our disbelief, or at least will assure us that any disbelief is misplaced.

This combination of the beliefs and desires that readers and writers bring to a piece of work emerges as a foundational aspect of considering autobiographical writing in terms of a pact, or contract, or agreement, or even bond. This is despite the fact that such desires and beliefs will usually be unknown to the other party. Discussion of such a relationship or contract between reader and writer appears often in theoretical discussion of autobiographical writing, to a significantly greater degree than it appears in discussion of writing in general. At this point I wish to further discuss how such a pact is conceived of and articulated, and what happens when it is not fulfilled.

For many people, one of the main allures of reading memoir and autobiography is the proximity they allow themselves to feel to the writer. There is something thrilling about feeling that the words we take in are a direct form of access to the mind and feelings of another individual, and a means for us to relate to the life and experiences of a person we (probably) have never met. Jill Ker Conway suggests that the reason for autobiographical writing's persistent appeal is that 'we *want* to know how the world looks from inside another person's experience, and when that craving is met by a convincing narrative, we find it deeply satisfying' (Conway 1995, 6). Of course, a 'convincing narrative' can be found in fiction, but, approached as fiction, would not satisfy the desire to read about 'another person's experience'.

Conway argues that because we human beings are 'stuck' in our bodies, we develop the desire to understand how others perceive and experience the world; our identities 'crave the confirmation of like experience, or the enlargement or transformation which can come from viewing a similar experience from a different perspective' (Conway 1995, 6). Because this desire for accessing and understanding multiple viewpoints is a persistent human quality, we will continue to seek ways in which to indulge it, especially since it will never be truly satisfied – as theorist Philippe Lejeune suggests, 'We do not really know how to get out of the self; that is to say, to represent, equally with our own, a point of view different from our own' (Lejeune 1980, 45). We also need not see this yearning or urge to see the inside of another person's mind, to experience the world as they do, as an indulgence or simple desire; our lives are built around our ability to relate to others, and the way we construct our perceptions of ourselves tends to rely on systems of measuring and judging ourselves according to the lives of others.

Because we simultaneously see and measure ourselves in relation to others but remain stuck inside our bodies, it becomes particularly seductive to image that we are in the hands of a writer who can transcend these divides, and present us with an entrance into their unique worldview. And because we approach these texts with what some might call a naïve desire – to be told a fantastic story that we yet believe, by someone *who was there* – there exists a particularly vulnerable relationship between reader and writer.

This desire to believe is problematic, especially when it turns into expectation. Understanding memoir and autobiography as truthful is sometimes described as an agreement between author and reader, but the different ways of understanding truth and the general danger of involving a reader's conception of authorial intention in any reading means that such

PACT

understanding can only really ever be a decision for the reader alone. Do they believe what they are reading, or not? The more autobiography is tested in terms of truthfulness – as in contemporary cases like *A Million Little Pieces* and Augusten Burroughs's *Running with Scissors* – the less precedent there is for any pact or contract with an author, regardless of genre. If we persist in assuming that, by writing (and publishing) a memoir or an autobiography, an author is entering into a contract with 'an intention to honor the signature' (Lejeune 1982, quoted in Anderson 2001, 3), we will encounter cases where there is disagreement between the terms of the contract, and the intentions of the parties. Anderson points out the slipperiness of this expectation: 'Trust the author, this rather circular argument goes, if s/he seems to be trustworthy' (Anderson 2001, 3).

Philippe Lejeune's body of work on autobiography is significant; the French critic has written extensively on the topic, and his writings track the development of his own ideas and theories regarding this form of writing. A discussion of this development process, and his efforts to pin down a definition of autobiography, is highly relevant here. For his 1971 *L'Autobiographie en France*, Lejeune attempted to define autobiography 'so as to be in a position to develop a coherent corpus of texts' (Lejeune 1975, 3). He tells us this in 'The Autobiographical Pact' (Lejeune 1975), an essay in which he outlines this definition, and discusses cases which complicate it. The definition is: 'Retrospective prose narrative written by a real person concerning his own existence, where the focus is his individual life, in particular the story of his personality' (Lejeune 1975, 4).

Lejeune offers four categories in which a text must satisfy criteria in order to be an autobiography. It is noteworthy that he distinguishes memoir from autobiography because the 'subject treated' (one of the four categories) of memoir is not the 'individual life, story of a personality' – presumably because memoir is most often the story of a particular time or sequence of events in an individual's life (Lejeune 1975, 4). Most important to note here is Lejeune's understanding of the difference between the autobiographical novel and autobiography. For Lejeune, 'identity between the *author*, the *narrator*, and the *protagonist*' was necessary to count a work as autobiography, and this identity rests largely on the author naming himself (Lejeune 1982, quoted in Anderson 2001, 2). 'Autobiography is not a guessing game', he says; the author either identifies himself as author, narrator and protagonist, or he does not – in which case, it is not autobiography (Lejeune 1975, 13). It can be, however, an autobiographical novel.

This strict criteria leads to the 'essential' element in identifying autobiography – 'the autobiographical pact': 'The autobiographical pact is the affirmation in the text of this identity [as author/narrator/protagonist],

referring back in the final analysis to the *name* of the author on the cover'
(Lejeune 1975, 13, 14). This identity can be represented to the reader
'*Implicitly*', by including the word 'autobiography' in the title or in an
introductory section, or '*In an obvious way*', by naming the author as the
protagonist and narrator within the text; or both methods can be used simultaneously (Lejeune 1975, 14).

As Linda Anderson points out, 'the difficulty is how to apply this
condition since the "identity" Lejeune speaks of can never really be established except as a matter of intention on the part of the author' (Anderson
2001, 2). Indeed, even in this early essay, Lejeune articulates the necessity of
involving authorial intention in an understanding of such a pact – a necessity
which seems highly problematic, and which he later revisits. He claims that
the pact is necessary because, at a purely textual level, there simply is no way
to distinguish between autobiography and novel: 'How to distinguish autobiography from the autobiographical novel? … if we remain on the level of
analysis within the text, there is *no difference*' (Lejeune 1975, 13). Authorial
intention is thus required, along with a reader's belief in this intention,
because, after all, 'All the methods that autobiography uses to convince us of
the authenticity of its narrative can be imitated in the novel, and often have
been' (Lejeune 1975, 13).

In his foreword to a collection of Lejeune's writing on autobiography,
Paul John Eakin speaks to this same difficulty, though he understands it
as something more of a paradox: 'To read autobiography in the manner of
Lejeune, one must be both sophisticated, alive to its imaginative art, *and*
naïve, believing in the sincerity of the author's intention' (Lejeune 1989, xiii).
In his later writing, Lejeune revisits his early essay and outlines the development of his ideas, noting that it was 'of value as hypothesis and working
tool' rather than definitive statement, and that the very terminology used
immediately led to ambiguity:

> The term autobiographical "pact" had fascinated me. It evokes some
> mythological images, like those "pacts with the devil" where someone
> dips his pen into his own blood to sell his soul. "Contract" is more
> prosaic: we are at a notary's office. The analogical use of the two terms is
> not without danger. If it were only a matter of indicating that someone
> is living up to his obligations, that he is referring to systems of conven-
> tions, fine. But the term "contract" suggests that it is a matter of explicit
> rules, fixed and recognized in a common agreement by authors and
> readers: at the notary's office, the two parties sign the same contract, at
> the same instant. No such thing happens in literature. (Lejeune 1986,
> 125–6)

Another important multiplicity he brings into his understanding is that of authorial intention:

> As far as the author is concerned, there can be a shifting between the initial intention and that which the reader will finally attribute to him … Finally, we must admit that different readings of the same text, different interpretations of the same proposed "contract" can co-exist. The public is not homogenous. (Lejeune 1986, 126–7)

This notion of an agreement between author and reader is found elsewhere, though not articulated as precisely as in Lejeune's early work. Francine du Plessix-Gray speaks of 'The Pact of Trust' that exists between reader and writer in all writing, not just autobiography. She explains that successful writing requires such a pact in order to 'create a tension … between the promise of gratification and the refined delay of that gratification – to intimate how much information I shall offer and how much I shall withhold' (du Plessix-Gray 1994, 7). This pact, merging trust, 'qualified, paradoxically, by a good measure of uncertainty, mystery and surprise', enables the reader to get close to the author, and the author to 'seduce' (du Plessix-Gray 1994, 7) the reader into his or her story. It is important to note that here du Plessix-Gray is talking about all writing, including fiction, and so here her words relate to the authenticity of voice that readers can assess in fiction. Although in the context of this quotation she is not speaking specifically about autobiography, she is still expressing the belief that some agreement between reader and writer is forged through reading.

If this agreement is broken, the consequences can be grave. 'The utter trust that exists between reader and author is like the trust between lovers', Erica Jong echoes, 'if I feel betrayed by an author, I will never surrender to him or her again' (Jong 1997, 69). We have already seen Vivian Gornick's view of this relationship, whereby the narrator must be 'reliable' in the eyes of the reader, in order for them to be trusted and for the reader to feel prepared to 'journey' with the author.

Gornick does not provide any firm evidence of why we might come to trust writers whose personae we respond to, or how she arrives at the conclusion that the voices she read as she formed her theory were indeed speaking the truth. But her words speak to a powerful effect that this feeling has – if we believe we can trust that a writer is speaking truthfully, we will allow ourselves to be taken in. This 'taking in' is a key aim of published writing, that of capturing an audience. As such, it is a very serious effort indeed.

Can we explain why we trust? The reasons are often frustratingly unsatisfying, and appear weak when probed. Because we want to, until we're let down', as Jong suggests. Because the voice is saying something interesting, as Gornick suggests. Speaking of the 'directness' in J. R. Ackerly's memoir of life with his father, *My Father and Myself*, she says that it 'dazzles', and that, through this directness, 'everyone and everything is made understandable, and therefore interesting. Because everyone and everything is interesting, we believe that the narrator is telling us all he knows' (Gornick 2001, 19). It is not easy to explain why we respond to some accounts and not others, and understanding reasons for trusting an author are complex, but the idea that 'interesting' writing leads to trust is frustrating – it clearly echoes Anderson's identification of the 'rather circular argument'. Also, by equating trust with interest, to me it makes the demand for truthfulness rather ridiculous, if we are actually just satisfied by something interesting.

John Sturrock, in a discussion of St Augustine's *Confessions*, touches on this tendency of the reader to believe, *to want to* believe, in the truth of autobiographical writing:

> Like all autobiography, the *Confessions* [here we can substitute any title we like] are a demand for attention, written with feeling and in the desire to prompt feeling in whoever reads them … in autobiography it is no longer misspent on the figments of an author's imagining because the story which is being told is true. (Sturrock 1993, 32)

It does not seem problematic for Sturrock to claim that autobiography 'is true', and this implied truth is closely connected to the 'feeling … no longer misspent' that is prompted by the writing. Sturrock goes on to claim that this truth is what 'seals the uniquely intimate bargain struck between the writers and readers of autobiography' (Sturrock 1993, 32).

Paul John Eakin refers to James Frey in his discussion of the pact between readers and writers. Eakin claims that what Frey faced in the aftermath surrounding *The Smoking Gun*'s article 'confirms … that the reception of memoir is contractual: readers expect autobiographers to exhibit some basic respect for the truth of their lives – break that trust and suffer the consequences' (Eakin 2008, 20). It is certainly questionable what consequences Frey suffered (especially in the long term), but Eakin's language echoes du Plessix-Gray's and Anderson's.

I believe the terminology used is inappropriate to the context. A contract implies binding regulations and the willingness of at least two parties to enter into it (the 'notary's office', in Lejeune's articulation). Such willingness cannot be confirmed or even expected for both parties. I believe the extent of the fallout over the Frey case reflects a public outraged at feeling tricked or deceived rather than outraged that the sacredness of truth had been threatened. Frey faced public criticism for his actions, but reimbursements requested from the publisher were minimal, suggesting much talk and little action. Interestingly, part of the outcome of the Frey affair was his publisher's decision to reimburse customers who wished to return the book; however, before money would be refunded, a 'sworn statement that they would not have bought the book if they knew that certain facts had been embroidered or changed' (Rich 2006) was required, as well as a torn-out particular page of the hardcover, or the cover of the paperback. This requirement served as proof of purchase, but has an undertone of suggesting that the destruction of the book was not only a proper response, but a requirement in order to object in an official capacity.

The Frey case is also a useful illustration of another aspect of the pact between reader and writer. Sissela Bok points out the way Lejeune's so-called 'intimate' kinds of writing – including memoirs, autobiographies and other personal narratives – result in an inverse reader response to that of self-declared fictional texts (Bok 2000, 314). This opposition means that

> the more autobiographers insist on their veracity, the more readers look for discrepancies between the written life and what they know of the author's life; whereas when confronted with autobiographical fiction, the effort of readers is, rather, to try to discern similarities between the author and the central character in the novel. (Bok 2000, 314)

This goes some way to suggesting that much of the reason Frey faced public outrage was because of his insistence on the factual truth of his book. According to Bok's statement, it may have been scrutinized precisely because he presented it as factually accurate. Had he been successful in publishing the manuscript as a novel, he might instead have been faced with a much kinder public, who perhaps thrillingly discovered links between author and character, rather than loudly objecting to the very absence of (enough of) such links.

Even after outright inventions were revealed in his text, Frey stood by the truthfulness of his book, using arguments that lend themselves to Gornick's theory of persona. In his author's note to the second edition (a condition of continued publication once the fabrications were admitted to), Frey writes:

> I embellished many details about my past experiences, and altered others in order to serve what I felt was the greater purpose of the book … I didn't initially think of what I was writing as nonfiction or fiction, memoir or autobiography. I wanted to use my experiences to tell my story. (Frey 2003, v)

Such language suggests a remove of Frey-the-person from the book, creating space for Frey-the-persona, who is not troubled by genre or accuracy, and whose priority is to express what he considers to be his story. In this way, the voice could be seen as 'Frey and not-Frey'.

This language also closely echoes the language used to discuss and understand testimonio, as I have noted. If Frey sought to write a book that could tell the story of drug abuse and redemption, and intended his text to speak for a community (again returning to authorial intention during criticism), then perhaps it doesn't matter that he claimed he was arrested, that he claimed he spent a certain amount of time in jail and that he claimed a particular number of police officers were involved in an altercation with him. We could instead read these descriptions, outed as inventions, in another way. To borrow Paul Lauritzen's words, we might say that 'If these things are not literally true about [James Frey's] life, they are certainly true of many [individuals in rehab] … what happened to [such individuals] could have happened to [James Frey]' (Lauritzen 2004, 27).

Frey did not use this potential defence. He argued that the book was about his own story: 'I wanted to use my experiences to tell my story about addiction and alcoholism, about recovery, about family and friends and faith and love, about redemption and hope' (Frey 2003, v). The themes are broad, but the voice remains individual. Interestingly, his explanation of some of his choices echoes Gornick's theory:

> I made other alterations in my portrayal of myself … People cope with adversity in many different ways, ways that are deeply personal. I think one way people cope is by developing a skewed perception of themselves that allows them to overcome and do things they thought they couldn't do before. My mistake, and it is one I deeply regret, is writing about the person I created in my mind to help me cope, and not the person who went through the experience. (Frey 2003, vi)

This process of 'developing a skewed perception' of oneself is not very distant from the process of creating a persona. In both cases, the identity is created to serve the purpose of storytelling, and in both cases the creation process involves a degree of shaping, pruning, selecting and therefore altering the material of one's identity. Above, Frey seems to see writing from this 'skewed perception' as a mistake, though this could very well be because he was under pressure from his publisher to write this note in the first place, and because his career appeared to suffer immediately following the discovery, making the appearance of penitence necessary (he seems to have quite recovered now). Rather than a mistake, Gornick sees this process as absolutely essential for good autobiographical writing. In her example of the woman giving the eulogy, writing as 'the person … created in [the] mind' rather than 'the person who went through the experience' is completely fine (Frey 2003, vi). In fact, creating a persona based on the 'experience' of being mentored, rather than speaking as the 'person who went through the experience' of her mentor's death, was key to the success of her eulogy.

We can understand Frey's text as employing a very located persona, rooted in a particular time and emotional state. Gornick's words above are slanted more towards believability and reliability than any form of externally verified factual basis; they speak to the author creating a voice with which to speak, rather than uncovering a voice from beneath layers of recorded lived experience. Frey's author's note states that he 'embellished many details about [his] past experiences, and altered others in order to serve what [he] felt was the greater purpose of the book" (2003, v). Such actions can easily be read as favouring believability of voice over actual recorded fact, for the purposes of connecting with an audience, and taking them 'on a journey' (Gornick 2001, 24).

In fact, Frey's text is very interesting to read in terms of approaching ideas of truth and believability. At one point, Frey recounts a pivotal conversation with a man who would become one of his closest friends in rehab and the subject of his second book. Listening to the man's unorthodox approach to convincing Frey of the value of sticking with the program, Frey thinks: 'I am listening to him and respecting him and respecting the words that he is speaking. They are true. They are from a place of experience and feeling. I can believe in those things. Truth, experience and feeling. I can believe in them' (Frey 2003, 230–1). In this man's eyes, Frey sees 'truth', which is 'all that matters' – a sentiment he frequently voices. This 'truth' that Frey sees, however, is explained as knowing 'by his eyes that he means what he says, that he will follow through with his words' (Frey 2003, 127), merging reliability, honesty and potentially even confidence and physical appearance in his voicing of his understanding of truth.

At another point, Frey's older brother drops off a copy of the Tao for Frey to read. Despite his initial scepticism, it becomes an essential element in his recovery. The writing activates something in him, and he calls it truth:

> The words and the words together and the meaning and the context are simple so simple and basic so basic and true and that is all that matters true. They speak to me, make sense to me, reverberate within me, calm ease sedate relax still pacify me. They ring true and that is all that matters the truth. (Frey 2003, 213)

His language merges ringing true and being true, and equates experience and feeling with truth. This is precisely the kind of language that can create a voice that I believe readers will experience as 'reliable', that they will want to take them 'on a journey', but it is also the kind of language that in fact showcases its prioritizing of self-determined notions of truth rather than 'correspondence between human thought and reality' (Barbour 1992, 26).

Gornick's position is particularly interesting to examine through comparison of her theoretical and autobiographical writings. Perhaps most well-known is her 1987 memoir *Fierce Attachments*, a book about Gornick's relationship with her mother. In *The Situation and the Story*, the text in which she outlines her theory of persona, Gornick speaks specifically about this book and how it helped clarify her views. *Fierce Attachments* is largely structured around conversations shared with her mother while walking the streets of New York. These conversations bring up memories of her past; the narrative shifts repeatedly from the present moment to her childhood and youth.

In light of her claim that a writing persona must be 'reliable', her later announcement that she had invented parts of *Fierce Attachments* surprised some. Gornick established a writing persona in *Fierce Attachments*, and saw it as 'me and at the same time not me'; this persona enabled her to believe 'with all her heart that her memoir is honest', yet it also enabled her to 'tell the truth as [she] could not' (Sterling 2003). This last comment is suggestively (and, I believe, deliberately) ambiguous: Whose truth? Was the persona able to tell this truth more truthfully than 'Gornick' could? Or just differently? Gornick admitted inventing a scene in the novel, combining multiple conversations into one and otherwise deviating from fact. This, according to Gornick, is acceptable in personal narrative. At a speaking event in 2003, she admitted to these fabrications and stood by her decision, arguing that the truthfulness of her memoir was uncompromised. When asked if she had considered informing her readers of these inventions, she replied that she had chosen not to include any note or preface, and that her readers were 'wilfully ignorant' (Sterling 2003).

Such 'wilful ignorance' seems to clash entirely with the notion of a pact between author and writer, and to contradict Gornick's statement that a reader responds to a 'truth-speaking' persona that they believe they can 'trust'. Indeed, it seems to stand at odds with the idea that the reader has consciously placed their trust in a writer. It does, however, suggest that Gornick is conceiving of, and commenting on, readers' intentions, similar to the authorial intention implicit in conceiving of an autobiographical pact or contract. Both practices are problematic, and result in deviation from focus on the writing itself. Once we move beyond the page and into intention, desire and belief, we are no longer only reading. It is worthwhile to bring ourselves back to the text when we find ourselves moving beyond it; after all,

The writer communicates with the page. The reader also communicates with the page. The writer and the reader communicate only through the page. Pay no attention to the facsimiles of the writer that appear on talkshows, in newspaper interviews, and the like – they ought not to have anything to do with what goes on between you, the reader, and the page you are reading. (Atwood 2002, 125–6)

2

Me and Not-Me: Dismissing Unity in Autobiographical Writing

It may seem counterintuitive, but this chapter takes something of a step back from the previous chapter. The contentious relationship between author and reader, when conceived of as an agreement or pact, presupposes that both author and reader are relatively stable identities. This chapters aims to destabilize that assumption and illustrate how identity in autobiography is fluid, as it is in life. I will offer various examples of writers articulating ways in which identity is not static within the same person, and how the passage of time can disconnect an author from his or her identity as it appears in a text, as well as from his or her own past. These articulations trouble the notion of a solid, lasting link between character and author.

Memoir and autobiography enact a paradoxical role, whereby the form exhibits and demonstrates a number of opposing features that co-perform in an effort to present a unified product. This form works with past and present, protagonist and author, truth (and truthfulness) and fiction, to produce an end product that is a fusion of these pairings. Multiplicity – multiple identities, multiple timeframes, multiple interpretations – are found everywhere in personal narratives (or sometimes made conspicuous by their absence) and yet these texts demonstrate the attempt, or at least the appearance of an attempt, at unity in presenting a single account, a unified whole.

Autobiography necessitates the removal of its author to a place outside the experience, in order to write about it. Yet it simultaneously illustrates his or her role in the experience, situating them within the described event. The writer must wear a multitude of masks in order to create the illusion of being both protagonist and recorder of the story, the character to whom we (hopefully) relate and have an interest in following, as well as the controller of the strings, the one who draws us along through the story even while knowing the outcome and writing from a time and space beyond it.

Something like a splitting of selves is required in order to feature within the text while constructing it. Or, rather, an embracing and manipulation of the splitting of selves we all experience over time. We all play multiple roles and change throughout our lives, and the writer of autobiography must embrace this, and work with this multiplicity. The changes we experience can be so pronounced, so fundamental, that we are arguably different people over the course of one life.

Writers are often associated with a certain fluidity of character, an ability to change identities and inhabit different forms. We speak of an author finding their 'voice', or of individual works embodying a distinct voice. This perception is deceptive; we are simply responding to an author's discovery of 'a way of writing words down in a manner that creates the illusion of a voice' (Atwood 2002, 48). If we hear a writer claim that one of her characters allows her to say things she could never dream of saying aloud, how do we understand that? We may perhaps imagine a division of identity, whereby the author sees (part of) herself as an instrument for these things to be said. The character itself is not speaking independently of the author, any more than the book itself demonstrates the discovery of an author's 'voice'. But it is inaccurate to read a text (solely) as an insight into the author's mind. The writing is entirely created by the writer, even as she herself is normally subject to forces and influences that go unexamined and/or unnoticed. However, once created, the work itself is assigned a certain agency, as in the example of a character who can say things the author would not say.

The work might also serve as a window into parts of the author's life that they are not consciously aware of, as though the writing acts as a palimpsest, recording information in different forms, about different things, perhaps only revealed from a certain angle, or at later times. This is precisely what Shoshana Felman describes when she recounts tracking elements of her personal life through her critical writing, seeing the patterns and themes only in retrospect. It is also what Søren Kierkegaard describes as the fact that 'life must be understood backwards ... But ... must be lived forwards' (Kirkegaard 1938, 127).

Contemporary novels deliberately probe the boundary and relationship between life and art, testing how thin they can stretch it. Jonathan Safran Foer's book *Everything is Illuminated*, released by Penguin as part of its 'Fantastic Fiction' line (distinct from other possible categories 'Viewpoints' and 'Real Lives'), features a character called Jonathan Safran Foer who embarks on a quest to discover information that happens to pertain to verifiable past events in author Jonathan Safran Foer's life. Bret Easton Ellis is well practiced at blurring the lines between reality and a novel, narrating existing actors, writers and other public figures interacting with his fictional characters in his novels: *American Psycho*'s Patrick Bateman shares a conversation with actor Tom Cruise in the elevator of the building they both live in (Ellis 1991, 71). Ellis's contemporary Jay McInerney shows up in Ellis's novels, as do McInerney's own fictional characters. Ellis draws on his previous work as much as he does his own history, blending both. *Imperial Bedrooms* (2010) tracks the lives of characters introduced in Ellis's debut novel *Less Than Zero* (1995), who are based on Ellis's peers from university. *Less Than Zero* was made into a film, which *Imperial Bedrooms* references:

> They had made a movie about us. The movie was based on a book written by someone we knew. The book was a simple thing about four weeks in the city we grew up in and for the most part was an accurate portrayal. It was labeled fiction but only a few details had been altered and our names weren't changed and there was nothing in it that hadn't happened. (Ellis 2010, 3)

Examining the boundaries between author and creation is by no means a postmodern approach, representative of an increasing preoccupation with challenging the relationship between art and reality. In one sense, the writer can *only* exist external to the work because anything written is a creation of the past, separated by time from its author and audience. However, the work and the author are bound by the process of authorship, connected forever.

In terms of recording past lived events, the process of translating sensation into language distances the two. Once the writing process is complete, the event hangs suspended between author and audience, trapped as though in amber. But, like amber, it never becomes truly fixed; it always has the ability to move and change shape. The experience itself remains the only fixed point, but the experience soon becomes untraceable, unreachable. Only our versions of it, expressed after transformation into language, exist in updated form. The memory is altered as it emerges in writing, and becomes connected to a particular time of writing, but this written event can be reinterpreted and reread (and rewritten) in countless ways. Even an over-the-shoulder reader is witnessing only the evidence of the changing of event into language; a slight delay removes them from the moment of transformation, distancing them further from the writer.

Perhaps it is because of this insurmountable distance, a distance that exists even if we feel that our stories can be told 'through others' stories' (Felman 1993, 18), that we crave insight into those other stories. We want to read and know about others' lives because we are interested in them, but this interest can stem from a crucial need we have as human beings – to understand who we are. In *The Waves* (1931), Virginia Woolf gives her character Bernard these words: 'But in order to make you understand, to give you my life, I must tell you a story – and there are so many, and so many – stories of childhood, stories of school, love, marriage, death, and so on' (Woolf 1992,

656). In fact, another character observes that 'Bernard says there is always a story. I am a story. Louis is a story', and 'the appalling moment' comes when the story stops, when 'Bernard's power fails him and there is no longer any sequence ... Among the tortures and devastations of life is this then – our friends are not able to finish their stories' (Woolf 1992, 481, 482). The story, the narrative, is the mode of making another person 'understand'; it is the (only?) way I can 'give you my life'. Language is the method of attempting to communicate the essence of one's existence to another person. It is also the method of articulating and attempting to communicate the essence of one's existence to oneself – we are telling our self the story of our life as much as, if not more than, we tell it to anybody else.

In *Living Autobiographically*, Paul John Eakin's main premise is that human beings live narratively. That is, by constructing narratives about our lives, we are constructing our actual lives. We live through narrative, and try to understand others though their own narratives and our narratives about them: 'story functions as the primary avenue to the self of another person' (Eakin 2008, 57). He also explores the alternative: the ways in which losing narrative powers can mean losing one's personality and self. For instance, he touches on the debilitating effect and profound loss experienced when an individual with dementia can no longer construct stable narratives about their lives (Eakin 2008). This loss of narrative ability can cause a resulting loss of identity and personality, and can disrupt or destroy previously established life narratives. The story is the instrument of selfhood.

This position supposes two things: that the inner experience of someone else can be accessed through reading their writing (or hearing their words), and that the inner experience can be (re)produced through language into a comprehensible account. These two assumptions are explored in depth throughout this book; at this point I want to linger on the desire, not to say yearning, implicit in Jill Ker Conway's claim that 'we *want* to know how the world looks from inside another person's experience' (Conway 1998, 6).

The desire to understand how another human being views and experiences the world prompts us to find ways to satisfy this desire – reading memoir for such a purpose indicates that the reader accepts, or hopes, that the writer of the text can be identified with its narrator and protagonist, precisely as articulated in Lejeune's concept of the autobiographical pact. In order to satisfy the craving for intimate knowledge of the world as seen through another's eyes, we must first be satisfied that their account is believable, and that there is unity between the person writing and the person living.

Considered in this light, the importance of truthfulness in autobiographical accounts may appear enhanced. We can perhaps better understand an angry reaction to the discovery that writing that was believed to be factually accurate was actually invented. If we read autobiographical writing in response to our urge to try and experience the world through another's eyes and as part of our construction of our own life narrative, the discovery that such writing, which we have approached almost as a tool for self-viewing and self-creating, is incomplete, false or dishonest, can be very damaging, largely because it is thus rendered useless for our purpose. As I have mentioned, readers turn to writing for many purposes, and we often turn to books to reflect on our own lives and learn about ourselves. We can do this through almost any writing, including fiction, but reading a novel to learn about ourselves is not the same as reading in the attempt to satisfy this craving for a glimpse of someone else's actual worldview and experience.

It may be intriguing to begin with an example of a writer whose most well-known autobiographical work appears to reject entirely the notion that such a text might provide authentic, intimate knowledge of its writer. I therefore propose a short detour into France. This brief section explores, though perhaps (very enjoyably) complicates, the issues introduced above, with reference to the autobiographical writing of Roland Barthes. *Roland Barthes by Roland Barthes* (1975) is a fascinating book with which to examine subversion of a pact between author and reader, and subversive approaches to writing autobiographically generally. Philippe Lejeune calls it 'the anti-Pact par excellence' (Lejeune 1986, 131); Paul John Eakin calls it Barthes's 'anti-autobiography' (Eakin 2008, 65).

The book starts with a collection of photographs and accompanying fragments of writing relating to Barthes's life, particularly his childhood and youth. The pages on which these photographs and captions appear are not numbered, one of many examples of Barthes's effort to disrupt conventional ordering or sequencing in the book. The page which appears as a facing page, or dedication page, is actually page one, including it in the main body of the text. What appears on this page is a sentence, in script that is a reproduction of human handwriting: '*Tout ceci doit être considéré comme dit par un personnage de roman*'[1] (Barthes 1975, 1). The placement of this sentence is interesting. Its location and formatting on the page suggest an introductory message, something like an epigraph or acknowledgement. However, this page is part of the main body of the text; it is page one rather than an introductory page. The first 42 pages of the book are not numbered, and only counting backwards from page 43 reveals the boundary between

---

[1] Everything herein must be considered as though spoken by a character in a novel (my translation).

front matter and body text, a boundary which is obviously blurred by this formatting decision.

Above all, however, the statement cannot but colour interpretation and reception of the writing that follows. Barthes's suggestion/advice appears to discredit the idea that the writer of autobiography has authority over his past, or can ever be more than the 'instance writing', an instance which is neither true nor false (Barthes 1977, 145). He later makes a claim in support of these ideas:

> What I write about myself is never *the last word* ... my texts are disjointed, no one of them caps any other; the latter is nothing but a *further* text, the last of the series, not the ultimate in meaning ... What right does my present have to speak of my past? Has my present some advantage over my past? (Barthes 1975, 120–1)

The introductory sentence speaks both playfully, to the uncertainty bound up in reading any autobiographical writing, and seriously, to the conscious rejection of a unified figure who speaks from some privileged position of the present about events past. The naming of autobiography as simply a '*further* text' alludes to the 'infinitely deferred' meaning Barthes describes in 'The Death of The Author' (1977, 147). It also speaks to the 'infinite succession of steps' that Nabokov identifies as being the path to 'reality', which itself is an unreachable destination (Nabokov 1973, 10).

Paul John Eakin reads Barthes's introductory sentence as slightly contradictory, where 'Despite the nagging implication of some personal connection between author and text that the facsimile of his handwriting generates, Barthes repeatedly undercuts any autobiographical self-reference that the title might lead us to expect' (Eakin 2008, 65). In a more direct way, Barthes actively challenges the link between the writer writing and the writer who lived the experiences being described. He reinforces and emphasizes the multiplicity of identity, where a present self cannot 'use' or be in any way superior to a past self.

A very real effort is made to disrupt any linear narrative, any hint towards a unified narrator and author. After the photographs, the remainder of the book is made up of fragments of writing, each with a title. These are arranged in alphabetical order, by title. The narrative voice employs a bewildering array of 'he', 'I' and 'RB' interchangeably; none is maintained long enough for us to establish a relationship with or understanding of the narrator in any fixed way. According to Graham Allen, 'Such a technique foregrounds the point that the person who speaks or acts and the person who writes are never identical' (Allen 2000, 41). A timeline of Barthes's life is offered, but this comes as part of the end matter, before an index of the photographs. The

FRAGMENTS

last page (unnumbered) is again marked with the handwriting. '*Et après?*'[2] it asks, and answers itself with two notes, formatted like dialogue between two speakers. One asks if anything can still be written; the other suggests that it can: '*On écrit avec son désir, et je n'en finis pas de desirer*'.[3]

These choices make the book present as something of an experiment, or even a treatise. It is particularly interesting to read comparatively with *Incidents* – a collection of short works released after Barthes's death (two of the four pieces in the collection were published individually before his death). *Incidents* is the title of the volume as well as the title of one of the four pieces. They resist easy categorization, especially as a collection – one is an essay on the landscape and light in Southwest France, the country of Barthes's childhood; 'Incidents' is a collection of short fragments of text (some as short as a sentence) that give the reader sensory flashes of a period of time spent in Morocco; the third piece is a short essay on the significance and atmosphere of the Paris nightclub Le Palace; and the final piece, 'Soirées de Paris', consists of diary-style entries about Barthes's daily (and nightly) life, dated only a few months before his death. There is no clear indication that Barthes desired or planned for 'Incidents' or 'Soirées de Paris' to be published.

In all four pieces, Barthes displays a very different approach to writing about himself than in *Roland Barthes by Roland Barthes*. I will focus on the first essay for two reasons. First, it was published before Barthes's death, which means it was released into his corpus of writing with his knowledge and permission. Second, it takes his own life as the focus, which is more suited to my purpose here than a reading of 'At Le Palace Tonight...'.

In his 'anti-autobiography' Barthes occasionally speaks to us plainly, in a style we might expect to encounter in traditional autobiography ('When I was a child, we lived in a neighbourhood called Marrac'), but just as often he frustrates a clear or steady narrative line ('His first, or nearly first text [1942] consists of fragments ... Since then, as a matter of fact, he has never stopped writing in brief bursts: the brief scenes of *Mythologies*, the articles and prefaces of *Critical Essays* ...') (Barthes 1975, 121, 93). In 'The Light of the Sud-Ouest', however, he writes at length about the relationship between time, memory, place and self, and he does so using a consistent 'I' that is clearly identifiable as Barthes. The voice does not engage in the destabilizing I/he/RB actions present in *Roland Barthes by Roland Barthes*. Throughout the first essay in *Incidents* he establishes and refers to links between his past and present, his childhood and adulthood, his memories and reality, and

[2] And after? (my translation).
[3] One writes with one's desire, and I have not finished desiring (my translation).

his physical location(s). He does this in sensual language that places us, embraces us:

> Today, July 17, the weather is splendid. Sitting on the garden bench and squinting so as to obliterate all perspective, the way children do, I see a daisy in the flowerbed, flattened against the meadow on the other side of the road. (Barthes 1992, 3)

From the start, we are provided with a location, a specific date (though the year is absent) and a landscape (which has been suggested more specifically in the title of the piece). We are introduced to a period of time in the speaker's life – old enough to look back on the habits of childhood and mimic those habits in adulthood. The text locates us in a body, which itself is located in a period of time and a physical space. The essay goes on to iterate its relationship to the subject of the essay suggested by the title, while also being itself the subject of the essay.

The first half of the 'The Light of the Sud-Ouest' speaks of 'My Sud-Ouest' (Barthes 1992, 4), and tells us at length what that is and how it is understood by Barthes. It is a space on a map ('a fourth of France'); a manner of speaking ('the Sud-Ouest accent has formed the models of intonation that marked my earliest childhood'); a sense of movement in, and by, the body ('Whenever I drive down from Paris … there is a signal that tells me I have crossed a threshold and am entering the country of my childhood'); a quality of light ('the great light of the Sud-Ouest … is a luminous light. You must see this light (I would almost say: hear it, so musical is its quality)'); and, finally, a more precise environment – the town in which Barthes grew up (Barthes 1992, 4–5).

The link between describing Southwest France and talking about himself is, in this essay, not a choice but a necessity: 'For "to read" a country is first of all to perceive it in terms of the body and of memory, in terms of the body's memory … Ultimately, there is no Country but childhood's' (Barthes 1992, 8–9). This method of embodying memory is not a limitation, but in some ways a destiny: 'I believe it is to this vestibule of knowledge and analysis that the writer is assigned: more conscious than competent, conscious of the very interstices of competence' (Barthes 1992, 8–9).

'The Light of the Sud-Ouest' ignores or dismantles the very obstacles that *Roland Barthes by Roland Barthes* builds up and then points to. I believe that the writing in this essay, and in the collection more generally, supports a reading of *Roland Barthes by Roland Barthes* as a statement or experiment. It can also be seen as writing done by a persona as articulated by Gornick – an identity created and used solely for telling the story, as only it can tell it. However, in this case, the persona is almost defined by its complete lack of a personality. By stripping away the characteristics that might make us more easily imagine the voice embodied in a person (as well as destabilizing the features of a typical autobiography), Barthes creates and uses a particular voice that seems almost inhuman. Beneath the timeline provided at the end of the book, he almost acknowledges this lack of personality or humanity when he writes that the timeline includes 'studies, diseases, appointments' but absents 'Encounters, friendships, loves, travels, readings, pleasures, fears, beliefs, satisfactions, indignations, distresses: in a word: repercussions' (Barthes 1992, 184). And yet these are not truly absent, for they appear 'In the text – but not in the work' (Barthes 1992, 184).

Roland Barthes by Roland Barthes very effectively displays a position, an approach to autobiography. It asserts, while the essay welcomes; the essay and the book can be read as having been written by distinct selves. There is no claim in the essay that the self writing has 'some advantage' over any other self, but as to the 'right' to speak of it, this does not seem to trouble Barthes throughout *Incidents*. Nor should it: to write of one's past is a right of all selves. *Roland Barthes by Roland Barthes* insists on its refusal to display standard autobiographical characteristics, and as such we are denied, from the outset, a way to connect to the writer in order to fix a narrator on which to place our trust and our desire for that narrator's true story.

This is why Lejeune identifies it as an 'anti-Pact'. There is no contract because one of the parties seeks 'maximum elasticity' in terms of self-identification (Lejeune 1980, 44). If Barthes seeks to 'escape from the weight of the "I" … theorizing and criticizing this practice as he goes along' (Lejeune 1980, 44), he cannot be party to any such contract or agreement, over and above his initial, explicit rejection of an autobiographical pact – the initial rejection being encapsulated in the opening sentence: *'Tout ceci doit être considéré…'* The autobiographical pact of trust discussed above is therefore not broken, since it never exists in the first place.

Writing about experience prompted by memory – even if assisted by later research into that memory – necessitates a division into selves based mainly on the passage of time: the writer writing is not quite the same person who lived the events being described. In the written account, the events also exist in relation to each other, in an order which does not necessarily mimic the order in which they occurred. Even if the memoir does not have a linear narrative, or such a narrative arc is deliberately shunned in favour of another structure, the events described in autobiographical work still occurred (in the past) and occur (in the text) in some sort of temporal arc. Something must, of course, have happened in order to be written about. But the person doing the writing is not the person who features in the events described, just

as a person who has written a book is not the same person as the one who
hands you a bound and signed copy.

In exploring various attempts at a definition of autobiography, Linda
Anderson quotes Lejeune's early claim that 'one condition for autobiography
was absolute: there must be "identity between the *author*, the *narrator*, and
the *protagonist*"' (Lejeune 1982, quoted in Anderson 2001, 2). John Sturrock
agrees that

> autobiography does indeed aspire to delineate the "features" of his
> personal history and character which its author believes as his claim to
> distinction, so that his text can finally take the place of his person, as the
> tangible evidence of his identity. (Sturrock 1993, 5)

John Barbour, in a study of the ethics of autobiography and the role
conscience plays in its construction, understands autobiography within a
context of its moral issues and implications, as 'not simply a description or
report on how the author's conscience operated in the past, but itself represents an act or exercise of conscience', thus fusing the written product and
the person who wrote it (Barbour 1992, 1).

This is the unity that I want to challenge here. In particular, I will show
how Gertrude Stein's *The Autobiography of Alice B. Toklas* complicates
Lejeune's requirement of shared identity between author and narrator, and
how Joan Didion and Natalia Ginzburg take deliberate steps to illustrate the
gap between the writer's experience at the time of writing and at the time of
experiencing the events they describe.

The descriptions of autobiography noted above, in contrast to Barthes's
'anti-autobiography', all point to a crucial and lasting connection between
writer and narrator. I suggest that this unity between writer and narrator
can be legitimately dismantled and indeed dismissed because of the time
elapsed between the writing and the events, and the changes the individual
has undergone in that time. Also, memoirs or autobiographies that focus on a
period of crisis, or very early childhood, can also be seen as undermining an
assumed unity between protagonist and author, as these events may happen
in, or create, periods of intense stress and heightened emotion, encouraging
a disassociation between the author of the memoir and the central figure
within it. As Felman suggests, writing about such periods may be part of
a process of understanding one's relation to such events, but can still be
understood as essaying, a period of artistic movement in multiple directions,
towards an understanding or version of the past, rather than an account of
facts. And, as a method of understanding or perhaps even healing, the artistic
project may be more valuable as a record of experience during the writing,
rather than a record of (or window onto) the events described therein.

The writer who begins a memoir may be very different from the writer who finishes one, and both selves can be distinct from the character in the text that they are describing. I now want to explore the ways in which the passage of time and/or crisis can cause what I refer to as multiple selves within one person. This multiplicity complicates an assumed unity between writer and protagonist, as well as making issues of truth and truthfulness much more nuanced.

'I have been a swallower of lives; and to know me, just the one of me, you'll have to swallow the lot as well. Consumed multitudes are jostling and shoving inside me' (Rushdie 1981, 9). The protagonist of *Midnight's Children*, Saleem Sinai, introduces himself to us with these words. He understands himself not as one person but as multiple selves, housed in the borders of his body; perhaps we can see here another version of Walt Whitman's declaration 'I am large, I contain multitudes' (Whitman 1999, 1209). Sinai also tells us that to know him, we must listen to him tell a story, echoing Bernard's words in *The Waves*, quoted earlier. Nathan Glass, protagonist of Paul Auster's *The Brooklyn Follies*, declares: 'All men contain several men inside them, and most of us bounce from one self to another without ever knowing who we are' (Auster 2005, 122–3). Writing about his own father, Auster repeats this image of uncertainty and multiplicity when his attempt to encapsulate his father's identity in a single way leads instead to a 'rampant, totally mystifying force of contradiction' (Auster 1982, 61). His father was not one man, or even one 'kind' of man:

> Impossible to say anything without reservation: he was good, or he was bad; he was this or he was that. All of them are true. At times I have the feeling that I am writing about three or four different men, each one distinct, each one a contradiction of the others. (Auster 1982, 61)

The story is the means of expressing the selves of which one is made, and can be a means of gathering multiplicity into one message, incorporating the many into one narrative. The story always involves multiplicity, always spills over into another story, and another, and another, as we all are in constant motion from one understanding of ourselves to the next, never static. Sinai understands the story of his life as extending outwards in multiple directions, not bound by the punctuation marks of his birth and death. Telling us his story is not straightforward for Sinai because 'there are so many stories to tell, too many, such an excess of intertwined lives events miracles places rumors' (Rushdie 1981, 9). As if to emphasize the 'commingling' (Rushdie 1981, 9) of stories and selves that make up the story of Saleem Siani, by the fifth paragraph he has moved to 'the early spring of 1915', more than thirty years before his birth, to a story that features Sinai's grandfather (Rushdie 1981, 10).

Beginning the story of the self by quickly reverting to the story of one's ancestors is common in much autobiographical writing – we can see it in *The Liars' Club*, in *The Autobiography of Alice B. Toklas*, in *Speak, Memory* and in Auster's *The Invention of Solitude*. Didion's *Where I Was From* (2003) extends this practice to writing the history of the state of California as she explores where she comes from. She moves backward from herself to her family to the land itself that she was born into, echoing Hurston's 'dead-seeming cold rocks' which hold great stores of information.

Another articulation of the inherent multiplicity of selfhood, which I believe offers a particularly evocative visual image of the impossibility of keeping identity to a straight, unidirectional path, comes from Adrienne Rich. The second stanza of her poem 'Delta' elegantly alludes to the difficulty of conceiving of a single, localized identity, and suggests the powerful transformation and movements we experience through the course of our lives.

> If you think you can grasp me, think again;
> My story flows in more than one direction
> A delta springing from the riverbed
> With its five fingers spread (Rich 1987, 135)

The image of the fluidity of water, combined with its force, alludes to the multidirectionality of our lives; the description of a delta conjures up the image of slowly collecting water, a primary source, a drawing out of buried resources that feed the movement. If some readers find this image too poetic, too figurative, we have another description of the multiplicity of selfhood in researcher David Eagleman's more scientific take on it: as he argues that the brain functions not as a single entity with one aim but rather as a 'team of rivals' (Eagleman 2011, 101), he suggests a view of selfhood that is not single but multiple, asserting that 'we are made of many neural subpopulations' (Eagleman 2011, 104).

This multiplicity that is inherent to Saleem Sinai's understanding of himself also applies to his writing process; he changes direction, settings and times in his effort to give us his story. This fictional character is embodying a recognizable splitting process, redoubled by the act of writing, and indeed blurred by it, because Sinai the writer is describing Sinai the child, the adolescent, the young adult – all the Sinais until the present moment. A similar division of selves is often referred to by authors. 'I began to rely so much on writing that I was living a double life – one in the world and one on the page', recalls novelist Susan Minot about her early life, where 'the [life] on

EVENT —> RECOLLECTION —> WRITING

the page was more intense, more satisfying and for a long time much more real' (Minot 2000, 50). 'I am after all a writer', says Margaret Atwood,

> so it would follow as the day the night that I must have a slippery double … All writers are double, for the simple reason that you can never actually meet the author of the book you have just read. Too much time has elapsed … and the person who wrote the book is now a different person. (Atwood 2002, 36–7)

Echoing Minot's division of her life into two parts, Atwood continues: 'When writers have spoken consciously of their own double natures, they're likely to say that one half does the living, the other half the writing' (Atwood 2002, 37). Author Natalie Goldberg articulates it slightly differently: 'Writers live twice … The one that lives everything a second time … sits down and sees their life again and goes over it. Looks at the texture and details' (Goldberg 1986, 48). She thus creates (at least) three categories of experience: the event, the later recollection of the event and then the event's written form, benefitting from both time periods but not fitting neatly into either.

In 'Borges and I', Jorge Luis Borges divides himself into a character with his name and a character he calls 'I', admitting to some similarities but an ultimate separation between them: 'I like hourglasses, maps, eighteenth-century typography, the taste of coffee and the prose of Stevenson; he shares these preferences, but in a vain way that turns them into the attributes of an actor' (Borges 1964, 282). The difference between the two is further shown by the claim that 'everything belongs to oblivion, or to him', indicating that while they may be two selves inhabiting one body, one can outlast the other. This indication, however, implies an untangling of a complexly intertwined identity: 'I do not know which one of us has written this page' (Borges 1964, 283).

In his study of doubles in literature, Karl Miller introduces his use of the term 'duality' with these words: 'an author may be thought to lead a double life, or to achieve a second self, an alter ego, in the art he creates, and he may also be thought to lose himself there' (Miller 1985, 22). This fluidity suggests the ability of one 'world' to change into another, and for human identity to shift between the real and the unreal world.

In discussing why she keeps notebooks, Joan Didion recalls a lifelong resistance towards 'dutifully … record[ing] a day's events', because the results of such an effort remained 'mysterious at best' (Didion 2006, 102). Instead, Didion's notebooks become a space where, instead of the 'pointless' type of entry just described, she embarks on the more useful course of

> what some would call lies. "That's simply not true," the members of my family frequently tell me when they come up against my memory of a

shared event ... Very likely they are right, for not only have I always had trouble distinguishing between what happened and what merely might have happened, but I remain *unconvinced that the distinction, for my purposes, matters.* (Didion 2006, 103, my emphasis)

Here Didion is articulating the same idea as Cinnamon did in Murakami's novel: that in some cases it doesn't actually matter if the event written occurred in real life, and often there is no way of knowing. Reality becomes subjective, and the border between the real world and the world of writing dissolves. 'The way I write is who I am, or have become', Didion claims (Didion 2005, 7). She is not acknowledging a split here between the real world and the created world; she is speaking to their unity: the real world *is* the created world. Didion is suggesting that, for her, this world creation happens through writing. If this is the case, then her confusion over the distinction between truth and fiction noted above is warranted. If the world is created by writing it into existence, the claim by outsiders that one's writing is 'simply not true' can cease to be meaningful.

By stating that her writing is who she is, Didion is imbuing written language not only with the power to define her but also to guide her through a process of self-discovery or self-formation, a process of becoming. If Didion exists only through, and because of, language, can any part of her exist outwith it? As she grows and changes as a person, into newer and newer selves, her writing tracks and records this progress/process. Her writing becomes the method of marking time, illuminating differences between her selves that emerge over time.

Indeed, writing may be the only means of marking time and noting change. After her husband's death, she becomes aware of the gazes of people outside her marriage: 'for the first time since I was twenty-nine I saw myself through the eyes of others' (Didion 2005, 197). During her marriage she 'saw [herself] through John's eyes', making her current self-image one 'of someone significantly younger' (Didion 2005, 197). When she writes these words, at age 69, she is writing her new self into existence. This does not make her self-image at 29 false, nor does it mean she existed for forty years under a false impression or a lie. Instead, it means that she is using her writing to record her process of change, and in this case she is recording the difficulty, or we could say crisis, of having forty years collapse suddenly.

This is the position from which Paul John Eakin begins his study of narrative and self-identity, *Living Autobiographically*. He quotes neurosurgeon Oliver Sacks, commenting on one of his case studies: 'It might be said that each of us constructs and lives a "narrative", and that this narrative *is* us, our identities' (Sacks 1985, quoted in Eakin 2008, 1). It is noteworthy that this suggestion comes on the very first page of Eakin's introduction, beginning a chapter called 'The Rules of the Game'. The 'Game' is both writing and life, since this understanding of narrative conflates them – we write ourselves into being.

Life (and communication) as a game requiring rules also appears in 'Slouching Towards Bethlehem' (1967), Didion's examination of the Haight-Ashbury scene. She describes her time in San Francisco through repeated scenes of self-destruction, apathy and confusion, painting a chilling picture of the young people she meets, the 'pathetically unequipped children' trying to 'create a community in a social vacuum' (Didion 2006, 93). The equipment they lack is language. '[W]ords are for "typeheads"', they are told, and, in the absence of 'the web of cousins and great-aunts and family doctors and lifelong neighbours who had traditionally suggested and enforced society's values', they 'do not believe in words' because 'a thought which needs words is just one more of those ego trips' (Didion 2006, 93). This lack of faith in articulation, resulting in an inability to articulate, means that these individuals become totally unable to understand the world around them, themselves, and any relation between the two concepts. They fail to produce narratives about who they are or what they experience, resulting in series of loose, meaningless encounters.

Here, language is the potential means through which these individuals could understand each other and, crucially, their environment:

> At some point … we had somehow neglected to tell these children the rules of the game we happened to be playing. Maybe we had stopped believing in the rules ourselves, maybe we were having a failure of nerve about the game. (Didion 2006, 93)

The game is serious; human relations and society hinge on it. Didion, who is 'committed to the idea that the ability to think for one's self depends upon one's mastery of the language', equates the dysfunctional relationships and pseudo-society ('they are less in rebellion against the society than ignorant of it') of these 'children' with their lack of language (Didion 2006, 93). She thus grants language the ability to create self-knowledge and foster productive interpersonal relationships. She describes the people she meets as 'an army of children waiting to be given the words' (Didion 2006, 93).

In her introduction to *The White Album* (1979), a collection of essays, Didion notes this same crucial function of language as the means of understanding the world, and she employs a term I have introduced earlier. She writes: 'We live entirely, especially if we are writers, by the imposition of a narrative line upon disparate images, by the "ideas" with which we have learned to freeze the shifting phantasmagoria which is our actual experience' (Didion 1979, 11). Returning to my brief discussion of Sarah Wilson's description of the term, here Didion echoes the idea that life, 'our actual experience', is too enormous, too chaotic, to be approached from a single viewpoint, or encompassed within a single story, and so requires us to organize our understanding of it into 'ideas', into separate stories, linking the 'disparate images' through, essentially, controlling and using language.

Speaking the story, establishing the narrative, creates a truly alive, living self. Nathan Glass's nephew in *The Brooklyn Follies*, shortly after hearing his uncle speak the words quoted a few pages earlier, reflects that 'When a person is lucky enough to live inside a story ... the pains of this world disappear. For as long as the story goes on, reality no longer exists' (Auster 2005, 155). If we believe in Eakin's, Didion's and Sacks's view of narration as a life-giving practice, there is of course no difference between living in 'reality' or 'inside a story'.

Virginia Woolf's *Orlando* is very concerned with multiple selves within one body, and the role of writing in the creation of identity. At one point, Woolf illustrates this multiplicity of selves in Orlando's many memories of times past, where her present experiences become confused with events long over:

> How strange it is! Nothing is any longer one thing. I take up a handbag and think of an old bumboat woman frozen in the ice. Someone lights a pink candle and I see a girl in Russian trousers ... indeed, it cannot be denied that the most successful practitioners of the art of life ... somehow contrive to synchronize the sixty or seventy different times which beat simultaneously in every normal human system. (Woolf 1928, 215)

Later, the many 'times' tangled in one body are articulated as 'selves':

> these selves of which we are built up, one on top of another, as plates are piled on a waiter's hand, have attachments elsewhere ... she had a great variety of selves to call upon, far more than we have been able to find room for, since a biography is considered complete if it merely accounts for six or seven selves, whereas a person may well have as many thousand. (Woolf 1928, 217–8)

The image of stacked plates suggests that these selves are always present in the body, where one might perhaps be at the fore at a particular time, but all co-exist. Jeanne Schulkind refers to such a collection of selves when she discusses Woolf's autobiographical writing in her introduction to *Moments of Being* (1976). She draws on Woolf's image of life as 'a bowl which one

WRITINGS & IDENTITY

fills and fills and fills' (Woolf 1976, 64). Because unemptied, each additional *[quote]* self and experience in this bowl 'displaces' existing ones 'ever so slightly and alters their previous meaning by forcing them into new combinations' (Woolf 1976, 13). This beautiful image suggests a gradual collection of selves and experience within a constantly swelling envelope of identity, whose contents are always shifting, exposing new planes and inviting new modes of understanding. This illustration speaks to a richness of memory and experience which can guide us and influence our present (and future) without ever leaving us, or formally substituting or eliminating our past – simply shaping and turning it, so that we see it from a different perspective.

Other writers speak of selves that come and go over time. Mary Karr writes about giving a reading of *The Liars' Club* in her hometown: 'I feel every school photo I ever took pass over my face to melt into the forty-year-old self I am now. Seen by so many pairs of old eyes, I become my every self' (Karr 2010, 360). Philip Larkin, introducing a reissue of his first collection of poetry twenty years after its initial release, writes: 'Looking back, I find in the poems not one abandoned self but several – the ex-schoolboy ... the undergraduate ... the immediately post-Oxford self ... this search for style was merely one aspect of a general immaturity' (Larkin 1986, 8). Here Larkin is also associating development of identity with development of writing style. By exploring different modes of writing, Larkin is exploring different identities, experimenting as he discovers who he is becoming, and looking back at who he was. In this quotation we get the impression that his different selves are recognizable to him, but that he does not hold them all within his consciousness, like Woolf's collection of stacked plates. Larkin's words suggest that he has come up against these former selves, as one might run into a former acquaintance at a party.

In *Orlando*, writing is a means of self-expression and self-knowledge, and remains a constant link between Orlando and the world. In some ways, Orlando's writer-self is the only constant self, remaining unchanged through the many shifts the body experiences. Like Didion and Larkin, Woolf engages with the idea of writing as a means of not only expressing oneself to the world, but also understanding exactly who one is. Schulkind follows this idea into Woolf's own life. She describes the way Woolf's maturing artistic skills and increasing confidence in understanding and describing her parents allow for different portraits of them to appear in different pieces of Woolf's writing. These changing views of her parents thus correspond to different periods in Woolf's life, and different stages of understanding. For example, in 'Reminiscences', Woolf's father appears a rather different personality than he does in 'A Sketch of the Past', with the difference in representation coming down to changes in Woolf's own life. In the differences between the two pieces we can read not only a development of writing style but also a corresponding development of self-understanding and identity formation.

A more obvious example can be found in Woolf's description of the way writing *To the Lighthouse* freed her of her obsession with her mother (Woolf 1976, 80). After decades of hearing, seeing and imagining her on a daily basis, the relatively rapid writing process liberated her of this presence: 'I no longer hear her voice; I do not see her' (Woolf 1976, 81), she wrote in 1939. Writing transformed Woolf's perception of her mother and profoundly impacted on her daily life, and, arguably, her identity.

The Year of Magical Thinking has much to say about the ways in which time can split us into multiple selves, and how the distance between living an experience and writing about it can trouble any assumption of unity between the author and protagonist of autobiography. Didion introduces the book as her

> attempt to make sense of the period that followed [her husband's death], weeks and then months that cut loose any fixed idea [she] had ever had about death, about illness, about probability and luck, about good fortune and bad, about marriage and children and memory, about grief, about the ways in which people do and do not deal with the fact that life ends, about the shallowness of sanity, about life itself. (Didion 2005, 7)

The book may also be read as support for her earlier claim that 'There is no real way to deal with everything we lose' (Didion 2006, 1103). Throughout *The Year of Magical Thinking*, Didion examines how the passage of time changes us, to the point where, contrasting memories with her present feelings, her writing presents us with multiple selves, distinct because of the vast difference between their reactions, beliefs and actions.

A notable instance occurs when she recalls her opinion of Caitlin Thomas's book about her life after Dylan Thomas's death, *Leftover Life to Kill*. Didion contrasts her scornful reaction after reading it at age twenty-two ('I remember being dismissive of, even censorious about, her "self-pity", her "whining", her "dwelling on it"' [Didion 2005, 198]) with her present attempts to handle her own husband's death. She uses language to understand her past response to the book and articulate her present feelings about it, the same way she uses language to try and deal with the trauma/crisis which has led her into a situation that is closer to Caitlin Thomas's than she could have anticipated. Although the way she writes remains who she is, in terms of coming to an understanding of herself through writing, the text still reveals how she has changed over time, and how time has changed her, so that her different selves becomes quite incomprehensible to each other. This articulation can be read as a mournful memory of a previous self, disconnected from the present self by the gulf of experience between them. Language is not the means of unifying these two selves, but rather of showing them to each other (and to us). As such, perhaps the only way these selves can co-exist is through language.

This motif of different selves is found elsewhere in Didion's work. Her writing style emphasizes it. She frequently adopts a cool and detached, almost clinical tone, which throws into relief the mysterious and almost eerie sense that she is finding herself in a situation that does not resemble, though perhaps is reminiscent of, any previous one, where everyone is a stranger, though perhaps, and slightly alarmingly, recognizable. 'I have lost touch with a couple of people I used to be', she states, 'one of them, a seventeen-year-old, presents little threat ... the other one, a twenty-three-year old, bothers me more. She was always a great deal of trouble, and I suspect she will reappear when I least want to see her' (Didion 2006, 107). Here she quite clearly rejects an image of an identity that encompasses all previous selves, as in Woolf's bowl image. This articulation of her past posits former selves as different individuals with whom one might lose all contact, or perhaps even be stalked by, as in the twenty-three-year old who might make an unwanted and unannounced appearance. In this quotation the different selves are given enough distance (and agency) that they might effect communication with each other, even if such communication is undesirable to one self. If we lose (track of) who we were at certain times, it may affect how we experience recognition or continuity, even if 'we are well advised to keep on nodding terms with the people we used to be, whether we find them attractive company or not' (Didion 2006, 106).

Didion's writing often highlights the edginess of imperfect communication, either between two individuals, or within one body. This miscommunication is evoked powerfully in her description of her marriage. Didion had an extraordinarily close relationship with her husband, in terms of time spent together, shared activities and drawing on each other for advice and support. Her brother-in-law, Dominick Dunne, has called it a 'superb marriage', and said that the two were 'ideally matched' and lived a 'life of total togetherness that was nearly unparalleled in modern marriage. They were almost never out of each other's sight' (Dunne 2004). Didion herself describes how

> During all but the first five months of our marriage ... we both worked at home. We were together twenty-four hours a day ... I could not count the times during the average day when something would come up that I needed to tell him. (Didion 2005, 194)

This exceptional closeness and communication sometimes enables her to feel as though she can read her husband with complete accuracy, or discern his intended meaning at all times: 'There was nothing I did not discuss with John ... There was no separation between our investments or interests in any given situation' (Didion 2005, 16). This quotation is also useful in supporting Eakin's argument that narrative is the way we live our lives, not simply write about our lives. In Didion's words, her relationship with her husband is reliant on their ability to 'discuss' things with each other, in being able to 'tell him' things, using spoken language, a narrative, to construct their relationship; their 'days were filled with the sound of each other's voices' (Didion 2005, 16). Indeed, her description of the moment of his heart attack is short and direct, and it identifies the stoppage of language as the moment of death: 'John was talking, then he wasn't' (Didion 2005, 10). That short line is the crossover from life to death.

Their union, however, can never be totally complete. Ultimately, they are two different individuals who cannot, despite what their intense closeness may suggest, know the inside of each other's mind. Their constant 'discuss[ion]' may function as a means of trying to bridge the gap between each other, but this gap can never be fully closed. This is well illustrated in Didion's reflection over a comment her husband made shortly before his death. After his death, recalling the comment sends her to his computer in search of context and meaning. She finds what she considers a relevant file and begins reading. 'I knew what he meant by that', she tells herself when she discovers a note relating to the comment, but this knowledge, which of course is determined by her, does not represent complete access: the file she reads was altered on the day of his death, somewhere within its 80 pages, but 'what he added or amended and saved ... I have no way of knowing' (Didion 2005, 186, 187). She grasps at clues but repeatedly comes up against evidence of the insurmountable boundary that is drawn between them. No matter how close they were, no matter how much time they spent working and thinking together, blending their lives, there is always a point beyond which Didion cannot pass. She remains herself, and stuck inside herself. This boundary was not created with Dunne's death; his death only threw it into relief.

Elsewhere, Didion describes a related event, where another comment made by Dunne is recalled by a mutual friend, years after he made it (but while he was still alive). Didion considers the friend's interpretation as a misunderstanding. 'I explained to Susan that John had meant something entirely different,' and explains her own interpretation, at which point John clarifies: "'That's not what I meant at all'", leaving Didion to wonder 'Had I understood nothing?' (Didion 2005, 173). Evidence of her misunderstanding does little to quell her insistence in various places that she 'knew' what her husband thought about a particular thing. Ultimately, this conviction only serves to underscore how removed they are from each other, as distant as the present Didion from her twenty-three-year old self, whose possible reappearance she dreads.

Muriel Spark alludes to an individual's division into multiple selves over time; she also refers to the idea of a multiplicity of selves that is particular to writers. She recalls each example of her body of work as foreign ('I read them as I would another's work') because each 'represents the convictions and humors of the writing personality I was at the time' (Spark 2001, 56). The 'writing personality' sounds very like Gornick's concept of persona, in that each book is told by a unique voice, linked to that particular project. This also makes re-reading difficult for Spark, and has the ability to make her question 'did I write that? I suppose I did' (Spark 2001, 56). The work bears her name and evidence exists of her having written it, but the passage of time and the becoming of different selves stands in the way of a clear and comfortable ability to identify herself as the author of the work.

This questioning of one's past actions recalls seeing baby photos of oneself, or indeed any photographs of an unremembered event. We recognize something about the person connected to the experience: in Spark's case, her name on the cover and accompanying memories of the writing of the book; in the case of the photographs, we recognize our bodies, our friends and family members, even our clothing. Yet there is a barrier to clear recollection of the event. We have to 'suppose it was' us, but time makes us different people, rendering the events in one's past sometimes unintelligible or distorted. The person in the photo is both us and not-us. We can recognize parts of the image but we cannot fully connect to the person and experience pictured. That this is a visual image does not diminish the analogy – any phrasing or understanding of the lack of recognition is expressed through language, through a narrative, and so the same effect is felt.

Such a lack of recognition is not only caused by temporal distance; we can become unrecognizable in other ways. Clinical psychologist and writer Kay Redfield Jamison's *An Unquiet Mind* describes her diagnosis and struggle with manic depression, a diagnosis that she initially resisted adequate treatment for and that severely disrupted her life, almost killing her. She describes a garden party she attended in a professional role, a few months before a period in which she became 'ravingly psychotic' (Jamison 1995, 63). At the party, she 'had a fabulous, bubbly, seductive, assured time', 'talking to scads of people, feeling ... irresistibly charming, and zipping around' (Jamison 1995, 71, 70). Another guest at the party, a man who would eventually become Jamison's psychiatrist, 'recollected it very differently. I was, he said, dressed in a remarkably provocative manner ... and seemed, to him, to be frenetic and far too talkative ... I, on the other hand, had thought I was splendid' (Jamison 1995, 71). After receiving treatment, and describing the event after some time, Jamison too sees it differently, and realizes the gulf that had existed between her perception of herself, and her future psychiatrist's. Both witnessed the same moment in time and the same physical body moving through the party and talking to guests. Their readings, however, are strikingly different, illustrating how our selves can be incomprehensible, indeed invisible, to others and unrecognizable to ourselves, so that the 'swallower of selves' might occasionally ingest something totally divorced from 'just the one' we sometimes think we are.

So far I have focused on a splitting of one body into multiple selves, exploring the notion that the body can be a sort of 'container' for these. I want to continue by looking closely at the way one author approaches the notion of a writing persona that opens the idea to include more than one physical body, alluding to, or perhaps questioning, whether multiple physical selves can share one persona. *The Autobiography of Alice B. Toklas* (1933) brought Gertrude Stein the international fame and recognition she had long desired and believed to be her due. When the book appeared it bore no name on the cover, and many people were taken in by its seemingly self-evident title – including some who claimed to be able to recognize Toklas's voice in the book (Sturrock 1993, 233). This, however, seems improbable, as Stein's authorship is explicitly stated on the book's final page, and her distinctive writing style is evident throughout. Stein makes a very rapid appearance in the text and acts as its central figure throughout; not only does the writing style suggest the book's authorship, but throughout it Stein's character is dominant. The writing serves to emphasize her actions and opinions, diverting focus away from Toklas and negating Lejeune's early criterion for autobiography – that of 'identity between the *author*, the *narrator*, and the *protagonist*' (Lejeune 1982, quoted in Anderson 2001, 2).

The chapter 'Gertrude Stein in Paris' marks a more formal indication of Stein taking the reins and directing the narrative away from a focus on Toklas's life – this occurs but thirty pages into the book. The introductory chapter, Toklas's life 'Before I Came To Paris', is less than a thousand words long, serving to reinforce the idea that there really couldn't have been much to a life without Stein's presence. Even in this chapter, the only one in which Toklas's life without Stein is given any space at all, Stein finds other ways to dominate the writing and influence the images readers have access to. After brief descriptions of Toklas's youth, the text directs us elsewhere for a more precise picture: 'In the story Ada in Geography and Plays Gertrude Stein has given a very good description of me as I was at that time' (Stein 1933, 2). Long, long before authorship is revealed, there is cause to doubt the title. This gesture towards Stein as an authority on representing Toklas in her own supposed autobiography is merely one of the first reasons why. This is a playful book, a venue for Stein to explore notions of authorship and what it means to write autobiographically. It is not the autobiography claimed in the title, but it is a work that can be understood as autobiographical. 'There is no fraud here', Lejeune notes, 'the reader is warned of the rules of the game' (Lejeune 1980, 46).

This book can also be read as an extreme example of creating a persona. Gornick's belief that the persona is created by the author and applied to the text at hand, becoming integral to the telling of the story, applies here. Stein is author and not-author of this text. The book is entirely controlled by her, it demonstrates many of the characteristics of her other writing and it serves as a platform from which to discourse on some of her favoured topics. Nevertheless, she is writing using a totally constructed speaker, advertising another voice as the author. These elements combine to suggest an authorial self that is neither Toklas nor Stein, only itself. The identity she assumes allows her to write this particular text, which is not going to adhere to the claim of the title, and at one point posits itself as being the story of 'how two americans happened to be in the heart of an art movement of which the outside world at that time knew nothing' (Stein 1933, 29).

The assumed voice also allows Stein to explain her position and opinions on a few choice themes, through imagined posed questions and/or narratorial space in which she can expound on her views. Examples include the difference she perceives between written language and spoken language, her criteria of what makes a genius and her reason for writing exclusively in English. 'When I first knew Gertrude Stein in Paris I was surprised never to see a french book on her table ... there were even no french newspapers', the narratorial voice says (Stein 1933, 77). (In an echo of the treatment of Toklas's life 'Before I Came to Paris', this information about Stein in Paris comes in the third paragraph of a chapter supposedly about 'Gertrude Stein Before She Came to Paris'.) The information about the French books and newspapers is merely a method of introducing Stein's views on writing and speaking languages. The visualization of 'words and sentences' makes English the only language she chooses to write in, while the 'tones and rhythms' of a language mean that 'it does not make any difference' to her what language she hears (Stein 1933, 77). Another example, where her views on art take center stage, occurs in a statement that once more closes by asserting Stein's authority. 'Toklas' describes the paintings in Stein's home, and the voice quickly shifts into a claim that

> Gertrude Stein always says that cubism is a purely spanish conception
> and only spaniards can be cubists and that the only real cubism is that of
> Picasso and Juan Gris. Picasso created it and Juan Gris permeated it with
> his clarity and his exaltation. To understand this one has only to read the
> life and death of Juan Gris by Gertrude Stein, written upon the death of
> one of her two dearest friends, Picasso and Juan Gris, both spaniards.
> (Stein 1933, 101–2)

Where Gornick describes the difficulty of fashioning a persona 'out of one's
own undisguised self' (Gornick 2001, 6), Stein's persona sheds its disguise at
the conclusion of the text, and what comes before is evidence of the persona
she has constructed for the purposes of writing. Despite the clarification
of authorship on the final page, the persona does not drop. The closing
paragraph states:

> About six weeks ago Gertrude Stein said, it does not look to me as if you
> were ever going to write that autobiography. You know what I am going
> to do. I am going to write it for you. I am going to write it as simply as
> Defoe did the autobiography of Robinson Crusoe. And she has and this
> is it. (Stein 1933, 268)

The final 'she' continues the idea that Toklas is indeed writing, despite
naming Stein as the writer of the book we have just read. We are left
with her comparison of this text with Daniel Defoe's creation of Crusoe's
'autobiography'. By indicating the two are analogous, she is challenging
what autobiography means, and who can write one. Stein and Toklas's life
is a story, just like Crusoe's. The fact that Stein and Toklas lived and Crusoe
did not is not relevant at all levels. The identities within both texts (Stein's,
Toklas's, Crusoe's) are constructed.

A few years later, in *Everybody's Autobiography* (1937), Stein elaborates
on the theme of identity, how it is determined and, particularly, how writing
complicates it. Indeed, she returns to the issue of identity over and over
again, talking about how 'funny' it is, about as 'funny' as things like money,
drinking and being a genius. 'It is funny about identity', she understates,
before claiming that one is who one is 'because your little dog knows you',
suggesting that identity is only confirmed, or conferred, by an external entity
(Stein 1937, 46). This claim also suggests that identity must exist through
some sort of witnessing, that even if created by the self, it requires the
agreement or at least presence of another party to be cemented. Shortly after
this statement, however, she alters her view:

> And identity is funny being yourself is funny as you are never yourself
> to yourself except as you remember yourself and then of course you do

not believe yourself. That is really the trouble with autobiography you do not of course you do not really believe yourself why should you, you know so well ... that it is not yourself ... You are of course never yourself. (Stein 1937, 70)

In this version, identity is never fixed, never permanent. In fact, it does not exist at all in a way that can be individually verified. Either it simply does not exist, or it is ever-changing, and cannot be understood in the present moment. This disconnects past from present from future, making it seem as though the person living is always a different person to the one who lived immediately before, and the one who will experience the future. This remove echoes the remove of the author from the text, the division that is inherent to writing the past. You always write from a distance, similar to the way (in Stein's articulation) that you live at a distance from your past selves. In some cases, the distance can be pronounced, as Didion's recollection of her youthful scorn for Caitlin Thomas shows. Sometimes the remove is subtler. The destabilization of identity mirrors the disconnection between the author of an autobiography and their appearance within the text.

It is also interesting to consider Stein's statement in contrast to commonly held perceptions of what memoir and autobiography entail. In Stein's words, 'you are never yourself to yourself', implying that genuine self-recognition is impossible. One does not know oneself in the moment. This lack of knowledge would make it impossible to establish 'identity between the *author*, the *narrator,* and the *protagonist*'. If 'you are of course never yourself', identity can only exist as an illusion, or as a constructed narrative. The only way one is in any way recognizably oneself is 'as you remember yourself'; that is, from a position that already implies two selves – the one who performed the action being remembered, and the self doing the remembering. In this reading, the construction of memory is the construction of identity, a slight echo of Eakin's position of living narratively. And even if one constructs a self through constructing a narrative, its inherent falsehood cannot be suppressed: it is invented, not really 'yourself'. This invention causes all the 'trouble' of constructing autobiography.

A final note on this topic compares Stein's words above with Woolf's 'moments of being' (Woolf 1976, 70). This is the term Woolf gives to those 'sudden violent shock[s]' where an individual experiences the 'realness' of reality, which is so often taken up with 'non-being', where one 'walks, eats, sees things, deals with what has to be done; the broken vacuum cleaner; ordering dinner; writing orders to Mabel; washing; cooking dinner; bookbinding' (Woolf 1976, 70). These 'moments of being' are precise; they address neither a person's future nor their past but pin them in the immediate present. Thus they can also be said to indicate a splitting of selves, into the self who experiences these moments and the self who is occupied with the 'non-being'. This defined locating effect of the 'moment' contrasts with Woolf's greater sense of identity, which is that it is never static but always in flux. Even the past is constantly changeable. As the time 'on which the identity of the present moment rests', it never ceases to be subject to different interpretations and viewpoints, rendering it flexible and, in some ways, as unknown as the future (Woolf 1976, 12). Vladimir Nabokov uses somewhat similar terminology and ways of understanding the passage of time and the effect of the present and past on each other when he claims that 'The present is only the top of the past, and the future does not exist' (Nabokov 1973, 184). Identity is always shifting, making you 'never yourself to yourself', and making even one's past a place of changeability, in Woolf's case, or uncertainty and even disbelief, in Stein's.

It is interesting to follow Woolf's explanation of what these 'moments of being' indicate to her, and the desire they provoke. She first suggests that perhaps 'the shock-receiving capacity is what makes me a writer', indicating the possibility that certain people are more perceptive to the very idea that life can be divided into 'being' and 'non-being', but also maybe that a particularly artistic temperament would respond as she does, which is with the 'desire to explain it' (Woolf 1976, 72). This explanation happens through words, through language; she is 'mak[ing] it real by putting it into words' (Woolf 1976, 72). Written language, once again, is shown as the means of establishing one's existence in, and relationship to, the world – a relationship that Woolf sees, during her 'moments of being', as one of supreme interconnectedness, where 'this vast mass that we call the world' is a great artwork – not the home or setting for art, but the art itself: 'we are the thing itself' (Woolf 1976, 72). Language is the unifying element for these disparate moments and selves.

Temporal duality

Successful memoir or autobiography (like successful fiction) usually enables us to experience what the protagonist does, and accompany them through the course of events with a level of immediacy. But the events described in autobiography are often decades in the past. They are new for the reader, unfolding in the moment of reading, yet the reader is also aware that these descriptions reference a time and place far removed from the moment of reading. This distance is necessary for the reconstruction and rearrangement

PAST & PRESENT

that is the writing process. The author knows the outcome of events. She is stepping out from, disrupting, the narrative line, in order to recall the past and reproduce it in a form new to readers. Even a memoir told in first person, aligned so closely to the narratorial voice that we seem to inhabit their body and develop understanding and awareness as they do, operates in this paradoxical space of recalled past and created present. Frank McCourt's *Angela's Ashes*, which abruptly switches to immediate first person towards the beginning, and stays like that for the rest of the book, comes immediately to mind as an example.

The Autobiography of Alice B. Toklas draws attention to this temporal remove repeatedly. Stein allows her story to follow various tangents and consciously draws herself back to the 'main' narrative by repeatedly using phrases like 'as I said', 'as I was saying', etc. She also alerts the reader to the distance between events and the writing with statements such as 'We were, in these days as I look back at them, constantly seeing people' (Stein 1933, 209).

I will look closely at a section in the beginning of the book which exemplifies the way this text plays with temporal distance. Right from Chapter One Stein alerts us to the flexible way she handles time. It is worth noting the extremely wide range of time periods encompassed in the very short first chapter. A rush of decades and people are, once introduced, immediately abandoned for the rest of the book. We read of Toklas's heritage ('polish patriotic stock'), childhood ('the gently bred existence of my class and kind') and life with Stein, in terms that widen out to a suggested future ('I have met several great people but I have only known three first class geniuses ... In no one of the three cases have I been mistaken'), before bringing us back to the beginning of Toklas's 'new full life' (Stein 1933, 1, 3). All these time periods are handled in the three short pages of Chapter One. It is as if Stein is flexing her narrative muscles, demonstrating the extensions and leaps that are possible, and making us aware that, in this book, we may need to move quite quickly to keep up.

The section I want to look at in depth begins Chapter Two, 'My Arrival in Paris', though it can be seen to represent a second beginning of the book as a whole, as it directly follows the closing lines of Chapter One: 'In this way my new full life began' (Stein 1933, 3). After the whirlwind first chapter, we are placed in a specific time and place, the arrival in Paris: 'This was the year 1907' (Stein 1933, 7). Following this placement, and despite the chapter title, we are immediately reoriented to the main subject of the book by being told what Stein was occupied with at this time ('seeing through the press Three Lives' [Stein 1933, 7]). We do not make it even to the end of the paragraph without a leap in time that alerts us to the time of writing: 'I remember not long ago hearing Picasso and Gertrude Stein talking about various things that had happened at that time' (Stein 1933, 7). By doing this Stein draws attention to the elapsed time between the events and her writing.

What I will call the 'Hélène sequence' is a good example of the ease and fluidity with which Stein handles the passage of time, and her refusal to adhere to any linear narrative. Hélène, the cook at 27 rue des Fleurus (Stein's house in Paris), is introduced on page 8. Toklas has been invited to dine on Saturday, 'the evening when everybody came' to eat dinner cooked by Hélène (Stein 1933, 8). This paragraph ends with 'I must tell a little about Hélène' (Stein 1933, 8). This indication of needing to tell 'about' Hélène's story before being able to proceed with Toklas's echoes the idea Felman, Gornick and Karr are earlier quoted as expressing – the need to tell one's story through others' stories, and the way in which telling the story of one's life must always necessarily include the story of other people. In this case, the story of Hélène is apparently critical to Toklas's story. To understand Toklas and the situation she was in at the time, these words tell us, it is necessary to first gain a suitable background through hearing the story of another person. This decision supports the idea that multiple stories must be considered in recounting the past. It situates the reader in a place where we can see down a number of roads – Toklas's, Hélène's and that of each additional person brought into the text. Only from this place of multiple vantage points can we form a confident picture of the events. This image almost suggests a panopticon, where the reader is located centrally and can see the story-paths of multiple characters, and is thus enabled to form a more complete picture. Any shift that is too emphatic in one direction, or towards only one story, can create an imbalance and affect the credibility and overall coherence and cohesiveness of the multiple stories that make up one account.

To return to the sequence: after Toklas pauses to introduce Hélène, we are taken further into the past ('Hélène had already been two years with Gertrude Stein'), and then through a more general time that probably seeps into the writing's present because mentioning more general character traits rather than information about a particular time or episode: 'She wasted nothing … She was a most excellent cook … Hélène had her opinions' (Stein 1933, 8). Following this snapshot of Hélène's character, the next time we are located is shortly after an anecdote about Matisse, which is actually repeated throughout the text. We are told that 'Hélène stayed with the household until the end of 1913'; we have moved from 1907 to 1913 in less than two pages (Stein 1933, 8). The reason for her departure from the household is given and we are then informed that 'much later, only about three years ago, she came back for a year' (Stein 1933, 9). The time of writing now becomes a measure, or reference point, for the events in the novel, and we are given another means of gauging when these events are happening in relation to the writing, i.e. three years before 'now'.

Connecting Hélène's return to her post with the time of writing also connects Stein as writer and Stein as character. 1930 ('about three years' before the book's publication in 1933) becomes another point in mapping the chronology of the book as a whole. This paragraph ends with a tactic which is characteristic of the book: after more information about Hélène's return, the narrator brings herself back to the task at hand with the words 'But to come back to 1907' (Stein 1933, 9). The very next line, however, once more leads us away: 'Before I tell about the guests I must tell what I saw' (Stein 1933, 9).

We encounter this technique repeatedly in the text: the slightly repentant, perhaps even flustered, voice telling us, and herself, that she 'must come back' to the story; in other words, that she must reorient herself to once again try and stick to a linear narrative, even though this attempt regularly leads her in other directions and into other times. This device highlights the way neither memory nor most stories operate in a linear fashion. Like Rich's 'five fingers spread', the story moves in more than one direction, and its retelling, manipulated and shaped by the events occurring between event and writing, insists on complicating the order of events. Indeed, the claim that to tell one story requires the telling of another ('Before I tell ... I must tell') reinforces the idea that there is no main story unconnected to others.

Another method Stein uses to draw attention to the non-linearity of time and the way a story can move backwards as easily as forwards has to do with an interjection briefly mentioned above – the anecdote about Matisse included in the Hélène sequence. This anecdote (the content is unimportant in discussing its function) appears several times throughout the text. Each time we read it, we read it anew, because our experience of reading has developed as we move through the book, and we bring our changed self to each page. Our knowledge of the people involved has also developed, as we learn more about them through reading. Every time she repeats the anecdote, it is a different anecdote because it has an additional layer of meaning, derived from its new context and our developing understanding. This repetition showcases the constant newness of the writing, the way even a repetition always brings new information with it, or at least a new way of looking.

Stein's text is a wonderful book with which to explore these ideas because of the real sense of play in the writing. The next text discussed in this chapter is rather more somber, mainly because of its subject matter. Although both books concern the period before and during World War Two, the authors were affected in very different ways. Natalia Ginzburg's *The Things We*

Used To Say provides striking (and heart-wrenching) examples of how the passage of time can release alternate truths, adding them in layers to events already lived, and alludes to multiple versions of an event or experience. Her memoir does very interesting things in terms of approaching an event after the passage of time has changed it. The book can be read on multiple levels, depending on how much research the reader does regarding the events she describes. Ginzburg does not provide crucial information she later learned about some events; in some cases, the relevant subsequently learned information is made conspicuous by its absence.

An account of her family's experiences during the rise of fascism and World War II in Italy, the book is, as the title suggests, structured around spoken language and dialogue. Ginzburg offers examples of oft-repeated phrases that demonstrate how these became a sort of family shorthand, and serve to construct a framework around the family that can be used to instantly recall shared lived experience, binding the family members together. 'There are five of us brothers and sisters', she writes, explicitly introducing the present moment of writing (this is one of the few times she does this):

> We live in different cities, some of us abroad, and we don't write to each other very often ... but among us a single phrase is enough. A single word, a single phrase is all it takes, one of those old sayings that we heard repeated endlessly during our childhood ... One of those words and sayings would be enough to make us recognize each other in the darkness of a cave or among a million people ... those sayings are our Latin, the lexicon of our by-gone days ... the basis of our family solidarity, which will exist for as long as we remain on this earth. (Ginzburg 1963a, 21)

This is a vivid illustration of the life-giving power of narrative, an example of living narratively. In this short passage Ginzburg establishes the importance of language as the means of constructing a family history and relationship. It is the family's foundation, their 'Latin, the lexicon of ... by-gone days'. It is also their present, in that 'a single word is enough'. And their future relies on it because it is effective 'as long as [they] remain on this earth' (implying that the death of language and identity are one). This is a family that tells itself stories in order to live. These stories are the very backbone of their existence, their means of identifying each other and the relationships that bind them, reinforcing them with each repetition.

In her short preface to the book, Ginzburg offers a dense amount of information, some of it paradoxical. She appears precise in her desired readership, makes requests of these readers and seems honest and willing to discuss the book. She begins by declaring the book's factual accuracy – 'the places, events and people in this book are real' – informing us that the tendency to invent, whenever given in to, was quickly rejected, with fabrications eliminated at once (Ginzburg 1963a, 1). Yet, she would prefer the book to be read as 'a novel; in other words, without asking either more or less of it than a novel can give' (Ginzburg 1963a, 1). Ginzburg, of course, has no way of knowing what one 'asks' of a novel, but it is significant that after informing us of its rootedness in fact, she prefers it not be taken as such, perhaps preferring the room for uncertainty or ambiguity that the novel form offers, and the absence of any implied obligations regarding the amount or quality of information she wishes to provide, and the amount she wishes to withhold.

'I have written only what I remember', she says, making a distinction between what she remembers and what indeed happened (Ginzburg 1963a, 1). The word is used in all its ambiguity – What she remembers now? What she remembers remembering then? It is also worth noting that she avoids saying she wrote what she knows. This distinction refuses to incorporate subsequently learned knowledge into the narrative. Events are related as she remembers feeling about them at the time, not as she feels about them at the time of writing. Ginzburg does not overtly use the present as a lens through which to view the past, and thus dilutes the relation between present and past. This is the opposite of Stein's actions described above, where the time of writing is invoked as a measure against which the past is discussed.

The language of her preface is deceptively simple. Within ten lines of her statement quoted above, she tells us 'there are many things which I remember but have omitted to write about' (Ginzburg 1963a, 1). She is creating a distinction between writing only what one knows, and all that one knows. This illustrates the memoirist's choice of what to leave in and what to take out, while simultaneously alerting us to the potential untruthfulness implied by deliberate omissions. How much room is there in a memoir for a narrator who confesses 'I have not really wanted to talk about myself?' (Ginzburg 1963a, 1) She says this because the book, according to her, 'is not in fact [her] story but rather … the story of [her] family' (Ginzburg 1963a, 1). This statement stands in contrast to any claim that one's story spreads into the stories of others; the suggestion that the story of her family could be distinct from her own story stands out. Even though she claims that the text is not about her, she must be part of it.

The memoir (if we persist in calling it such, it must be in recognition that this is against Ginzburg's wished designation for it) deliberately and consistently stays in its relevant time period. That is to say, she does not layer her recollections with information learned later; nor does she collapse time, as we can see in Nabokov's writing. Indeed, Nabokov blithely announces 'I do not believe in time' (Nabokov 2000, 109), and structures *Speak, Memory* in a way that accentuates his rejection of a linear narrative. He arranges events thematically rather than in temporal order, prioritizing his own pleasure of following the spirals of memory paths. 'I like to fold my magic carpet', he says, discussing the author's power to rearrange the chronology of events in a book, 'in such a way as to superimpose one part of the pattern upon another. Let visitors trip' (Nabokov 2000, 109). Ginzburg rejects his magic carpet metaphor and practice, refusing to dislodge events from their precise temporal place. We never 'trip' in this book. Instead, we walk slowly and very carefully, in a single direction, never coming abruptly up against a surprising juxtaposition, or looking over the precipice of sudden realization. Rather, we feel occasionally concerned about shadows we may glimpse or sense, without knowing their form.

The clearest example of the result of this temporal fixity is found in her description of Dino Segre, a friend of her brother's who was working as a spy for the fascist secret police and would eventually betray him. Ginzburg's description of this man remains firmly in the book's present, giving no hint as to his later actions, and refusing to mention the results of his entrance into their lives. Notes to the 1997 edition offer the following information after the first introduction of Dino Segre in the text: 'He was unmasked after the war when his letters to his spymasters were published. Ginzburg is here deliberately exploiting the gap between her ignorance at the time of [Segre's] complicity in the events … and his later notoriety in Italy as a spy' (Ginzburg 1963a, 207). This information dramatically changes the significance of Segre as a character, and sheds new light on his interactions with the Levi family. It makes us read very differently Ginzburg's description of his visit following her father's arrest, where he 'sat gravely in a chair talking soberly with [Ginzburg's] mother in tones of dignified sympathy' (Ginzburg 1963a, 93).

By making this decision, the text probes what it means to write the past, and once more raises the issue of truth and truthfulness. Does Ginzburg's refusal to amend events in the light of subsequent knowledge problematize her book as autobiographical writing? This would support her request for it to be read as a novel, which would carry no suggestion of owed truth to the reader, and no implied pact or agreement. Ginzburg might be said to be writing the truth, since her adherence to fact is stated, and her insistence on immediately eliminating any fabrications prefaced what we read (though of course it is up to us to decide if we believe her claim or not). But, if we accept her word for it, can we still claim that she is writing truthfully? Do these 'gaps and omissions', one of which is the Segre example, make her text untruthful? This is also a useful illustration of the division Murakami refers to in *The Wind-Up Bird Chronicle*. In this description in Ginzburg's text, we can see the way *'fact may not be truth, and truth may not be factual'* (Murakami 1998, 525). Her claims are that Segre came to visit, made 'polite conversation' and took a passing interest in some stories the young Natalia had written (Ginzburg 1963a, 93). That may well be exactly what happened on that evening. But is this representation truthful? It is debatable whether leaving such a crucial outcome obscured constitutes 'the most exact and insightful understanding of past experience' (Barbour 1992, 26).

It is striking that this note about Segre's subsequently discovered actions does not appear in an earlier version of the book. Indeed, for many readers there would be no hint as to another side of Segre's character. The 1967 version totally absents this information, instead simply noting that he was a 'popular writer of highly-coloured romances, very successful in the 1920s' (Ginzburg 1963b, 179). This comparison shows how the inclusion of additional information by editors, publishers and other individuals who are not the author can profoundly influence readings of (various versions of) the book.

The most significantly silenced element of the text is the death of Ginzburg's husband, Leone, who was tortured to death in captivity. He appears in the book infrequently, and his death occurs without direct mention. The ordeal is passed over in a few indirect lines:

> they arrested [Leone] three weeks after our arrival and I never saw him again.
>
> I found myself back with my mother in Florence [they had been living in Rome] … We didn't talk to each other much about Leone's death. She had been very fond of him, but she didn't like to talk about the dead. (Ginzburg 1963a, 154)

Elsewhere, she alludes again to Leone's death as seen through the eyes of a friend: 'Pavese hardly ever mentioned Leone … all the same, perhaps he suffered at times from having lost him. He had been his closest friend' (Ginzburg 1963a, 148).

On this topic, the reader is pushed firmly aside and away. This is not something Ginzburg wishes to speak to us about; it is something from which we are excluded. When she permits herself to speak of his death, it is at a remove, either from somebody else's perspective or in such a distant fashion that she is making a point of allowing us to learn nothing of her feelings about it.

Shown in the quoted matter above, the paragraph break between Leone's final moments in her life and her move back to Florence is the only space allotted to the experience. We know quite well that nobody 'finds themselves' in Florence, or indeed anywhere – they arrive after a journey which is more or less planned. She is unwilling to share any of the information that surrounds this time. Her mother's preference not to discuss the dead is stated, and allowed to be the reason why Leone's death is rarely mentioned, but Ginzburg omits her own feelings in this description. Not only do Ginzburg's feelings remain unrecorded, we are also denied her description of these crucial events, which become highlighted by their very absence. Likewise, her suggestion that Pavese possibly 'suffered' from losing his closest friend serves to underscore what must have been the intensity of her own suffering, without directly alluding to it.

This reading of the passage is also subject to formatting decisions, involving editors and publishers in the process, opening up the channels of how we determine the meaning of a book or passage. The paragraph break, which I read as crucial to Ginzburg's only direct mention of Leone's death, does not appear in the 1967 edition. In this edition, the paragraph opens with Ginzburg hoping the family's recent move to Rome will be 'the beginning of a happy time for us' (Ginzburg 1963b, 138). Leone's death occurs midway through the paragraph, which closes with her mother, with whom she now lives in Florence, 'bathing the children, combing their hair and keeping them warm' (Ginzburg 1963b, 138). The effect of opening and closing the paragraph with nurturing, domestic scenes serves to seal it off on both ends, and downplay the significant geographical shift that occurs during it. Leone's death sinks silently but heavily out of the images of home life, and this is effectively the last we hear of him. He departs from the text as Ginzburg suggests he dropped out of their lives – suddenly, unexpectedly, irrevocably. This example illustrates the myriad ways we glean meaning from a writer's words, and the subtle differences that can affect our interpretation of what we read. Formatting and translation decisions, possibly made without Ginzburg's input, or after her death, can significantly direct our reading in certain ways.

There are two notable exceptions to her resistance towards linking past and present. I have briefly discussed one above, when she states that her siblings continue to share this bond expressed and cemented by the repetition of phrases from their childhood. This moment not only joins the rest of the book to the present moment, because Ginzburg is telling us this practice is ongoing, but it also functions a little bit like the survival testimony mentioned by Karr and Felman earlier. Beginning the book by stating that she and her remaining family members continue to communicate in this way alerts readers to the fact that, no matter what events are described in the book, they at least have survived and are able to maintain their relationships.

The second example occurs towards the end of the book. Leone has been arrested, and Ginzburg's friend Adriano arrives to warn and help her. The paragraph is worth quoting at length not only because it links her present with her past, but also because the writing style is notably different from the restrained, detached voice used throughout the rest of the memoir:

> I shall always remember, as long as I live, the great comfort it was to me that morning to see his familiar figure, which I had known since my childhood, after so many hours of solitude and fear, hours in which I had thought of my parents who were far away in the north, and wondered if I would ever see them again; and I shall always remember his bent back as he stooped to collect our scattered clothing and pick up the children's shoes in a humble, kindly attitude of patient compassion. And when we escaped from that house, he had the same face as when he came to us to fetch Turati, the same breathless, frightened, happy face he wore when he was taking someone to safety. (Ginzburg 1963a, 161)

The whole paragraph is only two sentences long. The relief and happiness and fear Ginzburg recalls burst forth from the constraints of the rest of the book. In this passage, she references her present, and indeed her future, by claiming that this event is something she will never forget until her death. She thinks of her parents and her childhood, widening the circle of people involved in this moment, and the time periods considered. She also notes her children, including them (and their future, affected by Adriano's help) in the moment. It is a brief scene that stands out, largely because of the way it contrasts with the rest of the book. This is a rare instance in which we feel we are learning some intimate knowledge of Ginzburg's inner thoughts and emotions.

Keeping in mind Jill Ker Conway's suggestion that the reason for autobiographical writing's persistent appeal is that 'we *want* to know how the world looks from inside another person's experience' (Conway 1995, 6), we can read Ginzburg's text as deeply unsatisfying in one way, deliberately so. Apart from the two brief moments I have just described, she holds us away from certain intimate details of her life, so that the book does not satisfy our desire to know more. She presents a great contrast between the walled silence surrounding some events and the garrulous family chaos that makes up much of the rest of the story. The book is perhaps richer in terms of the reader's involvement because we must imagine the events and descriptions she notably passes over, but we are still denied Ginzburg's version of the story.

As noted in her preface, Ginzburg is not pretending to give us anything approaching the entirety of the story. She explicitly omits some information, and tells us she is doing so. The text is by turns almost suffocatingly embracing, thrusting us into the center of the large, excitable and shouting family, and impenetrable, closing around itself to keep its secrets. She closely guards the ways and contexts in which we can use her writing to see 'how the world looks from inside another person's perspective'.

Perhaps, also, there are some topics she wishes to keep separate from the voices of her family, whose story, after all, she claims this is. Perhaps the story of Leone's death is not open to discussion or debate, and should be protected from becoming a touchstone or codeword for her family to use to identify and relate to each other. By refusing to bring this story out into language, she keeps it sealed. Multiple viewpoints are perhaps undesirable on this topic. Ginzburg may feel that it should not be a story that meets the 'usual outburst of clamorous voices which always threatens ... to drown the single true utterance' (Woolf 1976, 50).

In this chapter I have explored two main ways in which autobiographical writing can be read as exhibiting and exposing the multiplicity of story and authorial identity that they may initially appear to unify. Not only does the construction of the story involve a profound temporal division in terms of the distance between events and writing, but the author herself can be seen to have experienced significant shifts in personality, rendering her present self almost alien to the self/selves that appear in the writing. Didion's writing on identity change and Stein's and Ginzburg's examples of temporal distance being explored and employed in autobiographical writing demonstrate why conceiving of the author as a constant identity is problematic, and why writing about past events always involves the present, which can bring with it very real changes to the past.

3

The Vortex Effect and the Tissue of Time

Keeping in mind the distinction discussed in Chapter One, between truth and truthfulness, this chapter will approach the topic of memory and its presence in memoir with specific reference to Vladimir Nabokov's *Speak, Memory* and Joan Didion's *The Year of Magical Thinking*. When John Barbour identifies truthfulness as comprising 'an active search for the most exact and insightful understanding of past experience' (Barbour 1992, 26), he is suggesting a particular way that past experience, 'returned' in the form of memory, is treated at the time of writing. In this chapter I will explore how memory can be used as a tool in the writing, and its characteristics as a resource.

When I call it a tool, I mean that I want to examine memory as something with a function, something that we (think we) can make use of, rather than simply an experience or force that visits and may guide us. Some authors speak of memory as something that can be employed, called upon and put into use, and it is such an approach that I want to consider in this chapter – memory as 'a tool, one of the many tools that an artist uses' (Nabokov 1973, 12). This conceptualization places memory on par with other devices, implying action on the part of the writer, and perhaps even skill; after all, we can practice using tools, and improve at it. 'Just give yourself a chance', advises Frank McCourt, in response to reader astonishment at the level of detail *Angela's Ashes* offers, especially about his life as a very young child (McCourt 1998, 79). This is a suggestion that many of us may be holding back from employing memory to its full capabilities, or may not even realize how much material our memories hold, having never tested them fully.

I believe Barbour's quote highlights the way a memory may appear in the mind of a memoirist, but is manipulated before being used in the writing. William Zinsser refers to this manipulation when he states that a memoirist must 'manufacture a text' from the raw material of memory (Zinsser 1998, 6). This practice illustrates the division of the autobiographical writer at the most basic level – before any writing is done, the self who experienced the event must find a way to merge with the self doing the writing, in a way that satisfies both. Both past and present self must be satisfied that the writing is an 'exact and insightful' treatment of the past event. This two-directional relationship already suggests the malleability of memory. It does not simply exist, waiting to be accessed and represented; like truth, it is not 'out there, hanging around, waiting for the [writer] to show up' (Buford 1990, 180). Instead, it is something that is altered and reshaped before being included in a written account.

Problems with memory

I do not believe that the notion that memory is an enormously powerful sensation and experience, which often visits us in response to no conscious stimulus and is occasionally undesired, needs to be debated here. This writing begins from the position that this notion is generally considered undisputable. Trying to harness memory in order for it to be functional and informative for autobiographical writing can be a difficult, some would say impossible, task. This task is made more complex and potentially problematic by the fact that memory can be extremely deceptive. We often misremember, or assign certain memories to incorrect places and times. Memory is altered or influenced by our current state. When we remember an event, we often do so as a different self than the one who experienced the event. As we change and age, repressed memories can return, or past events can morph into totally different events that we nevertheless think we remember, and can be convinced actually happened. The impossibility of verifying many memories does nothing to make it seem a more reliable and useful source. If we return to Woolf's image of life as 'a bowl which one fills and fills and fills' (Woolf 1976, 64), we can more easily see how past events, altered or shifted by subsequent events, can appear to the memoirist in a very different light than they may have when they occurred.

Paul John Eakin, in his search for an understanding of what happens when we remember, and how we use what we remember to construct our identity (or succession of identities), draws on the work and writing of neurologist and writer Israel Rosenfield. Rosenfield's *The Invention of Memory* is introduced by Oliver Sacks as a 'variety of clinical, linguistic, and psychoanalytic observations' (Rosenfield 1988, xiv) that explores ideas of how the brain works, and particularly how it perceives past events.

Rosenfield claims that 'Recollection is a kind of perception … and every context will alter the nature of what is recalled' (Rosenfield 1988, 89). As a kind of perception, it is subject to the conditions of the present in which it happens. This present 'updates' it, and each time recollection occurs it does so in a different context, and so presents differently. Elsewhere, Rosenfield suggests that 'the way we recall the past is … constantly changing over time … The brain normally reworks our recollections', again introducing an element of newness to any memory (Rosenfield 1995, 200). These arguments work to support Rosenfield's argument against 'localization', the idea that a particular, identifiable region of the brain is the 'site' of memory. Rather, Rosenfield argues that memory is a *process* that the brain is continually occupied with, because 'there are no specific recollections in our brains; there are only the means for reorganizing past impressions, for giving the incoherent, dreamlike world of memory a concrete reality' (Rosenfield 1988, 77). Other researchers share this 'anti-localization' view, including, more recently, David Eagleman, whose work I will draw on in this chapter.

Memory thus becomes something the brain can do, rather than something the brain can process or find: 'Memory … is not a set of stored images that can be remembered by an independent "I"; memory is a set of ever-evolving procedures' (Rosenfield 1995, 202). Drawing on Rosenfield's findings, Eakin concludes that, because memory can be seen as a process of constant reconstruction performed by the brain, it is 'one more source of fiction', and that autobiographies are 'fictions of a special, memory-based kind … fictions about what is itself in turn a fiction, the self' (Eakin 2000, 290). He notes that, with this definition, he is 'Steering clear of any pejorative connotations, any sense of untruths or lies' and instead 'speaking of fiction in its root meaning: that which is formed, shaped, molded, fashioned, invented' (Eakin 2000, 290).

A sense of continuity is crucial to both Eakin's and Rosenfield's arguments. The brain is continually occupied in these meaning-making construction practices, even when dealing with the past, and we are continually occupied in defining and shaping our identities, making use of these practices. For Eakin, an end to the narrative process equates with an end to our identity, because we continually alter who we are in response to our present circumstances. Rosenfield says the same thing about memory:

> Memories are not fixed but are constantly evolving generalizations – recreations – of the past, which give us a sense of continuity, a sense of being, with a past, a present, and a future. They are not discrete units that are linked up over time but a dynamically evolving system. (Rosenfield 1988, 76)

Here Rosenfield's view of memory is quite clearly linked to Eakin's view of narrative living. Rosenfield suggests that memory is in fact a creation that is based on previous experience, but is neither experienced the same way twice, nor understood by the brain in the same way twice. 'We recognize ourselves as persons in terms of our relation to others, and at each new encounter we reconstruct our identity' (Rosenfield 1995, 202). In this quotation Rosenfield both speaks to Eakin's thesis and alludes to Conway's belief that we feel the deep urge to understand and access the interior lives of others in order to structure our own understanding of our lives and relationships, because interaction with others profoundly influences our self-understanding and prompts us to 'reconstruct' our own identities. To return once more to Woolf's bowl image, 'each new encounter' can be understood to shift the contents of the bowl so that they present another face or angle, continuing our personal process of acknowledging and understanding the bowl's contents.

Instead of memory operating something like a movie that we can replay, Rosenfield's claims make it seem more like an always-new movie, but one with similar actors doing somewhat similar things, i.e. known elements constructing a new but familiar image. If the author's brain understands and experiences memory as a construction, how can the reader of autobiography read such a text as anything other than invention? This understanding desta-bilizes the authority of memory, and calls into question how we can claim that a memory is true or untrue – as an always-new invention, it cannot comfortably be considered within these categories. It also muddies, or at least complicates, the distinction between truth and truthfulness.

We can return to Mary Karr's words for illustration. If Karr, in the moment of writing, has a memory that has been shaped throughout her life and is presenting in its most recent form, it could potentially be divorced from all its previous forms. Because it concerns past events, it may feel like a complete image that is merely being accessed in order to include it in the memoir, and she may credit herself with having authority over how to represent it, especially if she sees herself as able to remember 'better than anybody else' how she felt at the time the memory was initially formed. But if she favours this memory, accessed decades after the event, at the cost of 'correspondence' between her memory and how the event actually occurred, the writing is being truthful but not factually accurate (Barbour 1992, 26). Likewise, if she finds, through subsequent research, that her memory of an event is not a factual portrayal of that event, she can include it in the text and be untruthful to her memory but true to her source of research.

I want to begin by considering memory as an activity rather than an experience of a 'visiting' sensation. I want to first turn to a brief incident described in Sara Maitland's *A Book of Silence* in order to illustrate the effect the present has on the past, and the impossibility of being certain of how some events occur. In this memoir, Maitland, a novelist and nonfiction writer, explores the ways in which she turned, in her middle age, from an extraordinarily noisy life to one governed by silence. She understands this as involving a strong element of solitude, and a celebration of natural noises (weather, birdsong, running water, etc.) combined with a muting or elimination of human sounds (speech, cars, radios, telephones, etc.), as well as a significantly reduced level of even silent human communication (email, for example). After a series of experiments and explorations that took her into various situations where she sought out and prioritized human silence and solitude, she now lives alone in a remote location, 'at the moment ... aiming for 80 per cent' silence in her life (Maitland 2008, 276). *A Book of Silence* describes a number of psychological effects resulting from her new lifestyle.

Four weeks into an early plunge into solitude and as much silence as possible, living in a remote house on the Isle of Skye, Maitland records an experience of seeing a shepherd who drives by her rented house, exchanges a few words with her and drives away again. Nothing out of the ordinary but for the fact that, as Maitland records in her journal (this is important as it was written minutes after the experience): 'the scary bit [about this meeting] is that within a couple of minutes *and still* I am not at all sure whether this actually did happen, or whether I hallucinated or imagined it' (Maitland 2008, 69).

The mind cannot always be relied upon to distinguish between what has actually happened and what is thought to have happened. Or, perhaps more specifically and importantly, there is no way of knowing whether what the eye sees matches what the mind perceives, and whether this agrees with what others see or perceive. As David Eagleman puts it: 'You're not perceiving what's out there. You're perceiving whatever your brain tells you' (Eagleman 2011, 33); and, as we will see, the brain sometimes takes some remarkable liberties. This clearly complicates the ability to ensure any 'correspondence between human thought and reality', and even troubles 'coherence among different ideas and propositions' (Barbour 1992, 26).

Maitland was unsure if the figure she saw was a living, breathing human being. In one sense, this matters very much – it's good to be aware of when you're hallucinating and when you aren't – but in another sense, the man was there and was real, if she saw and experienced him as such. A nightmare only becomes a nightmare when we wake up; until then, it is very, and terrifyingly, real. Like Didion's journal-keeping, in some instances the distinction 'between what happened and what merely might have happened' can be impossible to determine, and may not even matter (Didion 2006, 103).

Maitland is interested in the experience as a psychological and physical effect of prolonged isolation and silence, but it is also a useful illustration in a discussion of the accuracy of perceived experience. '[I]t never pays to be sure about what you can't prove', says Janice Galloway (Galloway 2008, 86), a principle that informs her approach to her childhood memoir *This Is Not About Me*, and opens up almost every event to multiple interpretations.

Maitland is demonstrably unsure about what she cannot prove. Her resulting examination of the memory and her response to the experience is intriguing. This instance in Maitland's book highlights the impossibility of proving something even to oneself, even when the event has only two possible narrators (Maitland and the shepherd, if he existed). This instance also serves to illustrate the disconnection between an event and any description of it. Because the writing process creates the account of an event, rather than a repetition of it, any link between the event and the description is ambiguous – their only link would be the language that serves to separate them.

In this example, Maitland's memory of the event is coloured by her circumstances at the time. She was experiencing a number of psychological effects from her increased isolation and silence, described as a general dissolution of 'accurate perceptions of all those external factors that shore up our sense of boundaries' (Maitland 2008, 66). She had also been reading rather extensively on such effects, which may have primed her to note them in herself. She is newly in love with silence; she knows she is 'safe', with 'every reason to expect someone to come and let me know if I had completely lost the plot and failed to emerge after the six weeks were over' (Maitland 2008, 68); she has a clock, car, telephone and, most importantly, interest and enjoyment in her undertaking. These factors all influence how she perceives the episode. In her diary entry, she acknowledges that the event's uncertainty is 'scary', but seems more interested in trying to come to some sort of clear conclusion of whether the event happened or not; it certainly was not 'scary' enough to make her seek any help, or cut her time on Skye short. In her curiosity, she feels her jacket to see if it is still wet from rain, recalls details about the shepherd's van and notes basic information about the event that she cannot recall. 'I honestly am not sure', she concludes, and there the diary entry ends (Maitland 2008, 69).

However, the elapsed time between the event and the writing of the book yields a different perspective: 'Perhaps more interesting', she notes, at the time of writing the memoir, long after the diary entry,

> is how little [the event] actually alarmed me ... I realize with what insouciance, even pleasure, I seem to have regarded episodes like this, which in my pre-silence life would have terrified me as signs of incipient lunacy. (Maitland 2008, 69–70)

Not only does she consider the event within a context that involves the temporal distance between writing the diary entry and writing *A Book of Silence*, she also understands it within an even wider context: her 'pre-silence life'. On Skye, the combination of circumstances creating her immediate present made the event only 'scary', and overall the diary entry reveals a desire to understand the event rather than fear at its occurrence. Considered alongside other events that occurred during the retreat, it represents one of her many new reactions to new sensations, and she recalls the trip to Skye as overall 'interesting, demanding, exciting, good fun and deeply joyful' (Maitland 2008, 79). However, seen within her previous life, which she is reconstructing through memory, it becomes a potentially terrifying experience. Maitland's story can be read as an illustration of Rosenfield's above claim. Events which we think we keep stable through memory actually keep changing as we adjust our beliefs, perceptions and ideas with each passing day. Remembered events are always constructed according to the present, are always shaped by it, sometimes subtly, sometimes less so.

Researchers Michael Ross and Anne E. Wilson write about the ways in which human beings perform a constantly developing construction process, not only of their perceptions of the present moment, but also of their understanding of the past. They suggest that 'people are motivated to view their pasts in ways that enhance their current self-view' (Ross and Wilson 2000, 253). Or, as Mary Karr puts it, 'We tend to overlay grown-up wisdoms across the blanker selves that the young actually proffer' (Karr 2000, 24). This 'reciprocal relation' (Ross and Wilson 2000, 252) destabilizes any fixed version of events, any fixed memory, since both past and present are ever-changing, and reliant on each other in our configurations of them.

We have seen an example of this in the last chapter's discussion of *The Autobiography of Alice B. Toklas*. When Stein claims that looking back on the days she is writing about shows her just how many people she knew and things she did, she is using subsequent knowledge to draw conclusions about a previous event or experience, and she is showing this process to the reader, making it part of the text. As briefly mentioned earlier, we can also see an interesting example of this relationship in Woolf's 'A Sketch of the Past' and 'Reminiscences'. The two accounts concern roughly the same time period, but were written at different times: the former when Woolf was approaching sixty (and the end of her life), the latter in her twenties. Not only does this provide an intriguing contrast in how she portrays characters and events, it also is evident in the form of 'A Sketch of the Past'. In this piece the sections are dated, and each entry begins with some brief information about Woolf's present life before following a thread back into the past. She describes making this structural decision after

> discover[ing] a possible form for these notes. That is, to make them include the present – at least enough of the present to serve as a platform to stand upon. It would be interesting to make the two people, I now, I then, come out in contrast. (Woolf 1976, 75)

She includes her present in her account of the past in order to draw out differences, but this decision also speaks to the effect one has upon the other. Her articulation of 'I now, I then' speaks to a larger identity that contains different selves; selves that can relate to each other, and whose relation can form a more complete picture of both past and present.

Ross and Wilson also write from a position that rejects the unity of an individual over a lifetime. In their discussion of the ways in which we change our self-view over time, they repeatedly use the term 'selves', and explain their understanding of the relationship between selves rather than, for example, between one's past and present. This terminology supports the view that, over time, one becomes different selves rather than maintaining a unified personality which itself changes over time. Ross and Wilson also assign enough agency to past selves to suggest that they may indeed act almost like a group of individuals collectively determining a current worldview:

> Presumably one can almost always identify other people who are better than a target individual on any specific attribute. In contrast, when people look backward in time they may see their current self as superior to any of its predecessors on that same attribute. (Ross and Wilson 2000, 253)

These remarks posit the individual as a series of selves that are potentially 'jostling and shoving' in their establishment of which is prominent at any given moment (Rushdie 1981, 9). This phrasing also suggests that former selves are equivalent to other human beings, and that the distance between our current and past selves is comparable to the distance we feel from another individual. Or, in Michel de Montaigne's words, 'There is as much difference between us and ourselves as there is between us and others' (quoted in Eagleman 2011, 149). Ross and Wilson's articulation makes clear the extent to which they believe someone can change over time, and echoes Didion's memories of experiences that seemed to literally have happened to different people, people she now regards as strangers. We also hear echoes of Larkin's looking back on his earlier work, and how reading it made him feel that he had run into people he had long ago left behind, and nearly forgotten about entirely.

If we are always constructing versions of the world around us and, through narration, telling it and ourselves into being, we must accept that we can only ever be somewhat sure of our own versions of things, both in the present and the past. Or, we can claim to be certain about our present understanding, but we must accept that such understanding can potentially contradict past perceptions, and can be contradicted by others' present understandings. This uncertainty is evidenced by Maitland's experience described above. The past, once lived, is not frozen and stored somewhere to be retrieved from a memory bank. It is ever-shifting and, when we try to call it up, we actually build it anew, influenced by our present life and the selves that stand between the event and its latest construction.

Now turning to Nabokov's *Speak, Memory*, frequently in comparison to *The Year of Magical Thinking*, I will explore the way it intentionally and explicitly engages with memory as a tool or conscious process used by the author. I will examine how these two texts employ and talk about memory, highlighting the ways in which it can fail us, the ways in which human beings can cling to it as a meaning-making process, and the ways in which it can function as an instrument we try to employ to access our past.

Vladimir Nabokov calls his memoir *Speak, Memory* 'a systematic correlated assemblage of personal recollections' (Nabokov 2000, 7). It was not composed in an uninterrupted fashion, and most of the chapters appeared as stand-alone pieces in various publications long before an assembled text appeared. The non-linearity of the book is mirrored by its method of composition, yet Nabokov claims that despite the 'erratic' schedule in which he wrote and released sections, from the first they 'neatly fill[ed] numbered gaps in my mind which followed the present order of chapters' (Nabokov 2000, 8). This claim, that the structure of the book was conceived of and confirmed before the contents created, is interesting considered alongside the way in which the text proceeds; as always, we never know how confidently we can believe anything Nabokov tells us.

'On *Conclusive Evidence*' appears as an appendix, and is presented as a review of the earlier version of the memoir. It was published in *The New Yorker* in 1950, by a pretended reviewer (actually Nabokov himself). This faux review appears as an appendix in the Penguin 2000 edition, marking the book's most recent incarnation. Filled with Nabokov's typical arch humour and wordplay, the review also serves as another platform from which he can (truthfully or not) make various claims about his book. 'A unique freak as autobiographies go', he calls it, it 'is easier to define in terms of what it is not than in terms of what it is' (Nabokov 2000, 238). (This statement echoes Barbour's claim that truthfulness is easier to define by absence rather than by presence.) Neither a 'garrulous, formless and rambling affair' reliant on extensive notes and diaries, nor a 'popular slick kind of reminiscence where the author keys himself up to the lofty level of grade-C fiction, and with quiet impudence sets down reams and reams of dialogue', the fictional reviewer instead calls it a 'meeting point of an impersonal art form and a very personal life story' (Nabokov 2000, 239).

This description stresses the union of the authenticity of the contents and the all-important style, insisting both are integral to the text. This is not surprising for a writer who claimed 'my style is all I have' (Bruccoli and Nabokov 1991, 382). Non-chronological and stepping across Russia and into Western Europe, with a few long looks into the America of his future, Nabokov's memoir shifts time and place in a calm rejection of any linear narrative. In fact, he early makes the claim that 'the following of ... thematic designs through one's life should be, I think, the true purpose of autobiography' (Nabokov 2000, 23).

This remark closes the penultimate section of the first chapter, and is made following the relating of two events in Nabokov's father's life that mirror and match each other across a divide of fifteen years. A friend of Nabokov's father comes to visit and tries to amuse young Vladimir by playing with some matches; called away from the house suddenly, this man resurfaces in the text fifteen years later (but on the same page) when, disguised, he bumps into Nabokov's father and asks for a light for his cigarette. Nabokov calls this the 'evolution' of the image, as though in its recurrence it develops, even strengthens (Nabokov 2000, 23). This 'evolution' 'pleases' him, perhaps suggesting that the repetition of the image, its spiraling outwards into time, lends both episodes an increased significance (Nabokov 2000, 23). The spiral itself, a shape that incorporates growth and extension in a form that turns back on itself regularly, has particular resonance for Nabokov. He described his life as a 'colored spiral in a small ball of glass', enclosing the imagined spiral in a larger structure, thus limiting its expansion, but in a structure that permits examination and, possibly, protection (Wyllie 2010, 125).

The general 'purpose' of autobiography can obviously not be definitively determined (not even by Nabokov), but his pleasure in these coupled events is evident from the number of such pairs he introduces. Another memorable pair relates to his student life at Cambridge University. Nabokov turns up for his first meeting with his college tutor and, upon entering the room, treads on a tray of tea-things that has been placed on the floor. Seventeen years later, during a visit to Cambridge he stops in to visit his old tutor:

> I crossed the dim room to where he sat near a comfortable fire. "Let me see," he said, slowly turning around in his low chair ... There was a dismal crunch, a fatal clatter ... "Oh yes, of course," he said, "I know who you are." (Nabokov 2000, 210)

The leaps do not always mirror each other in such a pronounced way. Often the repetitions are subtler, but he consistently exhibits the recurrence of themes or events over time, across decades or centuries. This technique emphasizes the connection between events in a way that collapses time, making the interim period disappear. Time, in this book, is less the means of measuring a unidirectional sequence of events, and more of a malleable substance that can be arranged according to one's own desires – an appropriate treatment of something the author has declared he 'do[es] not believe in' (Nabokov 2000, 109). At one point in the memoir, Nabokov slides into a prolonged and increasingly sentimental imagining of a sleigh journey taken by his governess. As the details flow forth and Nabokov appears to inhabit this past image fully, he abruptly pulls himself and us out to close the chapter:

> all is still, spellbound, enthralled by the moon, fancy's rear-vision mirror. The snow is real, though, and as I bend to it and scoop up a handful, sixty years crumble to glittering frost-dust between my fingers. (Nabokov 2000, 78)

This sudden shift makes the image less about following a memory to its closure (if such a place can ever be determined), and more about extending the sensations and emotions into the present, doing away with the sequence of events that led him from then to now, and letting the intervening sixty years melt away.

Nabokov's structural decisions support his idea that the 'purpose' of his authorial actions is to illuminate the ways in which his life has been a stage for these sorts of recurring motifs, rather than offering a chronological account of his youth and adulthood. Indeed, this process of discovering parallels is not limited to his own life; he finds echoes and matches among his ancestors. For him, 'reconstructing one's past' involves 'probing not only one's personal past but the past of one's family in search of affinities with oneself, previews of oneself, faint allusions to one's vivid and vigorous Now' (Nabokov 1973, 187). This belief speaks to the impossibility of telling a story which is not also the story of others' lives and histories. Nabokov includes his family history in his memoir because these stories are his as well. An extended history of his ancestors comes in Chapter Three, complete with such 'affinities', including an example of a physical manifestation:

> I see very clearly the women of the Korff line [including his paternal grandmother], beautiful, lily-and-rose girls, their high, flushed *pommettes*, pale blue eyes and that small beauty spot on one cheek, a patchlike mark, which my grandmother, my father, three or four of his siblings, some of my twenty-five cousins, my younger sister and my son Dmitri inherited in various stages of intensity as more or less distinct copies of the same print. (Nabokov 2000, 44)

(Lest we feel sorry that this feature skipped Nabokov himself, we can take comfort when we elsewhere learn that he possesses 'the Korff nose' [Nabokov 2000, 43]).

Throughout the book, flashes of his life in America intercept the spotlight on his childhood and youth, constantly disrupting any linear narrative. In addition to the dedication before the body of the text, we are continually reminded, through messages that break through the 'Now' (Nabokov 1973, 187) of the writing, that the book is not addressed to the reader but, very explicitly, to Nabokov's wife Véra: 'The years are passing, my dear, and presently nobody will know what you and I know. Our child is growing ...' (Nabokov 2000, 226). In these moments we as readers are more or less disregarded. We do not share the extensive history that he and Véra share. We do not know what they know, and any entitlement we might feel as readers is confused. We can, however, read in his structural decisions an effect similar to Woolf's prefacing her memories of the past with her present emotions and circumstances, providing a contrast that may illuminate the development of the story more richly: 'This distortion of a remembered image may not only enhance its beauty with an added refraction, but provide information links with earlier or later patches of the past' (Nabokov 1973, 143).

His approach makes plain his intention to refuse any 'dutiful line' of narrative (Zinsser 1998, 15) and instead to explore what he considers the most intriguing aspect of the genre: creating a space in which to present life as a series of echoing events, whose temporal order is unimportant, irrelevant or even non-existent, as we see from his declaration of not believing in time. This realignment of events into sequences in which they did not occur exhibits 'enhance[d] beauty' because arranged as a bouquet, with particular events deliberately set off against each other. In an interview, Nabokov makes the claim that:

> reality is a very subjective affair. I can only define it as a kind of gradual accumulation of information ... You can get nearer and nearer, so to speak, to reality; but you can never get near enough because reality is an infinite succession of steps ... and hence unquenchable, unattainable. (Nabokov 1973, 10–11)

The notion of reality as subjective is also held by David Eagleman, whose work on how the brain operates leads him to claim that 'the brain runs its machinations in secret ... It does not allow its colossal operating system to be probed by conscious cognition. The brain runs its show incognito' (Eagleman 2011, 7). So, while Eagleman would agree with Nabokov that reality is individually created and determined, he sees this subjectivity as extending far below our thin level of consciousness, deep into the recesses of the entity that is really 'run[ning] its show'. '[E]ach brain', claims Eagleman, 'uniquely determines what it perceives, or is capable of perceiving ... reality is far more subjective than is commonly supposed. Instead of reality being passively recorded by the brain, it is actively constructed by it' (Eagleman 2011, 82).

The 'infinite succession of steps' described by Nabokov need not be taken in only one temporal direction. The notion that reality is created, rather than simply existing, is intriguing. More intriguing is the idea that it is not actually created, but rather always in a process of creation; Nabokov's articulation suggests that reality is something that develops over time and results from accumulated time and effort, what Paul Auster describes as 'the-work-to-be-done-that-is-done-in-the-process-of-doing-it' (Auster 1982, 91). We do not exist in 'reality' because we are occupied with slowly constructing it, gathering ingredients over the course of years.

Creating the 'reality' of his father's death, Paul Auster views the task of writing about it like this:

> I have a sense of trying to go somewhere, as if I knew what I wanted to say, but the farther I go the more certain I am that the path towards my object does not exist. I have to invent the road with each step, and this means that I can never be sure of where I am. (Auster 1982, 32)

Here, too, reality is a process of creation, a process which can never end, and which indeed, one cannot measure in a meaningful way because one 'can never be sure of where [one is]'. Because this process is so serious, much more serious than simply a writing process, the fear of finishing is completely understandable, because it implies a closure of the process of creating reality, a kind of death. This reading returns us to writing as a response to the fear of death, and likens the process of writing to the process of living. Auster continues:

> The closer I come to the end of what I am able to say, the more reluctant I am to say anything. I want to postpone the moment of ending, and in this way delude myself into thinking that I have only just begun, that the better part of my story still lies ahead. (Auster 1982, 65)

It is frightening that the process of creating reality should stop; it is infinitely more comfortable to pretend and hope that much lies ahead. Auster finds the process fraught with tension, and recognizes his active desire to prolong it. In a parallel of his own experience, Auster recalls his last visit to his dying grandfather, who for some time has lain 'immobilized in bed', silently remembering his life (Auster 1982, 118). This silent memory, which we can read as Auster witnessing his grandfather's process of self-narration, is also a mode of resisting death: 'Memory was the only thing keeping him alive, and it was as though he wanted to hold off death for as long as possible in order to go on remembering' (Auster 1982, 118).

Despite *Speak, Memory*'s terrifying opening image of 'the cradle rock[ing] above an abyss', where life is 'but a brief crack of light between two eternities of darkness' (Nabokov 2000, 17), Nabokov takes pleasure in the life/reality construction process, perhaps because there seem to be endless pairings, images, paths to walk down. In his foreword, he indicates plans for a future memoir, prolonging the process: 'I hope to write some day a "Speak on, Memory", covering the years 1940–60 spent in America' (Nabokov 2000, 11). There is indeed a sense of the 'unquenchable' in Nabokov's treatment of time, his life and his memories. His pleasure in rearranging and comparing events is evident. He follows tangents and makes disparate events appear adjacent to each other, dissolving the stretches of time that occurred between them.

We come across something very similar in *The Year of Magical Thinking*, though without the sense of play and joy that Nabokov takes in these rearrangements of past events. In an interview, Didion speaks of the importance of language to her because of its function as a way of comprehending experience. She says: 'I've got no other way of understanding it. I don't really get things ... intuitively. The only way I really get it is by writing it down', and she recalls 'irritating deeply somebody [who] ... would ask me what I was thinking and I would say I was thinking nothing ... And it was true ... I was' (Brockes 2005).

She echoes this idea in her memoir: 'Long before I began to be published', she writes, 'I developed a sense that meaning itself was resident in the rhythms of words and sentences and paragraphs' (Didion 2005, 7). This 'sense' gives language the role of not simply expressing understanding, but actually being understanding; language is the way understanding exists rather than a way of expressing pre-existing understanding. However, in the face of her husband's death and daughter's illness, she craves a different approach to, or method of, organizing her experiences and trying to comprehend them. She finds herself wishing for 'instead of words and their rhythms a cutting room ... a digital system on which I could touch a key and collapse the sequence of time, show you simultaneously all the frames of memory' (Didion 2005, 7–8). Simply remembering things is of no help to her; what she now seeks is a way to combine memories, shift them into different places, compare similarities, and thus hopefully arrive at some deeper understanding of what has happened to her.

In some ways, we see the same reorganization of events and time periods in *The Year of Magical Thinking* as in *Speak, Memory*, particularly when Didion follows the non-linear but still sequential 'vortex' of memory links (Didion 2005, 107). But overall, her text is too deeply concerned with the one-way progression of life, specifically the unidirectional cross from life into death, to find bliss in rearrangement. Her book is rooted in research, methodical attempts at understanding, which she claims to be a response to difficult events throughout her life: 'In time of trouble, I had been trained since childhood, read, learn, work it up, go to the literature. Information was control' (Didion 2005, 44).

She cannot give herself up fully to the rearrangement, and her grief is too vast to manipulate, too raw for her to reach a place that Nabokov reaches, where 'nothing will ever change, nobody will ever die' (Nabokov 2000, 62). She does not take pleasure in it, but Didion also employs this layering of memory, this repetition of recalled events, following memory pairs or groups across time and space. She does so for different reasons, and to a different end, than Nabokov. For Didion, this reverberation of memory, this linking of images, is dangerous, sinister, hugely damaging and wounding. Far from offering the sort of wonder and joy that Nabokov revels in, Didion's recent experiences have so shattered her ability to withstand pain or shock that she steels herself against recalling too much in case it spirals around to include memories of her daughter and late husband. And yet she cannot stop pursuing memories because she seeks to understand, to learn. In order to try and cope with it, she needs to know what happened, how her husband died, how her daughter's illness developed, how things got so out of control. There is a constant tension in this book between pursuing memory in order to seek understanding, and avoiding triggers for memories that are too painful to bear.

Less than a month after her husband's death she becomes aware of what she terms 'the vortex effect' (Didion 2005, 107), a process whereby any memory, no matter how removed from her family life, finds a way to twist back into another memory involving them. In the hospital visiting Quintana, she tentatively thinks of her past job at *Vogue* magazine, a 'safe' memory as it does not directly involve her husband or daughter. She then 'venture[s] further' into a specific memory of a past co-worker, which flows into recalling a piece of fiction she wrote, influenced by that co-worker; she moves on to the house she was living in at the time, a house where she watched 'from the windows of the sun porch as Quintana ran through a sprinkler on the lawn ... I had been writing that book when Quintana was three ... There it was, the vortex' (Didion 2005, 110).

For Didion, the fluidity and interconnection of memories, the way her life has begun to operate as a network of stepping stones of linked memories that connect to each other in ways that she cannot always control or anticipate, has become unsafe and painful. Or perhaps the pain comes from her realization that her life has always been constructed of such interlinked events with multiple connections to each other – only when a violent gash is made in the fabric of her life does she see how every thread can somehow find its way back to the site of pain. Memory is a tool, one she uses to try and map her grief; paradoxically, it is also a force that she tries to protect herself from, with little success. The illustration of relatedness that Nabokov sees as the true purpose of autobiography features in Didion's text, but for her it becomes an agony of trying to unmesh her memories. 'The way you got sideswiped was by going back', she thinks, being sucked back into time through her memory-connections (Didion 2005, 53). This episode shows that there is almost no choice in terms of going back – the force of the 'vortex' is so strong that Didion must make remarkable efforts to avoid it; for instance, driving routes with huge detours to avoid passing a location of significance from her past. Despite these efforts, she can be thrust back into the past with no warning. This text illustrates the torrential force memory can have on us, and the way it can seem almost predatory, with Didion being hunted by her memories even while taking great pains to keep them in a hopefully safer, more bearable space. It also serves to highlight memory's unpredictability, because of the way it operates according to links that are often unclear to the person experiencing the memory.

Joyce Carol Oates describes a similar experience to Didion's 'vortex' when she identifies the 'memory pools' that become apparent after her husband's death (Oates 2011, 46). These 'memory pools' are 'treacherous as acid', and lie in wait for the unsuspecting griever who traces familiar paths through 'shadows ... stairwells ... elevators ... corridors and in restrooms' (Oates 2011, 46). The places become sites of pain which one tries in vain to avoid. Elsewhere she calls these pools 'sinkholes'; they are 'Places fraught with visceral memory, stirring terror if you approach them' (Oates 2011, 185). Approaching them is something she tries to avoid, altering her habits and movements in an effort not to evoke memories of the past. As in *The Year of Magical Thinking*, however, this effort is almost always in vain. As Oates explains,

> the terror of the sinkhole isn't that it exists. You understand, sinkholes must exist. The terror of the sinkhole is that you fail to see it, each time you fail to see it, you don't realize you have blundered down into the sinkhole until it's too late and you are being pulled down. (Oates 2011, 349)

This is an almost exact match of Didion's description: the hidden site of pain, the fear of the pain, the desperate attempts to outrun or avoid it, and the recurring lesson that such outrunning is not possible.

At this point it seems essential to draw upon Marcel Proust's *In Search of Lost Time*, in which we find a classic treatment of the power of memory, and an illustration of voluntary and involuntary memory. Proust, by differentiating between voluntary and involuntary memory, suggests a difference between those memories we can endeavour to have, through some effort on our part, and those which come upon us, without warning, as his famous *madeleine* scene sketches. As Didion records, the direction memory can take often cannot be anticipated, and the links it operates according to can be unconscious. Like Proust's *petite madeleine*, the initial stimulus can be distanced from the memory it initially brings up.

In the famous moment in *Swann's Way*, the moment of recollection does not actually happen immediately upon tasting the tea-soaked cake on the tongue; the first sensation is a non-subject-specific joy, which must be pursued until it unleashes the memories it has awoken. The passage comes after the narrator reflects that recollection of Combray was localized to 'but two floors joined together by a slender staircase, and as though there had been no time there but seven o'clock at night' (Proust 1913, 50). There is a sense of restriction in this image, both physically, with only two floors, connected in only one 'slender' way, and temporally, with the entire scene locked into a particular time. The narrator identifies his memories of the place as bordered by the confines of 'voluntary memory, the memory of the intellect', which 'preserve[s] nothing of the past itself' (Proust 1913, 50). There has been little cause to return to this limited memory for 'many years', making it 'in reality all dead' (Proust 1913, 51, 50).

What saves the memory from being lost forever is the taste of the tea-soaked *madeleine*, which at first causes an 'extraordinary thing ... an exquisite pleasure', a sensation which causes our narrator to feel first filled with a 'precious essence' and then to feel that he himself is the essence: 'this essence was not in me, it *was* me' (Proust 1913, 51). This moment can be read as a 'moment of being', where suddenly all the 'non-being' elements of life fall away to produce a 'sudden violent shock' which creates the sensation that 'we are the words; we are the music; we are the thing itself' (Woolf 1976, 72). All the cares of life fall away, and this sensation overtakes him. It is important to note, in a scene so celebrated for its treatment of the power of memory, that at first the sensation is not an immediate jolt of memory, but simply a sensation, 'isolated, detached, *with no suggestion of its origin*' (Proust 1913, 51, my emphasis). Without origin, the sensation cannot lead the narrator into recollection, though he greatly desires it: 'Whence could it have come to me, this all-powerful joy? ... Where did it come from? What did it mean? How could I seize and apprehend it?' (Proust 1913, 51–2). Nor can the sensation be recollection itself; subsequent bites are taken in an effort merely to maintain this 'exquisite pleasure', until suddenly the sensation changes form as 'the memory revealed itself' (Proust 1913, 53). Following from the initial connection of bites of pastry taken in his aunt's room as a child,

> in that moment all the flowers in our garden and in M. Swann's park, and the water-lilies on the Vivonne and the good folk of the village and their little dwellings and the parish church and the whole of Combray and its surroundings, taking shape and solidity, sprang into being, town and gardens alive, from my cup of tea. (Proust 1913, 55)

This is another articulation of Didion's 'vortex effect', though it also offers up Proust's differentiation between voluntary and involuntary memory. Proust's narrator suggests that involuntary memory is triggered by 'taste and smell alone, more fragile but more enduring', holding within them the 'vast structure of recollection' (Proust 1913, 54). This potential outlasts the voluntary memory of 'people' and 'things', and can be called up even after those are 'dead … broken and scattered' (Proust 1913, 54). The shift in Didion's memory, from the job at *Vogue* to the memory of her three-year-old daughter, is involuntary. It happens despite her efforts; it takes over her before she can do anything about it. And her involuntary memory also recalls in sensual, evocative language: the sense of warmth from the 'sun porch' (Didion 2005, 110), the visual image of what is seen through the windows, the image of Quintana running through a sprinkler, calling up laughter, cool water, grass beneath the feet. These sensual images return most forcefully, able to break through the preventative measures Didion tries to establish against them. Indeed, they resurface despite the fact that the people and things involved in the memory, apart from her, are now 'dead … broken and scattered'.

This association of sensual imagery with powerful, sudden recollection is echoed in *Speak, Memory*. Nabokov is frank about 'using' memory; his identification of it as one of the writer's many tools highlights this, but so does his frequent articulation of how his own mental efforts prompt or enable memory to function in his writing process. In his foreword he outlines some of the changes the manuscript has gone through, indicating that some errors were found in the previous version because he 'had not examined deeply enough an obscure but fathomable recollection' (Nabokov 2000, 11). This image of memory as a 'fathomable' space implies that it can be fully known, if sufficient time and equipment are provided. It also suggests a trawling, a methodical exploration of identifiable, measurable space. However, he acknowledges that he was also responsible for mismatching memories and times/places. He accepts that memory is not ultimately authoritative, but he recognizes it as a form of authority, and one he privileges, much like Karr's insistence on truthfulness being connected to her ability to remember how she felt better than anybody else.

Nabokov articulates this process of employing memory, calling it up and using considerable personal effort to draw information out. A notable example occurs in *Speak, Memory*'s brief seventh chapter, which features a youthful holiday romance between Nabokov and Colette, a somewhat socially unacceptable playmate with whom he recalls playing on the beach. Details come flooding back, but not fully: 'I remember the sail, the sunset and the lighthouse pictured on that pail, but I cannot recall the [little girl's] dog's name, and this bothers me' (Nabokov 2000, 118). Over the subsequent paragraphs, he paints the scene of their attempted elopement (getting no further than the cinema before being recaptured by Nabokov's tutor). He closes the chapter by recalling some souvenirs of this trip, and, in describing his favourite object, finds that

> the process of recreating that penholder and the microcosm in its eyelet stimulates my memory to a last effort. I try again to recall the name of Colette's dog – and, triumphantly, along those remote beaches, over the glossy evening sands of the past, where each footprint slowly fills up with sunset water, here it comes, here it comes, echoing and vibrating: Floss, Floss, Floss! (Nabokov 2000, 119)

In this section, Nabokov is illustrating the process of drawing upon memory, teasing open long-closed events, hoping to crack them open and reveal a preserved, glowing picture, an example of the process he describes in his foreword, where upon revising the first version of the text he

> tried to do something about the amnesiac defects of the original – blank spots, blurry areas, domains of dimness. I discovered that sometimes, by means of intense concentration, the neutral smudge might be forced to come into beautiful focus. (Nabokov 2000, 9)

In contrast to the suddenness of memory as seen in *The Year of Magical Thinking*, and indeed in other sections of *Speak, Memory*, this form of using memory is voluntary, and not very easy. It requires 'intense concentration' and often repeated efforts. The 'Floss' sequence acts out this process of concentration, allows the reader to witness the moment when the blur becomes 'triumphantly' focused. In his pseudo-review, Nabokov notes that this sequence

> retain[s] in the development of the story, as part of its texture, the actual difficulty he had, as he went along, of recalling the name of a dog – a name that suddenly was released from a secret cell in the mind during the process of writing. (Nabokov 2000, 239)

Alternatively, it has been suggested that in fact Nabokov, as usual, is operating on multiple layers, describing his efforts at recollection on the surface but in fact playing with this effort at recall throughout the chapter. The chapter is a neat flow through memory, moving swiftly from the train journey that takes the family to Paris, en route to Biarritz, where recollection of the beach cabin brings him to the attendant, who teaches Nabokov the Basque word for 'butterfly', a word he keeps 'preserved … in a glass cell of my memory' (Nabokov 2000, 116). The word, misremembered as 'miseri-coletea' (Nabokov 2000, 116), brings him swiftly to the episode with his young playmate, named Colette, mimicking the sounds of the foreign word. Moreover, the dog's name is revealed at the close of a paragraph replete with repetitions of the letters *o*, *s* and *f*, hinting at the sound of the dog's name.

Nabokov is certainly no less playful than Stein in his authorial decisions. When calling the text a meeting between his life story and 'impersonal' art, we should not suppose that his art form is not highly self-conscious and constructed. This episode is an echo, or another manifestation, of Didion's 'vortex'. The chapter illustrates the movement of memory, the (often delayed) way that links become apparent, and the way memory often expands in multiple, unanticipated directions rather than in any linear fashion.

It is worth a brief aside here to discuss a possible instance of what Nabokov calls 'farm[ing]' a memory 'out to my characters' (Nabokov 1973, 12). In the same interview in which he envisions memory as one tool of many, he draws a distinction between some memories which remain eternally vivid and fresh, and others, 'perhaps intellectual rather than emotional, [which] are very brittle and sometimes apt to lose the flavor of reality when they are immersed by the novelist in his book, when they are given away to characters' (Nabokov 1973, 12). To first exemplify this lending of past to fiction, we can find an easy example, which directly relates to the Colette episode.

In the opening of *Lolita*, Humbert Humbert recalls a formative event in his life: his relationship with a child named Annabel, while they were both children staying at 'Hotel Mirana', 'the luxurious hotel on the Riviera' owned by Humbert's father (Nabokov 1955, 11). Annabel is Lolita's 'precursor', and Humbert goes so far as to claim that 'there might have been no Lolita at all had I not loved, one summer, a certain initial girl-child. In a princedom by the sea' (Nabokov 1955, 11). (Here we also clearly hear Edgar Allan Poe's poem 'Annabel Lee', in which the youthful relationship takes place in a 'kingdom by the sea' [Poe 1999, 783].) Humbert and Annabel's 'affair' progresses 'madly, clumsily, shamelessly, agonizingly', until their activities are discovered and halted by various forms of adult authority (Nabokov 1955, 14). Annabel is 'half-English, half-Dutch'; Colette 'mix[es] governess English and Parisian French' (Nabokov 1955, 13; 2000, 117). Both girls are a few months younger than Nabokov/Humbert; both 'affairs' are almost entirely played out on the beach, where Annabel's hand, 'half-hidden in the sand', the 'soft sand on which they would sprawl all morning, in a petrified paroxysm of desire', creeps towards Humbert's body; Nabokov and Colette 'dig ... side by side in the sand' (Nabokov 1955, 14; 2000, 117).

Is this a memory that Nabokov has 'farm[ed] out'? Has the memory become 'brittle', lost 'its flavor'? Nabokov dismissed any connection between little Annabel and little Colette, and indeed the presence of what he called these 'telltale affinities' (Nabokov 1973, 24) can indicate a conscious attempt at parody in *Lolita*. But considering these questions becomes more interesting when we read how Humbert and Nabokov distinguish between memories, in terms that call up Proust once more. 'There are two kinds of visual memory', Humbert Humbert tells us,

> one when you skillfully recreate an image in the laboratory of your mind, with your eyes open ... and the other when you instantly evoke, with shut eyes, on the dark innerside of your eyelids, the objective, absolutely optical replica of a beloved face, a little ghost in natural colors. (Nabokov 1955, 13)

Here we have a familiar distinction. The first kind of memory is 'recreate[d]', a practice that one can be skilled at, and which takes place in the 'laboratory of [the] mind', bringing to mind the image of a workplace, an almost clinical, or perhaps medical, setting, a place where 'tools' might be necessary. The other form of memory is 'evoke[d]' rather than created. It is called forth, implying its pre-existence, its greater independence from the mind. 'The more you love a memory', claims Nabokov, 'the stronger and stranger it is', explaining how some memories do become brittle with lending out, while some are unaffected by this weakening process: only 'a certain type of intellectual memory' is weakened when placed into fiction (Nabokov 1973, 12). As an example of a memory which cannot be weakened and always remains immediate and vivid, he offers the following scene:

> the freshness of the flowers being arranged by the under gardener in the cool drawing-room of our country house, as I was running downstairs with my butterfly net on a summer day ... the red sand, the white garden bench, the black fir trees. (Nabokov 1973, 12)

The more permanent memory is recalled in very visual, even sensual terms: the heat of summer and the cool drawing-room, the sensation of running, the sudden perfume of flowers, the bright colours of the objects he passes outdoors, the passion of butterfly-hunting. In contrast, the descriptors Humbert uses when recalling Annabel according to this former, more intellectual (and more prone to weakening) type of memory are her 'thin arms

... brown bobbed hair ... long lashes ... big bright mouth' (Nabokov 1955, 13). These are still visual images, but they lack the specificity and immediate sensory nature of the descriptions of a less 'intellectual' type of memory. This difference is aligned with Proust's 'voluntary memory, memory of the intellect', as opposed to another form of memory, which lies dormant in 'taste and smell' (as in the fragrance of flowers with which Nabokov introduces his example of an 'unbreakable' memory) but which can cause whole worlds to rise up suddenly (Proust 1913, 50, 54).

Nabokov desires the recalled memory of the dog's name. He creates an image of summoning it with effort, and through (paradoxically) trying to activate the involuntary memory. Didion does not want to activate this process, and indeed seeks ways to close it off, sealing herself in a 'safe' zone that has no potential connections to her pain-free past. Proust's narrator is surprised by the process, but it brings him bliss. In all three cases the strong onset of memory is posited as a sudden illumination provoked by (thinking of) a physical sensation, and in all cases this sensation has the ability to 'open up' the memory, which swiftly becomes expansive and all-encompassing. The passage that ends Proust's *madeleine* chapter is an excellent example: we move quickly from the morsel in the mouth outwards, almost cinematically, taking in the gardens, the houses, the town, always enlarging our scope as the vast structure grows around us.

Israel Rosenfield refers to *In Search of Lost Time* during a 'literary interlude' in his *The Invention of Memory* (Rosenfield 1988, 81). Identifying the importance of involuntary memory in Proust's writing, he points out that in those cases when it occurs, the rush of memory is still a new creation, not simply the onset of a replayed past experience. He provides the following example from *The Past Recaptured* (*Time Regained*): 'as I compared these diverse happy impressions ... I experienced them at the present moment, *so that the past was made to encroach upon the present and I was made to doubt whether I was in the one or the other*' (Proust 1954, quoted in Rosenfield 1988, 82). This quoted passage continues with the suggestion that the nature of this meeting between past and present means 'the one and only medium' in which to enjoy and experience 'the essence of things' is 'outside time' (Proust 1954, quoted in Rosenfield 1988, 82). The narrator notes that the 'extra-temporal' nature of such experiences, which have 'in them something that was common to a day long past and to the present', means that he too was 'an extra-temporal being' during the experience, and so was 'unalarmed by the vicissitudes of the future', since the concept of a future, or a past, does not exist (Proust 1927, 904). It is now worth briefly returning to Kierkegaard's notion of living life forwards but understanding it backwards; he concludes that this proposition so complicates temporal order that it

Re read

'becomes more and more evident that life can never really be understood in time' (Kierkegaard 1938, 127).

Rosenfield suggests that this fusion of past and present 'transcend[s] any temporal relation' and that 'Proust is describing the ways in which we create and recreate our categorizations of events, people, and things' (Rosenfield 1988, 84). Ordinary notions of time do not apply to memory because we are by definition negotiating between past and present to establish the fusion that is the memory. Indeed, as a relevant aside, we may query exactly what might be meant by 'ordinary notions of time', since there is evidence that there is nothing ordinary or commonly understood as time at all – time is merely one more way in which we are subject to the decisions made by our brains for us. 'The perception of time is also a construction', argues David Eagleman, adding one more item to the list of ways in which the brain 'runs its own show' (Eagleman 2011, 51). The brain takes no notice of our attempts to overlay hours and minutes, weeks and years, onto our experience of the world. Rather, 'our sense of time – how much time passed and what happened when – is constructed by our brains. And this sense is easily manipulated' (Eagleman 2011, 53). This explains, for instance, why in moments of danger or panic, things seem to happen in slow motion, and why experiences many years old can feel fresh, eternally new – timeless.

'Memories', says Rosenfield, 'manifest themselves in the immediate, and therefore differ greatly from the occasion on which they arose' (Rosenfield 1988, 75). In the present, 'recollections of events depend on the perspective from which we view them'; because our perspective is obviously in the present, the 'recollections *now* have a new meaning' (Rosenfield 1988, 83). As Rosenfield states, even events long past can 'have a new meaning' in our present life and 'therefore are not really past events in themselves vividly recalled. They are different in both their emotional and intellectual significance' (Rosenfield 1988, 83).

'We are time-bound creatures', claims Jill Ker Conway, arguing for the importance of understanding and acknowledging the 'causation' of our actions (Conway 1995, 56). Narrating our lives into existence reinforces the idea that we are 'time-bound creatures' precisely because our narration always builds upon past experience. But, paradoxically, memory and the newness of recollection can have such a strong pull towards the past, while being so rooted in the present, that the very meaning and understanding of time can be blurred, and its linearity, its effect of causation, ceases to be clear.

In *The Invention of Solitude*, Paul Auster considers the death of his father alongside the life of his own infant son. He reflects on the changing relationships as son becomes father, and, in moments of intense wonder and sorrow, feels as though 'he were going both forward and backward, into the future and into the past. And there are times … when these feelings are so strong that his life no longer seems to dwell in the present' (Auster 1982, 81–2). The past, bound up with his father, and the future, bound up with his son, are simultaneously pulling him in opposite directions and yet collapsing into one timeless space. 'Memory: the space in which a thing happens for the second time' (Auster 1982, 83), he writes, a suggestion that includes both the connection between past and present fused through memory, and also the newness of memory, as a place where a second occurrence is experienced, rather than a replay of the first occurrence.

　Didion's account is very much about going forward, progressing through the year and charting changes she experiences as she moves days, weeks and eventually a complete year beyond her husband's death. She frequently situates herself within that year, writing from a specific, named date and orienting us around that day. Nevertheless, her tracking of her movement forward often brings her up against events in the past; her attempt not to go backwards is rendered impossible. There is no clear-cut forwards and backwards, but rather a constantly growing interconnection between her present and her past. Her fluid movement across decades, even while working within a clearly stated present, illustrates Nabokov's articulation of the 'tissue' of time: 'The Past is also part of the tissue, part of the present' (Nabokov 1990, 186). (Elsewhere, he identifies the present as 'only the top of the past' [Nabokov 1973, 184].) The 'tissue' of time is so densely interwoven that past and present almost cease to have real meaning. The links can easily span large periods of time, and the movement and duration of time itself is destabilized. As a tissue, time is considered as a whole, as a tapestry on which one can move one's eye from one place to another, rather than, for instance, walking along a length of string, which stretches out in both directions but is only connected to the individual in one small, precise place. The notion of time as a 'tissue' echoes Barthes's 'tissue of signs' (Barthes 1977, 147), and aligns text with life – past and present mean little to either, and each imitates the other. For Nabokov, the past exists in the present, but the present also exists in the past, as his son Dmitri's beautymark existed even when it was only present three generations earlier. Virginia Woolf, in recalling the unwanted sexual advances of her half-brother, remembers 'resenting, disliking' the feeling of his hand on her body, even while being unable to articulate precisely why she knew this action was wrong (Woolf 1976, 69). This knowledge, she suggests, 'seems to show that a feeling about certain parts of the body … is instinctive', which, to her, 'proves that Virginia Stephen was not born on the 25th January 1882, but was born many thousands of years ago; and had from the very first to encounter instincts already acquired by thousands of ancestresses in the past' (Woolf 1976, 69).

Likewise, for Didion, the past is the present, and her attempts to block out the painful parts are therefore in vain. Trying to manoeuvre away from painful memories does nothing but bring her up behind some other site of pain, and her current project of mapping one year becomes about every single year prior, and indeed extends before her marriage, before her birth, as far back as King Arthur's tales, where Gawain claims 'I tell you I shall not live two days' (Didion 2005, 26). Didion uses this sentence almost as a refrain throughout the memoir; it becomes shorthand for her attempt to recover her husband's thoughts in the days before his death, a recovery which might help clarify her own reactions. She brings the present into the past as much as she brings the past into the present. She continually asks herself whether he knew, whether he had any premonition of his death, remembering events over and over again in an effort to glean some new knowledge from them, trying to see if she can reinterpret them as having more significance than she initially thought they had. 'Did he have some apprehension, a shadow? … was something telling him that night that the time for being able to write was running out? … What did he mean? Did he know … ?' (Didion 2005, 23).

Various manifestations of this uncertainty, the inability to pinpoint exactly when a particular event happened or how it happened, haunt her throughout the text. She fixates on times and dates, mapping the chronology of her grief and relating events to each other until a network of despair, a structure, rises up from the text, enclosing her. The structure is made up of fragments, individual pieces of experience which are now coming together and binding her within them. '*These fragments I have shored against my ruins*' (Didion 2005, 190–1) she thinks, invoking Eliot's disorienting shards of image and experience, recalling these segments of the past and seeing that the fragments have done nothing to stop disaster, but merely confine her in endless recollections.

Joyce Carol Oates invokes this same line from Eliot, but suggests that this is the best we can do, that these shards and fragments are all we have. 'Words may be "helpless" – yet words are all we have to shore against our ruin, as we have only each other' (Oates 2011, 310). Here words and human relations are given equal weight, though both are ultimately unsuccessful in keeping us from 'ruin'. Both Didion's and Oates's phrasing seems to suggest that trying to use language as a barrier to devastation is normal, a human tendency. It is a method we use to stall disaster, and bind us to each other. Oates suggests that 'for all who are grieving, there is no way to survive except through others' (Oates 2011, 158). Survival, in both women's memoirs, is closely bound up with communicating memories and stories, and possibly even surviving 'through others' stories' (Felman 1993, 18).

When Didion and Oates attempt to use language and memory in ways that might heal or even staunch pain, they do so with their own ability to self-narrate more or less intact. Although they have suffered huge losses and are going though periods of trauma after a severe rupture in their daily lives, they both revert, eventually, to language as a means of re-writing the narrative and corralling the memories. Linda Grant's memoir of her mother's experience living with dementia illustrates how, when this ability to self-narrate is also stripped away, there is no longer any way to reliably construct a version of reality; unsurprisingly, this has catastrophic effects not only on the diagnosed individual, but also on those close to them.

Rose Grant's condition deteriorates throughout the memoir *Remind Me Who I Am, Again*, in ways that clearly show memory not as a stylistic tool that one can choose to employ when making art, but rather an essential means of self-narration, a way of asserting selfhood and stability. As Rose loses the ability to, for example, reliably identify her family members, recall where she lives and relate to those around her in an appropriate and consistent manner, memory is revealed as not just a tool that can be used if an author wishes; rather, 'Memory is … everything, it's life itself' (Grant 1998, 17). This is what Rose's illness teaches her daughter Linda; memory is an essential part of maintaining not just social and family relations, but one's very humanity: 'without [memory], we are animals … without the past we're nothing, we belong to nobody' (Grant 1998, 28).

So while Didion and Oates grapple with their memories and attempt to find some new way of understanding the world around them, revisiting the past and trying laboriously to make some sense of it, they can at least do so with a weakened, but not destroyed, sense of who they are. Linda Grant, on the other hand, witnesses Rose lose that sense entirely, and this perhaps helps her understand why the Head of Residential Care at the institution where Rose is moved to suggests to Linda that 'In a way your mother is dead, and in a way she's not dead' (Grant 1998, 268). Rose's experience shows Linda the clear links between memory and survival, and of course between memory and the greater process of self-narration to which it contributes: 'Because we do not remember everything that has ever happened to us, because we must filter and select and edit the experiences and information that enter our senses every day and transform it into a meaningful narrative, our lives are essentially stories' (Grant 1998, 293).

Here of course she clearly echoes Eakin, and highlights the importance of the past, as well as our ability to sort through it, to our current stories. She also understands the eternal newness of memory, as a product of people whose identities are constantly in progress, never complete. That means memory is 'a fabrication, a re-interpretation, a new reconstruction of the original', and yet, or perhaps because of all that, it is 'a miracle' (Grant 1998,

294–5). It is miraculous in part because of its life-giving property: 'Without memory there's chaos. Without memory we don't exist' (Grant 1998, 268). '[I]f I am not my memory', Grant asks, 'who am I?' (Grant 1998, 294). Grant's exploration of how memory is cruelly and permanently destroyed for her mother does much to illustrate how crucial memory is for our very identity, and that of those around us – she is forced to consider, for example, the terrifying question: 'If you live in the memory of someone else and their memory starts to fade, where are you?' (Grant 1998, 268). And yet her memoir also reveals the multiplicity of memory, and the way it refuses to actually remain in the past, but moves from present to past smoothly, suddenly, not requiring our consent. Memory, in this account, bleeds into everything: personal identity, family relationships, historical significance, cultural understanding. Its many forms become bewildering; maybe this is appropriate if we believe Eagleman's view that 'The conviction that memory is one thing is an illusion' (Eagleman 2011, 126).

In a much less extreme way than with Rose Grant, some things escape Didion's memory, nevertheless causing her uncertainty and anguish. She clings to these 'blind spots' and obsesses over them, vainly trying to employ memory as a tool, as though arriving at a definitive conclusion could lend some certainty to the events, or possibly alter the final outcome (this thought process is the 'magical thinking' of the memoir's title, which is referred to as 'if thinking' in the one-woman play developed from her memoir). She can recall the words of a conversation with her husband shortly before his death, but cannot pin it down in time precisely: 'he said these things in the taxi between Beth Israel North and our apartment either three hours before he died or twenty-seven hours before he died, I try to remember which and cannot' (Didion 2005, 82). Didion's anguish echoes Maitland's frightened wonder. These blank spots do not persist for lack of 'intense concentration'; she does not keep forgetting because she is not trying hard enough to remember. Her book is as much about failing to remember as it is about the sudden force of unwanted memory. It shows how memory is something that we are not in control of, an effort we may claim to turn on and off without appreciating that it is a mode of thinking in the present, a mode of thinking that calls up the past, but which can only ever use the lens of the present. Didion in *The Year of Magical Thinking* seems very, very far away from a younger Didion, writing at age thirty-three that her memories are 'so clinically detailed' that she 'sometimes wish[es] that memory would effect the distortion with which it is commonly credited' (Didion 2006, 173).

Speak, Memory and *The Year of Magical Thinking* are about memory as much as they are about their authors' lives. They both occasionally treat memory as a functional practice, which the authors can choose to employ in order to better present the writing, but the memoirs also offer occasions where we can see memory as an independent force that can withhold information, or provide false information. Memory may be a tool, as Nabokov indicates, but it is an imperfect one. At any opportunity it moves independently, changes direction, connects images with no regard for their temporal order or highlights meanings and significance never before appreciated. And the results it provides are always products of the present, though they contain glimpses of the past.

4

Inventing the Road with Every Step

This final chapter builds on the arguments constructed in the three earlier chapters. I will continue using Paul John Eakin's suggestion that works of memoir and autobiography are 'fictions about what is itself in turn a fiction, the self' (Eakin 2000, 290), and also draw on John Sturrock's view of autobiography as a process of conversion. Sturrock uses this term with particular reference to Augustine's *Confessions*, which he refers to as 'the paradigm of all autobiographical stories' (Sturrock 1993, 20). Addressed to God, the *Confessions* tell the story of Augustine's religious conversion, a process which changes him fundamentally, therefore profoundly affecting his self-view. Sturrock employs this term to also refer to a fundamental changing of the present, or life events, into a narrative, drawing a parallel between the two acts. The conversion of events and experiences into a written account is a permanent change of great significance, and here it is connected to the kind of change in personal identity that a religious conversion entails. Sturrock is using the powerful connotations of religious conversion, and indeed referring to this process by drawing on Augustine, to describe the process by which a written account is formed out of the material of lived events.

Understanding conversion in a secular sense as well, we can read much autobiography and memoir as deeply concerned with the events contributing to the formation of identity, and indeed certain particular events which can have a lasting, even permanent, effect on one's notion of selfhood. Sturrock's use of the term alludes to both the process of change and development charted in the individual who is the subject of autobiography, as well as the process by which life events become written narrative. It also connotes an essential element of transformation: the changes made by a conversion are near-total. Religious conversions do not often appear in contemporary autobiographies, but the same sense of rupture, struggle and large-scale alteration on the most basic level of identity does, and autobiographies continue to exist as records of such changes and conversions.

I have suggested that human identity in terms of understanding oneself changes constantly, in a continual process that involves interpreting experiences and events in such a way as to renew who we think we are after each one. I have shown that narrative is the mode of such understanding – telling ourselves, our reality, into being. I have also discussed how memory is a new construction that always changes to reflect one's previous selves and experiences, and therefore, while *like* a past event, is always a new event. In this chapter I speak in greater depth about the way this troubles definitions of memoir and autobiography as works of either fiction or nonfiction.

To begin, I'll use an example of an author who appears to reject the idea that the writing of memory entails the creation of a new fiction out of the material of older fictions. W. H. Hudson's *Far Away and Long Ago* was largely written during a period of illness, when the 76-year-old author was laid up for some time. This illness was the result of a combination of emotional and physical pain; Hudson was already 'feeling weak and depressed' when he became more gravely, physically ill (Hudson 1918, 2). This was at the close of the First World War, an event which was partially responsible for Hudson's depressed state, and this depressed state became complicated by physical sickness. Hudson himself joins the two bodily responses when he recalls how 'the bright colours of the afternoon kept me too long on the front in an east wind in that low condition' (Hudson 1918, 2). The 'low condition' was exacerbated by the 'east wind', and Hudson experienced a period of illness which can be seen as a physical and mental response to trauma, depression and physical weakness. It is intriguing that such a book would come out of a period characterized by pain, and Hudson himself marvels that he looks back on writing it so fondly. The book is full of energy, and Hudson seems to have found writing it deeply therapeutic.

The manner in which he wrote it is very interesting. During this period of ill-health, he discovered an almost magical ability to recollect his past at will, with extraordinary vividness. Hudson tells us that prior to this experience, it was 'never [his] intention to write an autobiography', because he previously believed that 'when a person endeavours to recall his early life in its entirety he finds it is not possible' (Hudson 1918, 1). However, the 'very serious illness' presented him with reason to change his mind, for, during the long, idle, bedrest hours of his recovery, he found that his weakened state somehow granted him the ability to recall his past with total clarity and, furthermore, he found himself possessed of the ability to select 'this or that point to dwell upon, to examine it in all its details' (Hudson 1918, 3). Throughout his six-week recovery, Hudson recorded these recollections, or, rather, deliberate journeys through his past, continually surprised at how 'marvellous' it was that his 'mental state' allowed for this kind of re-living (Hudson 1918, 3).

The book is a record of these mental exercises, or journeys, where Hudson leads us through the Argentinean pampas of his childhood, taking extreme pleasure in the sense of life, movement and abundance of nature. He brings his childhood to life for us, through detail and a rush of emotion that spurs on each chapter.

What are we to make of Hudson's claims? Does his illness, or his claim of his resulting ability to voyage through the past with perfect clarity and ease, imbue his experience with any added validity, or his account with added veracity? I argue it does not. While it had the happy side effect of releasing this flood of memory for him, and enabling him to explore his past with excitement and relish, there is no guarantee or even support for the assertion that a particular state of mind (which we must trust he indeed experienced) means his narrative is more true, or even more truthful. His writing is simply another version of events, written at a particular point in time and subject to Hudson's circumstances at that time.

In fact, this situation is no different from the circumstances around the writing of each of the books discussed in this book. Hudson's situation was simply somewhat more singular because of his claims of being in an almost supernatural state. He may well have found that this state of mind permitted something which hitherto he had not thought possible, i.e. writing memoir, but every memoir is a product of a particular place and time, as is every novel. We might, however, less easily recognize the geographical and/or historical context of a novel. In this way, the historical context of a memoir is perhaps more relevant when considering it, but, because time and place are integral to every memoir, Hudson's wartime depression and period of ill-health are no more or less important than Didion's post-millennium, New York setting. Setting and time are important for autobiography, but no setting or time is especially important, or more important, than another. The fact that much of Stein's book is set in the interwar period in Paris is essential to understanding the text, but not more or less important than understanding the atmosphere of overall excess that characterized New York City in the 1980s when reading Dani Shapiro's memoir *Slow Motion*. In fact, looking back over the works discussed here reminds us that *The Year of Magical Thinking* was written during a time of such profound grief that Didion claims she was 'demented' (Didion 2005, 125). Natalia Ginzburg was also dealing with the trauma and loss she suffered during World War Two. Hudson's state becomes less unique when we consider comparable examples of mental anguish and activity.

Hudson's claims are, however, interesting in how they endow illness with a certain power to bring forth greater or clearer self-knowledge. He explicitly names the illness as giving him the ability to return to his past – returning his past to him, in a way. Virginia Woolf's classic essay 'On Being Ill' is useful in exploring this idea. We can find echoes of Hudson's words in this essay. Woolf suggests that a person who is ill discovers nothing less than that 'the world has changed its shape' (Woolf 1930, 8). She suggests that illness has the ability to reveal the world in a new way to those who 'cease to be soldiers in the army of the upright' (Woolf 1930, 12). Hudson describes how he was possessed of the ability to choose which moment to focus on by hovering overhead, looking over his youth as though it was laid out beneath him, and then selecting the moment to explore, swooping down into it. In Woolf's essay, this image is inverted. She describes ill people as those who can, 'perhaps for the first time in years' look up at the sky (Woolf 1930, 12) because they have ceased to stand and walk though their day. This sight is 'strangely overcoming', mainly because the 'endless activity' therein has been going on unnoticed for so long (Woolf 1930, 13). In both cases illness allows one to see vistas previously concealed or ignored.

Woolf also speaks to the liminal state that illness creates, one that Hudson also describes. There is 'a childish outspokenness in illness', according to Woolf; it is 'the great confessional' where 'things are said, truths blurted out' that would remain silent in our healthier, more guarded states (Woolf 1930, 11). Illness bestows greater openness of communication, and may also remove inhibitions. Illness also encourages language and the creation of new language. Without adequate words to describe physical discomfort, Woolf suggests that those who are ill are reduced to taking their 'pain in one hand, and a lump of pure sound in the other ... so to crush them together that a brand new word in the end drops out' (Woolf 1930, 7). Rather similar descriptions begin *Swann's Way*, where sleep, rather than illness, causes the liminal state. The narrator describes moving between sleeping and waking, and the loosening sensation this provokes, where he is unsure where he is, or which is more real between his recent dream and the reality in which he fell asleep.

Hudson's claims as to his powerful control over his memory echo Nabokov's earlier willing of the dog Floss's name, suggesting that there are means and situations in which buried memories can be unearthed, particularly through human effort, or 'intense concentration' (Nabokov 2000, 9). However, keeping in mind that Nabokov's book is dedicated to a woman who has lived her life alongside his and knows his history, a history that he dips in and out of while always remaining firmly in the present, even looking towards the future, illustrates the way that recollections are always considered in the context of the present and shaped accordingly. Even stating that a period of illness in adulthood brought about Hudson's memoir is to acknowledge the relationship between selves and the effect time has upon memory, and to suggest a relationship between the two periods of time that is integral to the present product.

This is to say that, despite the overall appearance of memoir and autobiography being one of a return to the past, or even bringing past events into light, they are actually newly created accounts, whose transformation from mental image to written text completes the process of change into a new form. The events within memoirs and autobiographies are new both for the reader and the writer. Despite having lived through the events, reconstructing them will result in a narrative that is also new to the author. We recall William Zinsser's claim that 'Memoir writers must manufacture a text', which involves 'imposing a narrative order on a jumble of half-remembered events' (Zinsser 1998, 6). Even if, according to the writer, these events are not half-remembered but recalled accurately, their (re)arrangement, the process of manufacturing and 'imposing a narrative', still makes a new product, necessarily influenced by the present. It is also but one of many possible such products, a unique version of the past.

The process, says John Sturrock, of beginning with a memory and ending with a written account is one of conversion rather than adhesion (Sturrock 1993). This is an important point; it relates to a fundamental difference between two ways of handling material and language. Autobiography is not the layering of language over history, ending with two related but still distinct entities. It is instead a process of converting the memory, through language, into the written account, changing it and ending up with a new product. 'If you describe a dream', says Annie Dillard, 'you'll notice that at the end of the verbal description you've lost the dream but gained a verbal description' (Dillard 1987, 157). This aptly illustrates the conversion process – language becomes the tool with which memory is transformed into something new: 'All that we can share of the past, even with ourselves, is what we are capable of saying or writing about it', argues Sturrock, naming language as the only possible means of effecting such a process. This is a natural extension of his position that all we can share of ourselves in any time frame is what we can narrate (Sturrock 1993, 24). Sturrock claims that the 'pre-textual' life, that 'potential nebula of thoughts and sensations' (what William Zinsser calls the 'jumble' [Zinsser 1998, 6]), can provide the material from which this new account is created, but the narrative is distinct from this material because converted, fundamentally changed (Sturrock 1993, 24).

Creating a narrative becomes the only way we can express our own lives and get close to accessing and trying to understand the lives of others. In line with Didion's claim that we 'tell ourselves stories in order to live' (Didion 2006, 185), Sturrock indicates that the only way we can express a life of any meaning is through narrative: 'A human life can be brought to display a meaning only on condition of being turned into a story ... A life storied is a life made meaningful' (Sturrock 1993, 20). The lack of a narrative is, in many ways, a lack of an individualized, personal life, as we saw in the case of Rose Grant in the previous chapter. Even 'thoughts and sensations' need to be articulated, if only through a mental narrative, in order for us to order them, comprehend them and react to them. Writing autobiographically is a greater externalization of this narrative process. Instead of simply narrating a life in our minds, silently and individually, we are externalizing this narrative and sharing it. But when we transform an event, which we have likely already narrated to ourselves or even to others through spoken language, into a written account, we still convert it into a new form.

Conversion changes the memory, and the change can be both positive and negative. 'The sharing of our lived experience verbally with others entails loss as well as gain, when the autobiographer must shape his past to the constraints of language equally with shaping his language to the constraints of his past' (Sturrock 1993, 25). Memory experiences another incarnation when it is expressed in language, and language moulds to form an approximation of our memory. Both processes alter the original kernel of memory that exists as an image, or flash, or odor, or snatch of sensation. We may lose the immediacy of the sensation or the precise, unnameable understanding of an experience when we articulate it. However, we may gain connection to others through the shared experience, and we may gain the power that comes from making one's life and experience more meaningful and palpable through linguistic expression. Cultural historian and author Rebecca Solnit illuminates this idea of fundamental change with a vivid image:

> Sometimes you hear of murals and miraculously preserved bodies buried, sealed, protected from light for hundreds or thousands of years. Exposed to fresh air and light for the first time, they begin to fade, crumble, disappear. (Solnit 2006, 38)

Solnit provides a personal example. She remembers a particular blouse she had as a child, and is shocked when one day her mother retrieves it and Solnit sees how 'tiny' it is, 'with arms less than a foot long, with a tiny bodice for a small cricket cage of a ribcage that was no longer mine' (Solnit 2006, 37). She cannot make the connection between the two because 'the continuity of memory did not measure the abyss between a toddler's body and a woman's' (Solnit 2006, 37). The memory of wearing the blouse 'vanished' (Solnit 2006, 37).

The writing process can be traumatic for a memory. Not only does it fundamentally change the memory, it can have far-reaching effects on the writer's present and future. Mary Karr writes of being shown the photographs of two children by her grandmother and being informed that the two strangers were, in fact, her half-siblings. The experience was so traumatic that she simply blanked it out, immediately: 'an erasure that held for nineteen years' (Karr 1995, 79). As she began returning to her childhood in her adult years, and writing about it, the experience came back – and not only to her: 'I later learned that [Lecia had] been shown the same pictures by Grandma. She had also promptly forgotten them. In this way, we entered amnesia together' (Karr 1995, 79).

Karr states that she forgot the experience, but, reading between the lines, we can see its effect. The time during which her grandmother lived in their house was a time of crisis for Karr. She experienced tangible effects of psychological stress – for example, sleepwalking, physically violent behaviour – and we can understand this as another form of expression of the experience, though not a linguistic one. Nineteen years later, during the writing process, the event 'comes back', i.e. is transformed into a narrative. During this transformation, it changes properties, finds a new mode of expression and becomes a story, enabling her to draw meaning from it.

This is another example of the crumbling, fading image introduced above. In Solnit's case, revealing some physical evidence of the memory destroys it; in Karr's, revealing the memory returns it to her and makes it a meaningful part of her book, and life. We can recall Nabokov's differentiation between memories which are weakened by lending out, and those which remain bright. How can we know which memories may withstand the change of being written, and which will crumble? Solnit's 'vivid memory included what it felt like to be inside that brocade shirt but not the fact that inside I had been … something utterly other than my adult self who remembered' (Solnit 2006, 37). This realization leads to the loss of the memory, because the memory and the blouse she holds in her hand are 'irreconcilable' (Solnit 2006, 37). This memory may have withstood transformation into language, but the introduction of a physical element – the blouse itself – shatters it.

The process of change, however, was not complete; some time later she again takes out the blouse and holds it, noting that 'my memory had turned it into something more familiar, a different style of blouse altogether' (Solnit 2006, 38). I think this process can be read as an illustration of Nabokov's steps towards reality, that unreachable place. The story of the blouse is never completed or attained; it merely changes, just as the memory of the blouse can be seen to also develop and change. And in this case, the change weakens the initial experience (wearing the blouse as a child) but does not halt or even impact the progression of the story of the blouse.

'When I first began to write … my childhood memories were vivid and potent', Solnit continues, 'whenever I write one down, I give it away: it ceases to have the shadowy life of memory and becomes fixed in letters; it ceases to be mine' (Solnit 2006, 39). In this case, in contrast to Nabokov's childhood memories, which he claims are the strongest, Solnit's are subject to the weakening effects of time, and become diluted when shared with an audience. The memory is irreversibly altered when 'fixed' in the language, and in this case we can clearly see the 'loss' involved in her sharing her childhood experiences, though presumably there is also some 'gain' in their inclusion in her writing.

Things held privately assume power and significance. This is precisely why we keep secrets secret. We still narrate them, of course, to ourselves, or to one or two trusted people, but a secret is strong when it remains secret. Even if powerfully destructive when publicly known, it loses some of its momentum and strength when it ceases to be secret. Writing down childhood stories can therefore be tremendously difficult, letting loose events that have perhaps been narrated only to the self or a small circle, or even kept as unarticulated sensations for years, into written language which is then shared. Even if this is the only way to glean meaning from such stories, their transformation is not always smooth.

Kay Redfield Jamison touches on this issue when she discusses her reluctance to record her experiences with manic-depressive disorder:

> I am deeply wary that by speaking publicly or writing about such intensely private aspects of my life, I will return to them one day and find them bleached of meaning and feeling … I am concerned that the experiences will become remote, inaccessible, and far distant, behind me; I fear that the experiences will become those of someone else rather than my own. (Jamison 1995, 202)

Here she suggests that publicly sharing her stories will erase their meaning, which stands at odds with the notion that sharing a story is the way to imbue it with meaning. Her fear echoes Solnit's experience of sharing a story making it fade, crumble, rendering it powerless. Jamison is concerned her stories will lose their power by becoming something new, although, paradoxically, if they become unrecognizable and thus lose some of their meaning for her through sharing, they will potentially become meaningful for a reader. The writing process may take away her ownership of the story, cutting her connection to it and turning it into 'someone else['s]' story rather than hers, a clear articulation of fundamental change. The memory sometimes cannot bear this change of environment. Recreating it in our present destroys its earlier configurations. Some authors find this an empowering practice; some are wary of its destructive power.

The distinction between conversion and adhesion, which relies on the understanding that to write a memory is to fundamentally alter it, is an important one, because of the way it orders events and processes. Adhesion presupposes (at least) two entities that exist before a process binds or connects them, whereas conversion makes no such presupposition – the conversion process is one that creates, ending with (at least) one more entity than one began with. Seeing the writing process as a creative one, a process that ends with a new entity, is accurate, and supports the images of distorted, damaged or even erased memories. Conceiving of writing autobiographi-cally as a conversion process highlights the way it results in a new product, as well as its crucial, flexible relationship to the events being written about. Some of the descriptions above speak to a weakening of the original by the creation of the new, converted description. The connection between an event and its description is literally self-destructive: by losing its vividness, potency, power or its actual selfhood (in Dillard's description the dream is replaced), the distance between an event and its description/recounting is reinforced.

The writing process can also serve as a farewell to the original experience, a willing release of one's story. In her introduction to Natalia Ginzburg's *The Things We Used To Say*, translator Judith Woolf remarks on the lexical choices Ginzburg makes, and how they affect her text: 'Experience is never crystalline, it is only our later formulations of it that make it appear so. The lexicon, superficially a means of preserving the past, is really a means of leaving it behind' (Ginzburg 1963b, xiii). In this figuration, the construction of the text, down to word choice, is the means of creating a new product, but also marking a formal division between the text and the writer's memories of the subject matter.

Ginzburg's refusal to admit readers into her story of Leone's death, an absence discussed earlier, is a fundamental rejection of the process of recre-ating events into an autobiographical narrative. John Sturrock argues that 'the only medium in which such states of "conversion" are feasible is that of language' (Sturrock 1993, 24). Rejecting this process of converting her experience into words allows the story of Leone's death to remain unaltered and un-'converted'. We are not aware of how she has narrated this event to herself, but as readers we note the lack of narrative provided to us about this experience. Sturrock's understanding that 'loss as well as gain' (Sturrock 1993, 25) are necessary to arrive at a written account – possibly entailing a corruption of the original memory, along the lines of Dillard's losing of a dream coinciding with the gaining of a story – is firmly sidestepped in Ginzburg's case, with no attempt to recreate or convert the story, and therefore no evident loss or gain.

Perhaps her memories of her husband's death would 'fade, crumble, disappear' if exposed to the light of the present, or perhaps the process of transforming them into something different and new is impossible, unbearable, for Ginzburg. Alternatively, maybe the refusal to record the story, thus involving it in the constant recreation process that is a life, is some attempt to leave it in a place where it cannot renew its pain. 'Sometimes we only escape by abandoning [stories]', says Solnit, rather than 'increas[ing] them by giving them away' (Solnit 2006, 181).

As a method of escape or abandonment, this is the opposite of Didion's approach. For one author, the experience of a husband's death is plunged into silence, kept unwritten, not allowed into a public space in which it could multiply, increase, take on new forms. For the other, the only way of dealing with it (even though 'There is no real way to deal with everything we lose' [Didion 2006, 1103]) is through obsessive recording, questioning, probing and, above all, recollection that leads to her desire for 'all the frames of memory ... the marginally different expressions, the variant readings of the same lines' (Didion 2005, 8). Didion writes speculatively, beseechingly, constructing her account as a search for meaning. She wants to examine the fragments of memory, the 'variant readings' of her experience, hoping some arrangement or particular juxtaposition will shed some light on her pain. Conversely, Ginzburg mutes the event itself, and therefore halts description of her personal search and her personal successive steps through the development of this experience. In the context of her memoir, she denies this particular story full development and extension into its future.

Ginzburg's approach to the narration both exemplifies and complicates the position of the narrator in relation to the events being described. She resists any evidence of standing outside the events; she does not include any conclusions drawn or lessons learned. This contrasts with *Speak, Memory*, or any of Mary Karr's memoirs, where the authors seem to make a point of periodically speaking from the moment of writing, drawing attention to their position beyond the main narrative. Ginzburg's story stays in the moment, and the reader must draw upon history and secondary sources in order to contextualize what they are reading, if indeed they become alert to the fact that some potentially significant information is absent. Her omissions mean that, as she says in her preface, if the book 'is read as a factual account, it could be objected that it is full of gaps', but the filling of any gaps is something Ginzburg leaves entirely up to the interested reader, giving no clues or hints as to what gaps she is speaking of (Ginzburg 1963b, 1). These gaps indicate not only the absence of information she has chosen to keep private, but also places where subsequently learned material changes the significance or meaning of events described.

At this point it seems essential to discuss the presence of the translator – a presence which will have had an effect on other texts discussed here, including Murakami's, Proust's and indeed Nabokov's, though he acts as his own translator in *Speak, Memory*. Even my own translations of Barthes's writing affect my reading of the original French, and my reading obviously affected my translation. The translation of a text can be understood as another form of construction and a source of further ambiguity. The choices a translator makes can alter a piece of writing significantly, and, in autobiographical writing, especially if the author is uninvolved in the translation, the translator assumes a degree of authority that may not always serve the writing in the best way. The same way the author of an autobiography will display one version of many possible versions, the translator similarly puts forth one translation out of many possibilities, and these decisions can have a huge impact on how we read. Issues of truth and truthfulness are complicated further by a translator, who may be able to ensure 'correspondence' or 'coherence' between the two languages, but may not, or may not be able to, go forth on 'an active search for the most exact and insightful understanding' of the subject matter, or the meaning expressed in the original language (Barbour 1992, 26).

The Things We Used To Say is the title given to the 1997 version, translated by Judith Woolf. In 1967, a version 'revised from the original tanslation [sic]' by D. M. Low was released. Ginzburg's original text is called *Lessico Famigliare* in Italian, suggesting a direct translation of something like 'family vocabulary'; the 1967 version was titled *Family Sayings*. Comparing the 1967 and 1997 editions provides good examples of the profound changes that can be wrought upon a piece of writing by the decisions of a translator. A close comparative reading of the two prefaces displays some interesting differences, which arguably alter the general voice of each preface, thus setting a different tone for the rest of the text.

In the 1967 version, Ginzburg felt 'impelled at once to destroy' any fabrications that found their way into her text; in the 1997 version, she 'felt compelled to erase' these. The difference is significant; in one version she feels motivated by an inward force, while in another, the implication is that some outer or external force is responsible for her actions. The differences between 'erase' and 'destroy' are also intriguing and noteworthy. In discussing her decision to use the real names of those who appear in her account, the 1967 version declares, for those who might not be happy about this decision, 'To them I have nothing to say'. The 1997 version somewhat more gracefully states that, should anyone be 'displeased … there is nothing I can do about that'.

Such subtle, and not so subtle, differences can profoundly impact how we read, all the more so if, as we read, we become accustomed to a voice and absorb its level of aggression, defensiveness, kindness, ambiguity, etc.

I have looked at the prefaces in particular because I believe this portion of a book can have an enormous influence on how we approach the rest of it. Also, in a genre where we are often primed to read as though gaining direct, honest insight into the author's life, such initial pieces of writing (prefaces, introductions, acknowledgements) offer the seductive image of even more direct contact with the writer, an even closer relationship to them because they appear to speak from some closer, more immediate space than the rest of the text. Consider the sentence that opens Barthes's 'anti-autobiography' (Eakin 2008, 65), and how persuasive and powerful his directive may be. It is no accident that the sentence appears on its own page, and in 'handwriting'. These decisions affect how we read, and what we do with the information we have read as we continue through the book.

In Ginzburg's book we can see instances where translation may be seen to complicate or cloud her intended meaning. The text opens with a description of her father and his particular notions of how people, especially his children, should behave. The descriptions are slightly ridiculous, and he is painted as a fussy and stubborn man whose opinions appear comic to the reader. He has specific ways of naming and identifying undesirable behaviour, and in the opening passages he appears primarily as a figure who encourages his family to adopt his own favoured practices and attempts to stop them from behaving in unacceptable ways. In the 1997 version, Judith Woolf translates this image of a person who practices such unacceptable behaviours as a 'yahoo', using Swift's word, with its connotations of brutishness and uncouth behaviour, to indicate his frustration and slightly old-fashioned attitude without eliminating comedy from the description of him:

> To my father, a "yahoo" was anyone who had gauche, awkward and bashful manners, anyone who wore the wrong clothes, who didn't know how to climb mountains or who was ignorant of foreign languages … "Don't be such yahoos! Stop being so yahooish!" he would shout at us all the time. The gamut of yahooishness was wide. (Ginzburg 1963a, 3)

In 1967, however, Low translates this rather differently:

> A stage worse than silly men were "negroes." A "negro" for my father was one whose manners were gauche and lacking in assurance; one who dressed inappropriately, who was no good at mountaineering, and was ignorant of foreign languages. (Ginzburg 1963b, 9)

As a record of the past, this is valuable. This kind of comparison is useful in illustrating how choices of translation can influence a reader, and indeed how language changes over time. For a contemporary translator (or reader), Low's version suggests a degree of racism in the character that, if it does not appear elsewhere in the text, or in other aspects of the character (which I do not believe it does), can easily be read as an offensive misrepresentation of Ginzburg's father. Judith Woolf's word choice suggests no such element of his character, and such questions are thus absent from the text.

It is unclear which translation gives us a more accurate or truthful rendering of Ginzburg's childhood, but this straightforward comparative reading highlights a particular element of the text's construction, and shows how decisions that come long after the initial writing process can continue to change a book, and possibly its reception. Even after the decisions made by editors and translators change them, we as readers continue to change books. We bring our own views to them, which might explain the different reception Low's edition would likely receive if it was published now rather than 45 years ago.

While I agree with Sturrock's view that an autobiographical piece of writing marks a process of fundamental change from memory into text, I believe the word 'construction', rather than 'conversion', more clearly explains my view of the process. I believe Sturrock's view of a conversion process as necessary for a sensation to become language is accurate, but I think the construction of autobiographical writing is an important element that needs to be taken into account when discussing it. To me, the word speaks to the newness of any writing, and the series of actions involved in its formation. Sturrock's 'conversion' clearly indicates the new form that the writing takes, but it is important not to lose sight of the actual construction of the memoir. The memory may be converted from 'sensations' into language, but the book itself is constructed from nothing into a book. Word follows word, paragraph follows paragraph, and the writing eventually becomes a whole, where before there was nothing, even if an internal narrative conversion process began before the book's construction.

This construction process is where we can locate and discuss choices such as layout, narrative order and chapter divisions, and the comparisons of the two versions of Ginzburg's book show how neither this discussion nor this process necessarily ends with the author. The construction of memory is the primary means through which I understand autobiography as 'fictions about what is itself in turn a fiction' (Eakin 2000, 290), but the more literal construction of the written account is another important element. The ordering of the narrative, and the linearity or lack thereof of events presented, constitutes a form of construction that can deeply influence a reader, or present events in a particular light.

While bringing readers into the progression of events, a progression hopefully engaging enough to keep us turning pages, the writer is meanwhile positioned outside the narrative, ordering those events in a way that reflects their version of accuracy while still crafting an engaging story. No matter how swept up we may feel, how immediate the writing, it still exists from a place of consideration and planning. The autobiographical writer (re)constructs the events in a manner of their choosing. Because they work from an often significant temporal distance, a linear version of events is not required, though many memoirs employ a linear narrative. A non-linear narrative can be a more effective mode of storytelling, however, and can emphasize the intention to express a particular approach to autobiography, or to comment on the writing of the events as much as to express the events themselves.

Vivian Gornick's *Fierce Attachments*, a text briefly discussed earlier, is particularly useful in examining autobiographical writing that deliberately challenges the linearity of events, moving swiftly across time and space. Her memoir swings back and forth repeatedly between Gornick's past, growing up with her mother, and her present, in which she meets her mother for walks through New York City, having conversations through which she can both reflect on her past and move her story forward. This back and forth construction allows her to illustrate her story, her 'tale of psychological embroilment', which required the construction of a 'solid, limited' persona to tell it (Gornick 2001, 21, 23).

For Gornick, the story of *Fierce Attachments*, the 'flash of insight' around which it was created, is that she 'could not leave [her] mother because [she] had become [her] mother' (Gornick 2001, 21). This development, this becoming, can be illustrated more clearly in a narrative that shifts back and forth through time. Also, as Virginia Woolf found, prefacing the story of past events by making reference to the author's present can be an effective means of drawing out or illustrating the author's development. In this way, the construction of *Fierce Attachments* serves the story best, and also highlights the discovery which, for Gornick, was key to developing the writing persona behind the book.

Likewise, in *Speak, Memory*, Nabokov can more effectively illustrate 'the true purpose of autobiography' (Nabokov 2000, 23) by organizing his book so as to emphasize the collapse of time that allows echoing events and images to appear next to each other. He forgoes a strict temporal arc in order to move fluidly through time and space, linking the sequence of events according to a narrative arc that prioritizes thematic coherence.

This approach is in direct opposition to Jill Ker Conway's understanding of temporality relating to autobiographical narratives. For Conway, the desire to complicate temporal order and 'fold' (Nabokov 2000, 109) time so that events line up in a way that prioritizes symmetry of experience rather than reflecting the manner in which those experiences happened contradicts the very way we live and understand our lives. 'We experience life along a time continuum', she argues, 'things happen sequentially in our lives, and we need to understand the causation' (Conway 1995, 56). For Conway, this rearranging process, which takes attention away from the 'causation' that might otherwise more clearly be traced through a life, is 'frustrating' (Conway 1995, 56).

Conway's own autobiographical writing can be said to support her views. Her two memoirs, *The Road from Coorain* and *True North*, follow her childhood and young adulthood, and her professional development, respectively; they can be read as tools to help us understand how she sees 'the causation' of events in her life. She begins with her childhood, spent on an isolated sheep farm in Australia, and moves on to describe how, propelled by academic study and work, she moved to North America. She seeks to understand why her life has taken the form it has. In this search, close examination within the confines of the ordered steps she has actually taken in her life is more useful to her than manipulation and experimentation. This can be clearly seen in, for example, her structuring of an event from her childhood that occurs as she and her mother travel by train away from the sheep farm that has been the only home she has known, now rendered uninhabitable by years of drought:

> We who rode in comfort looked out at the ragged children and tired women who inhabited the burlap and tin shacks, as though we were comfortable spectators of the action in a Dickens novel, the forlorn waifs gazing in upon us merely sign of some other person's social imagination. Much later, at Sydney University, I learned about the social scientist's concept of social distance. To me it always recalled the cool carriages and the hot plains, the desolate shacks, and the uplifted faces of the undernourished children. (Conway 1989, 83–4)

Here, she brings in her more recent past to understand and underscore the significance of an earlier event, with an emphasis on using one to understand the other. Her experiences at university enabled her to more fully understand (this event in) her childhood, but she is as interested in showing how her childhood propelled her into a life of learning and teaching. Introducing a more recent self to comment on her experience does trouble a strict linearity, but she does this only briefly, and immediately returns to the primary narrative of her past.

In *True North*, she describes her training as a historian during her PhD studies at Harvard University. Her doctoral supervisor approves of her choice of a research project that involves studying women who have made

professional and academic choices that Conway sees as crucial to the development of her own life. Conway seeks to know more about these women,
whose choices and life patterns can help her map and understand her own.
'It only counts if it's really close to the bone', says her supervisor (Conway
1994, 39). It's close to the bone because her research and writing act as tools
to help her track her own movements, and the closer to the bone it is, the less
she seems inclined to play with the forms her research and narrative take.
This desire to track and map shows itself in the construction of her memoirs,
which both adhere to a linear pattern, carefully moving through her history
with an eye to illustrating how one experience led into another.

We can see her carry over this sentiment, and articulation, from her thesis
supervisor to her own thinking when she describes writing her first memoir,
The Road from Coorain. She explains the differences in approach between
her academic and professional writing, and her memoir: 'So I thought, "I'm
going to have to write something that's really close to the bone and see if I
can rediscover my own style"' (Conway 1995, 45).

If Conway seeks to understand by retracing and examining the strand
of her life, Nabokov, in throwing off the constraints of linearity, emphasizes
the enormous implications in the way the autobiographical writer stands
outside the text while also featuring within it. In the book, he moves between
childhood to adulthood and back again before our eyes, but we never stop
being made aware of his presence as (adult) controller of the story, who
orders images and events in a particularly illuminating way for us. From
his position of control, his book presents as a kaleidoscope of summoned
visions, a repeated plunging into history.

Speak, Memory is a useful book to consult as I move from examination
of the more literal construction of a memoir to the construction of the
memories within. Nabokov appears to take such pleasure in reconstructing
his past that his memories often flood from the page in waves. '[T]he act of
vividly recalling a patch of the past is something that I seem to have been
performing with the utmost zeal all my life', he tells us (Nabokov 2000, 60).
However, this act occasionally becomes difficult, requiring 'intense concentration' (Nabokov 2000, 9); perhaps this is why we see him outraged when
faced with a contradictory version. In typical Nabokov fashion, he can be
quite cutting when his version of events is called into question. His past
governess, treated as a somewhat ridiculous and pathetic figure in *Speak,
Memory*, encounters Nabokov once he has passed out of her care, and
bombards him with her past.

> Those good old days in the *chateau*! The dead wax doll we once buried
> under the oak [No – a wool-stuffed Golliwogg.] And that time you and

Serge ran away and left me stumbling and howling in the depths of the forest! [Exaggerated.] … My, what a spanking I gave you! [She did try to slap me once but the attempt was never repeated.] … And the way you whispered your childish troubles! [Never!] (Nabokov 2000, 84)

Elsewhere, she happily recalls a gift she gave him: "'How you hugged me, how you danced with joy!" she exclaimed ten years later in the course of inventing a brand-new past' (Nabokov 2000, 101). He is fussy in insisting his version is correct, but of course there is no way to determine where the truth lies in those exchanges, particularly the first one. Likely, it lies somewhere between the two versions, as we saw with William Zinsser's recollections of his grandmother discussed in the introduction.

We are perhaps primed to accept Nabokov's version as authoritative because of the way he paints Mademoiselle as a ridiculous figure, and because of the control he exerts over the story, but his indignant response does not indicate that his own memories are more accurate, any more than Hudson's exhilarating sensation of hovering over all aspects of his childhood indicates that his memories are more accurate. The quoted passage works to reinforce Nabokov's authority by positioning him as the source of accuracy, who can clear up somebody else's misconceptions, and even correct them, as we see from his insertions. Nabokov's confidence in the face of Mademoiselle's version seems to discourage the suggestion that Nabokov himself is 'inventing a brand-new past', which is exactly what he is doing.

The construction of a 'brand-new past' is an apt description for memoir and autobiography generally. Influenced by the past, the author first constructs the memories that are converted into written language, and then constructs their arrangement into book form. I have previously discussed how memory always contains an element of construction because it is created in the present, and how some studies suggest the brain experiences memory as a new event, profoundly affected and coloured by the present. This element of invention, or creation, can be read as essential to living narratively. If we construct stories or life scripts as the very means of living our lives, we are motivated to make the story a good one.

'Perhaps it's because events leave so much to the imagination that people seek an imaginative response in order to best understand them', suggests novelist Rhidian Brook (*Thought* 2011). It is not always necessary to stick to a researchable truth to 'best understand' something, nor to 'search for the most exact and insightful understanding' (Barbour 1992, 26). We all perform this imaginative aspect of remembering and narrating, which to me suggests that it is a normal part of memoir and autobiography. As a recognizable, human activity, imaginative interpretations of reality seem perfectly truthful. Brook continues: 'storytellers … writers and poets … help depict the ambiguities and complexities of reality and bring to light the hidden things that can reveal a bigger picture' (*Thought* 2011). This bigger picture can be the 'substantial truth' told by Rigoberta Menchú (Lauritzen 2004, 28) or the 'subjective truth' told by James Frey (Frey 2003, vii), or even an individual truth like the one Zinsser suggests is the only one a memoirist can 'work with' (Zinsser 1998, 12). Brook's words suggest that, to make the world comprehensible, some invention is necessary, and to communicate 'the ambiguities and complexities of reality', or perhaps simply the ambiguities and complexities of our successive steps towards reality, we must be, or draw upon, storytellers. We must use imaginative narration as a fundamental way of understanding and communicating the world to ourselves and to others.

The invention involved in constructing a memoir or autobiography is also a reflection of the imagination involved in memory, and the process of construction that remembering something implies. 'I will remember Paris, 1985', writes Dani Shapiro in her memoir *Slow Motion*:

> We are walking along the Boulevard Saint-Germain on a cloudless spring day. The rooftops of the Left Bank are creamy against a rare blue sky, and the air outside Café de Flore smells of croissants and the acrid smoke of Gitanes, but I don't notice. It is only years later, as a grown woman, that I will take in the rooftops of Paris, the extraordinary sky, and so I am supplying this scene with a collage of my own memory. (Shapiro 1989, 58)

Here she openly adjusts her earlier memories with more recent information, articulating a construction element to memory that is not usually as deliberate or conscious as it is here. Shapiro is describing consciously performing an action that the brain often performs undetected – this filling in of information. Driven by 'the attempt to find structure in meaningless data', the brain will fill in such information as is required to create a narrative, because 'Minds seek patterns' (Eagleman 2011, 138). For Shapiro, this is a stylistic decision; it serves to highlight the solitude and immaturity of her earlier, '1985' state (she is not yet 'a grown woman', she is with the wrong man, in a relationship that permits her to see 'only what is within one square foot of [her]' [Shapiro 1989, 58]), but it also suggests the way memory is not accessed but constructed, and the way the brain very often takes the liberty of filling in gaps, or collapsing multiple memories into one, or abstracting common themes from repeated actions, dulling specific instances, or otherwise incorporating false elements into our memories. Shapiro is not adding supplementary information in an 'attempt to find structure in meaningless data', but rather to illustrate how this memory fits into a greater narrative, a bigger picture. Her conscious actions mirror totally unobserved (and unobservable) actions performed by the brain almost continually.

I understate when I say that the study of human memory is very complex. A tool that we rely on daily is not well understood scientifically. 'Although [scientists] have made tremendous advances on many fronts, the main "discovery" to date has been that memory is extraordinarily complicated' (Tulvig and Lepage 2000, 208). I am not a scientist, nor is this a scientific text, and, fascinating as it may be, my new knowledge on the topic will not find a very comfortable home in this work, but I believe some very basic evidence and working hypotheses are relevant and illuminating here.

'Our memories virtually always contain information that we don't really remember', says cognitive psychologist and memory researcher Martin Conway (*Memory* 2011). Often this happens because, in his view, the brain does not operate according to our commands. In Eagleman's description, we are barely aware of a fraction of the decisions and actions taken by our brains, and are very much observers of its 'show'. Echoing Eagleman, Conway sees the brain as essentially 'a kind of device … that is more concerned with making sense of things than it is in representing them accurately' (*Memory* 2011). We make sense of things through explanation and thinking them over, through constructing a narrative about them, understanding them in some sort of context, with reference points; this is true even if the brain has taken the liberty of supplying additional information to help fit experiences and sensations more easily into a pattern or narrative. This position entirely supports Eakin's view of living narratively, and suggests that the brain acts in ways that support this goal as well, regardless of whether we 'allow' it or not. Conway suggests that our brains will make choices that reinforce or further a comprehensible narrative rather than merely collecting experiences or images to add to a growing bank. More useful to us as human beings are stories that can make sense of the world around us, rather than mirrors which exclusively reflect it. In an attempt to understand what we are experiencing, and connect the various selves we are and have been and the different periods of our lives, our brains might enable this narrative process by making it smoother, emphasizing configurations that make sense to us, even if some invention is required to fill the gaps.

Conway describes a simple experiment that neatly illustrates this process. Given a list of related words and asked to remember them, participants are often surprised to find that, when they are asked whether a highly related but unmentioned word was on the list, they claim to remember hearing this word, despite the fact that they did not. The word makes sense and fits the rest of the list, and so the brain will often 'remember' it, and the person will 'actually experience an item as having been seen before when it wasn't' (*Memory* 2011). If the word fits the narrative that the word list suggests, the brain seems willing to recall having previously experienced it even if it didn't. Of course, the brain may not consider items on a word list the same way it does more significant life experiences, especially if these experiences are particularly traumatic or intense, and such an experiment should not 'be simply translated into real world experiences', as memory researcher Chris Brewin advises (*Memory* 2011). But this experiment does highlight the almost intertwined relationship between imagination and memory.

Another example of the brain's prioritizing of a narrative over simple reflection of events can be seen in memories of repeated events. Professor Chris Brewin, an expert on memories of trauma, discusses childhood abuse trials that rely on an individual's memory of events, and suggests a discrepancy between what is convincing for an audience (or jury), and what is being discovered in memory science. Noting that many areas of human memory are 'relatively unstudied', including 'memory for repeated experiences', he states that those studying memory 'think that when experiences are repeated, people abstract the common elements of a set of different experiences, but they may forget the details of individual experiences' (*Memory* 2011).

The implications of such a hypothesis in witness testimony are very significant, especially when we consider Martin Conway's description of testimony which, for many memory researchers, will 'ring alarm bells' (*Memory* 2011). Such memories are extremely precise and detailed ones, especially from early childhood. They often include a degree of detail that makes Conway sceptical, but which, he suggests, people are often primed to consider more believable, in the belief that the more detailed a memory is, the likelier it is to be true. Conway suggests that in legal cases which rest only on witness testimony and concern childhood memories, a jury may be presented with an extremely detailed account. The level of detail suggests that the veracity of the memory is 'impossible' in his and other researchers' eyes, but 'those are the exact sorts of memories that people are easily convinced by' (*Memory* 2011). So, if a witness is supposedly remembering events which happened many times, such as repeated instances of abuse or sexual assault over a given period of time, it would be entirely normal for specific details to fade while common elements remained vivid. This kind of brain response would indeed make highly detailed memories of repeated events irregular, especially events experienced at a very young age. However, such detailed memories are often, ironically, seen as more believable because so detailed.

We can see a clear example of this relationship between repeated events and loss of detail in Kathryn Harrison's memoir *The Kiss*. In this memoir Harrison describes an absorbing, manipulative, overwhelming and dangerous relationship growing between her and her estranged father during her young adulthood, when he re-enters her life. Consider her language as she describes the obviously traumatic experience of beginning a sexual relationship with her father at age twenty:

> Five, ten, fifteen years later, the only thing I can remember is my father's undressing … In years to come, I won't be able to remember even one instance of our lying together. I'll have a composite, generic memory. I'll know he was always on top and that I always lay still … I'll remember such details as the color of the carpet in a particular motel room, or the kind of tree outside the window … But I won't be able to remember what it felt like. No matter how hard I try, pushing myself to inhabit my past, I'll recoil from what will always seem impossible. (Harrison 1997, 136-7)

Although she can remember 'every tiny thing about him' in general, this repeated instance of trauma can only be accessed as a 'composite, generic memory' (Harrison 1997, 136). Detail comes forth only in remembering singular events, such as a particular carpet, a particular tree. The repeated action is muted; her response to the event is, appropriately, sleep: 'The sight of him naked: at that point I fall completely asleep' (Harrison 1997, 136). She physically expresses the response that will remain with her throughout her life, a literal closing of the eyes to the experience. Yet this 'composite, generic memory' that Harrison claims to have, bled of any detail, is, according to Martin Conway, just what would present as less believable to a typical jury.

Why might we be convinced by detail? 'Perhaps it's because events leave so much to the imagination that people seek an imaginative response in order to best understand them' (*Thought* 2011). Detail is imaginative; even the noting of detail can be an imaginative act because it by definition implies moving beyond the basic, opening the mind to additional layers of information, and joining these layers into a picture of greater depth and greater potential meaning. Our brains may allow detail to fade in the interests of establishing and maintaining a comprehensive basic narrative, but our conscious minds may also desire and respond to detail which we may see as enriching these narratives.

Conway links invention and memory inextricably; in fact, memory *is* invention to a great extent. To attempt to divide what really happened from what we remember may be simply impossible because of the way our brains deal with information and experiences. Therefore, an exercise like Mary Karr's instances of seeking out and consulting the memories of her sister and other relatives in order to assess the accuracy of her own writing is interestingly pointless. All accounts will involve invention, and the blending and clashing of so many memories and versions will provide rich material for a memoir, but not necessarily a truer story.

In fact, trying to seek out a single version of what happened, a single correct memory, is impossible no matter how many people one asks. This is because we may very well have multiple memories inside of our own minds, instead of a single, personal version of events that we share with others. David Eagleman argues that 'Nature seems to have invented mechanisms for storing memory more than once' (Eagleman 2011, 126). Memories of daily experience under normal circumstances are stored in one way in the brain, but 'during frightening situations … another area … also lays down memories along an independent, secondary memory track' (Eagleman 2011, 126). The result is two memories, with different characteristics. Eagleman drives the point home: 'We're not talking about a memory of different events, but multiple memories of the *same* event – as though two journalists with different personalities were jotting down notes about a single unfolding story' (Eagleman 2011, 126).

If we understand some events as capable of prompting us to recall the same thing differently from our *own* other versions, it becomes even clearer why the notion of a single true version of history matching one particular memory and not another is unhelpful and inaccurate, and it also highlights why finding corroboration in somebody else's version does little to ensure or reinforce the veracity of our own recollections.

Perhaps the most intriguing hypothesis applicable to this chapter comes from developmental psychologist Katherine Nelson, whose work focuses on how human beings develop episodic memory, and how we can measure and understand the ways in which we develop this ability. Episodic memory is the kind of memory which 'enables the individual to mentally travel back into the personal past' (Tulvig and Lepage 2000, 211), and as such is drawn on heavily when writing memoir and autobiography.

Nelson sees 'The child's emerging capacity at about 4 to 5 years of age to use language as a medium of mental representation … as the key to unlocking' their potential to 'entertain … simultaneously two (or more) different representations of reality' (Nelson 2000, 260). It is not totally clear how early and at what age episodic memory develops, but the 'unlocking' that Nelson speaks of represents a junction between the development of memory and the development of language, linking them importantly.

> [P]rotoepisodic fragments and scripts may turn into full memories when elaborated into narratives through talk with parents. Effects of these different processes can be seen in memories from childhood

recalled later by adults, resulting in some cases in false beliefs about events from early life that are held with strong conviction. (Nelson 2000, 264)

This position indissolubly connects language to formation of memory. In this hypothesis, language acts as a catalyst, transforming 'fragments' into something more significant and permanent. It makes these events more lasting in an important way; Nelson writes of experiments with children who can technically recall some prior event that they participated in, but do not seem to really connect to that experience, or find such memories interesting or meaningful. Nelson's last point will ring true for anyone who has experienced the disconcerting feeling of discovering a remembered event never indeed happened, but it also evokes the sensation of 'remembering' something that one can only actually remember hearing discussed, rather than actually happening.

This hypothesis returns us to Didion's early sense 'that meaning itself was resident in the rhythms of words and sentences and paragraphs' (Didion 2005, 7). This sense came to her early, 'even as a child' (Didion 2005, 7). Both statements suggest that language is not simply a means of expressing a previously developed mental action, but an integral part of such development. It suggests that to develop language is to develop memory. Nelson's hypothesis is exciting because it suggests that language and communication will activate this particular kind of memory.

Paul John Eakin pursues similar avenues of study when he examines the joint development of language and the concept of the self. He draws on work by David Bleich, who emphasizes this co-development when he notes that 'the child learns to name things *to* someone' (Bleich 1978, quoted in Eakin 1985, 196), linking the act of developing speech to an audience. The 'someone' is a crucial part of learning language and developing memory. Acquiring knowledge and asserting individual voice and identity are fused here. Language becomes the means of understanding one's life and existence, from the 'very dawn of the "I" to more complex notions of multiple selves and lifelong identity development' (Eakin 1985, 197). Eakin suggests that 'The history of the self, then, would be coextensive with discourse itself' (Eakin 1985, 198), and supports this view with Bleich's claim that 'without language, it is not possible to distinguish between awareness and self-awareness' (Bleich 1978, quoted in Eakin 1985, 197).

What I find especially interesting about these hypotheses is the way they rest on shared communication, or at least interaction, with others. Nelson in particular articulates the relationship between discussion 'with parents', or presumably peers, and the establishment of memory. This includes, indeed necessitates, multiple accounts in the formation of a memory. It is intriguing that something as highly personal and individual as memory might develop through the discussion and sharing of stories, but this is precisely what may occur during 'talk with parents'. Developmental psychologists Robyn Fivush and Elaine Reese view 'both the child and the adult as playing active roles in the construction of autobiography' through this dialogue process (Fivush and Reese 1992, quoted in Eakin 2000, 296).

Catherine E. Snow traces an even more intriguing development when she studies children who are essentially learning how to remember. By analyzing discussions between parents and children, she can note differences between

> memories located in the parental mind, which are transferred to the child but not actually shared by the child, and memories which children have some access to, though they are undeniably enriched and structured by parental intervention. (Snow 1990, quoted in Eakin 2000, 296)

This description suggests something like the implanting of memories from adults into children, and, almost as a form of learning through imitation or by example, paves the way for children to develop, store and express their own memory reconstructions. In this quotation, it is impossible to divorce language from the process of memory development. Talk and verbal sharing, then, may have a double power. It can work to enable the formation of memory, and encourage the development of this ability, but it can later work to destroy these memories, as we can see from Solnit's example above. Memory and language are closely bound together, and the relationship can be an explosive one.

At one moment in *The Autobiography of Alice B. Toklas* Stein mentions the visits of Wyndham Lewis, 'tall and thin' and looking 'rather like a young frenchman on the rise' (Stein 1933, 134). At this point in time Lewis is well-liked by Stein, and

> she particularly liked him one day when he came and told all about his quarrel with Roger Fry. Roger Fry had come in not many days before and had already told all about it. They told exactly the same story only it was different, very different. (Stein 1933, 134)

We get no more information about the quarrel, and we do not learn how the versions were different. Stein embraces the paradoxical way that the stories were very different and yet exactly the same. It is an easily recognizable situation and an accurate description, as anyone who has been in a position similar to Stein's will recall. So much of what we remember is constructed, and so much of what we reconstruct in narratives is embroidered with imagination. We may consider this invention as our way of understanding the complexity of the world around us. No matter how we see it, it is important to consider the multiplicity inherent in forming and recounting memory.

Kathryn Harrison writes of her estranged father visiting her and her mother for a week. The two parents had a brief, explosive relationship, and the visit comes nearly twenty years after their marriage ended; it is only the third time in her life Harrison has seen her father. As they spend time together discussing the past, Harrison writes,

> I watch and listen as my parents begin to argue. They can't reconstruct a year, a season, or even a week from the past without disagreeing. Whatever they talk about – their wedding day, my birth – it's as if my mother and father experienced two separate, unconnected realities, a disjuncture that allows no compromise, no middle ground. The picture that I form of their courtship is one that I have to piece together; no matter how hard I try to make things fit, it will always have the look of an incomplete collage – some details too large, other too small, many missing. (Harrison 1997, 54)

Here her memory 'collage' echoes Dani Shapiro's memory 'collage', which was 'suppl[ied]' with memories from different years (Shapiro 1989, 58). This excerpt also clearly illustrates what Stein expresses when she recalls the same, yet entirely different, stories told by Lewis and Fry. The inability to compromise is echoed in the certainty each party feels about the veracity of their version. This inability is an expression of the belief that there *can* be a single way something occurred, that there is no need to compromise because one individual sequence of events corresponds to reality, and all other possible sequences do not.

Harrison's reaction is also interesting as an expression of how she is imagining the situations, and forming them in her memory. The varying 'sizes' of the images and the way they awkwardly fit together in unnatural positions, suggesting an amateurish attempt at coherence, illustrate the supreme individuality of memory. Her parents clearly have their own versions of the past, which they argue over, but as they do, Harrison forms a third, distinct version, affected by the two versions she hears, but different from them. It seems paradoxical, but this version of the past is utterly new, as it is newly created by Harrison. Here she is enacting what Linda Grant describes as the way 'the past goes on re-arranging itself in surprising new ways. It is not over, never finished with. It keeps returning. And always to surprise us' (Grant 1998, 302).

If, as Nelson suggests, our development of memory is a collective act, the multiplicity bound up in it is totally overt. By forming memory through discussion, multiple voices become not only essential to making memories, but become the very act of memory-making itself, for children. But even as adults, when we remember, we are juggling a variety of voices: those of our past selves meeting our present self, that of our uncertainties, unsure of how something happened sequentially, perhaps the voice of later knowledge, adding subsequently learned information, and perhaps even a voice raising concerns over how the memory might be received by others.

In such an understanding, memory is always negotiated and always collaborative. This remains true when we write what we remember, after we have constructed it. As John Sturrock suggests, we do not simply layer a written account on top of the bank of memories and impressions we wish to share. We perform one more process of change in the sequence of changing impressions that memory represents. This process can represent a profound alteration, but can also be seen as one step in a chain of like steps.

Conclusions

There is a scene in the movie *Biutiful* (Iñárritu 2010) where Javier Bardem's character Uxbal is giving his children dinner. They complain about the milk and cereal that he serves them. The daughter would prefer omelet, the son a hamburger with French fries and a milkshake. Uxbal spoons cereal into the bowls. 'Here's the hamburger', he tells his son; 'this is the omelet', he says to his daughter. He pours milk on top, calls it a milkshake. His kids smile at him and eat their milk and cereal. Their apartment is not clean, cared for or well-lit; the film has already highlighted some of the serious financial and health problems in Uxbal's life, and his children's.

I think this scene is a sad one, an illustration of their relative poverty (relative because it is so minor compared to that of others in the film) and Uxbal's reaction to it. I think he would be happy to give his children omelets and hamburgers every night, but can only provide imagined versions of them. Rather than express anger or frustration or sadness, he turns his unhappiness into a game, or joke, for the children, and we see his pain alongside their lack of complete comprehension. It is a tender scene, with tension in it. We can see that his daughter, the older child, who gradually becomes aware of the many sources of pain in life and matures visibly throughout the film, both knows this is a game and yet eats her food with greater relish; the son, who is about six or seven, chews his 'hamburger' solemnly.

This reading, according to my father, is totally incorrect. Uxbal did not cook hamburgers or omelets for his children because he did not like cooking; he did not like cooking because he was a man, and men do not normally like cooking. This scene is an accurate reflection of Uxbal's maleness, and suggests one of the drawbacks of living in a house with a single father.

A third viewer disagreed, and thought the scene was an illustration of what it is like to be around children, to have children, to communicate with children. The magic of this kind of playacting, the way you can get away with this sort of explanation or response with children. Yet another viewer saw it as a life lesson, a parent's attempt to teach his children that, if some imagination was allowed into their outlook on life, they might live more happily and enjoy more pleasure than if they remained loyal only to what their eyes (and mouths) told them.

This is the collaborative act of reading, or interpretation. We bring ourselves into whatever we look at. Food is one of the ways I measure excess or lack of money. I am bewildered by bounty when I open a fridge and see seven kinds of cheese; three opened jars of olives (of different colours and from different regions); boxes upon boxes of frozen steaks, salmon filets, chops; ripe tomatoes glowing with sun; a precarious balance of fruit. I can also remember finding change on the sidewalk and instantly, before even picking up the coin, equating it to a can of kidney beans; saving money for a weekend splurge of a single rock-hard tomato; carrying a bottle of olive oil up and down the aisles of the grocery store before swapping it for vegetable oil at the last moment; sudden tears when a longed-for avocado, which amounted to a week's worth of tinned soup and was carried tremulously home in a sweaty palm, turned out to be black and slimy inside, the worn pit lying wrinkled as I slowly parted the two cut halves. I brought this with me when I saw the movie, and I will bring it everywhere, adding to it but almost never taking away.

My father hates to cook; he brings this with him. He buys food that lives in his fridge for years; he frequently has nothing in his house with an expiration date shorter than one month away; expiration dates on principle make him scoff. He avoids fruits and vegetables because they need preparation not normally involving a microwave and because they go bad too quickly. He can eat once a day, when it becomes imperative, and tries to eat enough to stall the next session for another 24 hours. Unless, of course, he is in a restaurant or someone else's house. He loves to eat, and he loves food. The preparation of it, however, is usually a black hole. He brings this with him.

At one point I had a plan to bookend these four chapters with two sets of stories: the initial group, which served as a launchpad for the research and critical writing, and another group, written after that work. At another point, I thought about revisiting and editing the stories, which had lain patiently in wait, untouched for over a year, and sandwiching the four chapters in between the two versions. Both possibilities now seem, in fact, impossible. I now see the value of the stories as lying in the way they presented an opening, an entrance, for the reading and writing that came after, and I also see value in the way they stay fixed, still, allowing me to see more clearly how I have changed in the interim, how my own channel of viewing things has been influenced, and how I bring this updated channel with me to each subsequent consideration of the stories. Perhaps one day I will eagerly revisit them, depending on how my view changes. For now, I am pleased to leave them alone, appreciating their power of beginning. The work done after the writing of the stories has changed the channel, or tunnel, through which I view them, widening the space between us. In Woolf's articulation, it has added more to the bowl of life; in Larkin's or Didion's, it has split off another self that I will perhaps meet unexpectedly one day.

Are the stories fiction or nonfiction? For some reason I keep returning to this question, perhaps because it involves the kind of authorial intention that I find so maddening, which keeps appearing in many of the understandings of autobiography I have encountered. Beyond a moral imperative not to lie, if indeed I feel such an internal command (you will never know whether I do), there is no objective in determining this distinction. This lack of an objective renders the distinction meaningless, or at least problematic. As Lejeune said, 'there is *no difference*' between the novel and autobiography if we keep to textual analysis. And why move beyond 'the level of analysis within the text?' Indeed, how can we? I may insist on the veracity of the stories in this project, and I may even draw upon others for support, as Mary Karr makes a point of doing. If a reader disagrees, perhaps because they too were involved in the events and their memory tells them another version, my insistence is ultimately meaningless.

Perhaps this is why I feel myself drawing away from the stories. I have no desire to insist on anything about them other than my own feelings towards them, but this is a state of affairs I recognize from writing fiction. A word like veracity, angular and imperious, now appears to me Wizard-of-Oz-like in masking its littleness. Veracity is meaningful at an individual level, subject to one's own worldview and moral compass, if you want to involve morality. If a reader disbelieves my stories happened, it matters not at all if I swear they are true, nor if I can get a team of fifteen other readers to agree with me. Likewise, if a reader connects to some individually determined vein of truth, or truthfulness, in the stories, I don't see why I would want to inform them of the site(s) of invention, if I can even accurately identify these. Because of my discomfort with involving authorial intention, the division between fiction and autobiographical writing has dissolved. These stories are 'fictions about what is itself in turn a fiction, the self'.

The self as a fiction. Something about this causes rebellion to flicker, perhaps the idea that our selves have weight and meaning, exist in a way that is more solid and significant than the word fiction implies. We sometimes like to think that we have a permanence that roots us, and that we move through a life which parts to meet us, rather than constructing our lives one moment at a time, forever reconstructing.

My father fixates on the past, revels in it. He chooses the same restaurant again and again, eating in memory of former meals. We revisit places we've been to before, and he sketches out the past with his arms. 'You were standing here, remember you had those shoes? And we had gone to that store with the dishes'. He describes places with reference to their past significance: 'the place where we ate the enormous steaks'; 'the place we met your friend from school, and his parents'. A hotel transformed into a new restaurant nearly disarmed him: 'we used to sit here and eat ice cream and look at the water, here, and we stayed in that room, where they put that antenna, do you see it? Do you remember?' It occasionally becomes a plea, a form of begging that can almost never be satisfied. I often encounter him 'in the course of inventing a brand-new past'; it is brand-new because I do not share it, and it is brand-new because what seems most important to him is not that I remember my version, but that I share his, which I never can.

As we live them, our lives slowly construct a channel through which we view the world. The channel constantly changes shape, which is the impact of the present on the past, but we can only see through this channel, which is the impact of the past on the present. One day we drove in the car together and talked about a particular period of time in my childhood. To say we remembered it differently is to understate. Eventually, he suggested, and then indeed argued, that I had invented the memories I was describing, that the things I was saying had happened had never actually happened. He had reasons why this must be so, evidence that he thought proved it. I thought of Janice Galloway writing of her mother looking at old pictures and investing them with a single, true version of the past, despite Galloway's own memories:

> They were not slips of paper to her, however … They were absolute reality. If I continued to know that the garden was a field and what a torn lip tasted like, I was on my own. Collusion or loneliness. (Galloway 2008, 28)

Loneliness did not bother me in that moment; in fact, nothing about the situation bothered me very much. It was oddly appropriate, considering the reading and writing I was doing, and it was even more odd and even more appropriate that he drew on some knowledge of testimony of childhood memories in cases of alleged past abuse. It was appropriate because I was reading about this topic, and how we can assess the accuracy of memories in these situations. It was odd because he introduced the topic by asking if I knew that such testimony was being disallowed in more and more court-rooms 'because it was false', as though our relationship was about to be legislated, and as though such a legal decision amounted to getting to the bottom of something.

'[I]t never pays to be too sure about what you can't prove', decides Galloway (Galloway 2008, 86). I agree, to a certain point. I can't prove most of my memories, but I don't actually want to. I am comfortable in my own certainty, and I am equally comfortable in that of others. Perhaps this is another reason why insistence in dividing novels from autobiographies is increasingly irrelevant to my reading. I prefer to draw my own conclusions and be guided by my own compass, and I prefer authors to do the same.

The situation in the car was perfect. It was a perfect moment of communication, miscommunication, tragedy, hilarity, destruction, finality and continuity. There is no way to return to the past, and both our understandings of it are necessarily coloured by the period between then and now. Even in the present, this present, where I am writing, the experience influences the past and is influenced by the past, and how I view it keeps changing. To spend too much energy trying to determine which version is closer to 'what really happened' is like a dog chasing its tail: exhausting, pointless, comical. What is really important in this experience, and what I value in it, is the light it shines on the essential individuality of determining truth and truthfulness. I do not see it in an individualistic way because I am self-centered, or because I like to practice dishonesty so long as I can convincingly lie to myself. Determining truth, and truthfulness, is an individual experience because, as this incident in the car shows, there is often no way, actually no way, to arrive at a conclusion when two versions of the past are in conflict.

Maybe this is part of my own channel. Maybe I have spent enough time witnessing other versions of the past that I cannot access, corroborate or even share, that I have been well primed to steer away from drawing in someone else's claims or intentions (assumed or otherwise) when trying to understand what I see and experience. The very notion of involving assumed authorial intention to understand a work of art, which I have clearly indicated my discomfort doing, is yet another element of this channel, a form of looking around the world which, over time, has settled into a form of discussing movies, books, behaviour, anything at all. I draw away from asking What did the person mean? and I draw closer to asking What does this mean to me? That someone might ask me these questions about the stories is interesting in a very limited way – as the writer, I am sometimes happy to discuss them (happier and happier as more time passes and I move further away from them), but I reject entirely that my views might influence or even direct the way they are read. In the case of *Biutiful*, this approach stands in the way of wanting to know what the director intended in order to assess his success or failure, and instead structures film analysis in terms of the ideas and connections prompted in me.

Truthfulness is not relegated to autobiography, nor is truth. As Sissela Bok (Bok 2000, 314) suggests, defining a book as autobiography might actually invite excessive hunting for clues and 'correspondence'. The lack of such a designator might save a book from this dreadful fate, and instead encourage readers to spend their time interpreting the book without a pre-existing set of criteria to which it must measure up, criteria which themselves are often individualized and personal (for example, composite characters are permissible; invented characters are not, or, reported dialogue is acceptable;

telescoping time is not). This absence might make it easier for a book to present its version of truth, and truthfulness, to a potentially more receptive audience.

Even after this short time, the way I see certain events which feature in the stories has changed. I would not write them the same way because I would not see them, and myself, the same way. To use Barthes's words about his own autobiographical writing, they were not '*the last word*' when I wrote them, they are not '*the last word*' now, and the stories will never be '*the last word*' because my self at the time of writing had no 'advantage over my past', nor any advantage over my present (Barthes 1975, 120). The stories are fixed in the time of writing, and in this sense they are permanent, but they continue to change and develop because seen through changing and developing eyes. Should I see *Biutiful* again as a parent, in a period of poverty or financial instability, as a film critic or while suffering from a terminal illness, I expect it will be a very different film for me, and my interpretations will begin from, and indeed stay lodged in, my own viewing channel, without drawing on the intentions of the director.

As Didion described, as Auster described, I am resistant to stopping, because it indicates a more important stop. But one way to resist the tendency (temptation?) to make the writing stand for more than itself is to reject the difficulty in stopping, and simply stop, for now.

Appendix

I have chosen these fourteen stories because I think they best demonstrate the ideas and questions that led to, and are discussed in, the preceding chapters.

Job Interview

When my mother and father moved they had no stuff. There was no stuff anywhere. No stuff in the refrigerator, no stuff in the closets, no stuff in the car – for the first short while there wasn't even a car. No stuff whatsoever. At the very start there was no stuff because there were no jobs, but this was soon remedied and after they started working they started to acquire stuff and soon enough they got a car which could carry more stuff more easily, over greater distances. Sometimes the best stuff is a little ways out of town. Stuff makes my father happy, makes him buffered, makes him pleased as punch when someone says, under their breath, maybe more or less to themselves, that they could really use a three-hole punch, or that they wish their European electronic adaptor hadn't gotten lost in the airport, or that they quite feel like some fresh-squeezed orange juice. These moments are when my father shakes off his cloak of everydayness and steps forth like a wizard. He sorts through his stuff, sifts through the piles and boxes and drawers and cupboards and shelving, and emerges with a three-hole punch, a European electronics adaptor, a squeezer of oranges.

If you are from here you call it junk but if you are born without it, it is blessed, blessed stuff. My mother has since crossed over to the other side, somehow corrupted herself; now she walks around calling it junk as though she never used to mend the ladders in her cheap tights, nearly blinding herself trying to make the seam invisible, as though she has never washed a plastic fork and put it in the cutlery drawer. She gives herself away every now and then: unwraps the aluminium foil off a casserole and folds it neatly away back in the kitchen cupboard, washes out plastic take-out containers because they're useful, loops ribbons around her finger and pins them together with a bobby pin for next Christmas.

The stuff came after the jobs, and the stuff made them a little more from here, in a way they were not from here before. People who are from here don't say things like 'what do you mean there's a microwave in the children's lunchroom? A *free* microwave?'

When my mother needed a job my father went through the phone book and chose the company that most suited her. My mother knew he was right because his finger was placed so authoritatively on the page. The page was yellow and so the book was called yellow pages. These small things you learn day by day. He pressed the numbers into the phone and straightened the knot in his tie as the phone rang, even though he wasn't wearing a tie. When he was finally talking to the person he wanted to talk to, my father asked him what he would do if he knew someone with enviable work experience and very desirable qualifications, well-suited to the company this man worked for. There was a pause. My mother gripped the arms of the chair. She was impressed with his knowledge, and his accent, so much slighter than hers. How had he learned to do that? When I bring schoolfriends home to play and they ask me where his accent is from I am confused. I look around. Whose accent?

The voice on the phone admitted that as happy as they were to hear that someone was demonstrating such an interest in the well-being of their company, they had to ask how exactly they could be of service. Knowing this was a trick question, my father did not answer, instead turning the tables and asking what this person would do if they had the good fortune of being able to be put in touch with this same person, the one with the enviable qualifications. The voice cleared its throat and said they guessed they would welcome the opportunity to talk to this accomplished individual, as they had a strong interest in developing the company and a commitment to working with like-minded people.

When my father hung up the phone, my mother had an interview later that week. She tried to swoon. The prospect of being spoken to in English for any length of time over a minute and a half was only slightly more appealing than water torture. She wasn't from here. They would know in less than one second. My grandmother had warned her. This is where trying leads to. End of discussion. My father invoked the promise of stuff, the stuff they could easily have if only my mother had the good sense to take the first step towards it. Didn't she care about stuff? My mother had nothing to worry about. After all, these were people who wore tennis shoes to dinner and ate food in their cars. Out of a paper bag. That had been handed to them through an open window. (It was beyond my father how one could use a knife and fork while driving a car.) She had nothing to fear from these paper-bag-eaters; she didn't even own tennis shoes anymore.

In the end my mother memorized, painstakingly, the twenty-five likeliest questions and their most desirable answers, as determined by my father. She closed her eyes and listened to the sounds of the words, the waves of long E's and A's and sharp consonants. She practiced endlessly, learning to pick up which question my father was asking even when he changed his intonation. When my father tested her by asking a new question and she simply smiled brilliantly and carefully enunciated the words 'Can you please repeat?' my father knew it was in the bag.

The day came. My mother set her hair and dressed as solemnly as if for a funeral. They walked to the office together, murmuring the questions and responses to each other. My father kissed my mother on the cheek and went across the street into a coffeeshop to wait. What a lot of people wearing blue jeans with holes in them. When my mother came back outside, she was acting a bit funny. How had it gone? Alright. How did she do? Alright. Had he asked the questions? He had. Had she answered the questions? She had not. What? Why on earth not? She had forgotten every single word that she had memorized. Right out of her head. So what had she done? Smiled. Smiled?! Yes, smiled and nodded. Smiled and nodded and said the few words that had somehow broken through. *Thank you. Yes. I see.* More smiling, more nodding. My father sighed. They would try again. It was not the end of the world. Was the man polite up until the end, at least? Very polite, my mother said. So nice and polite that he had given her the job.

Geneva

The first time my father went back to Romania it was a different country. The fall of the Iron Curtain had in effect hoisted up another division, between his life then and his life after 'then'. He took one of his children on his first visit. My brother was older; he was listed on my father's own passport. My father did not take passports lightly, took comfort in the two names on the one document, found it connected the two of them in a way he hoped might withstand any nasty surprises; he knew he was going somewhere experienced in nasty surprises. He left his daughter behind. She was not bound in such an official way; she did not even have a passport. In those days she didn't officially need one to travel, according to the rules of the new country, the country that understood families.

He left his daughter in Switzerland, in his mother's flat. It was a place of greenery and feminine workmanship. Every surface was covered in handmade lacework or embroidery, or a well-tended plant, or ceramic dishes painted by hand, or a combination of those things. The kitchen was a greenhouse in which cutlery and plates were cannily tucked away. The floor and walls of the living room had long since vanished, receding behind plush peach carpeting, framed prints and artwork, furniture that climbed the walls, sprouting out tiny cunning wooden shelves on which knick-knacks were placed. Even particularly beautiful chocolate wrappers, shining gold and decorated with images of Mozart, or exotic birds, or pretty European streets, were worthy of display, after being painstakingly smoothed out with the flat of a fingernail.

The hushed drama of the apartment provided a satisfying counterbalance to the anxiety of my grandmother's company, a space in which sweets were ever-present but previously unknown rules were enforced, such as the correct position of one's knees when seated in a chair, or the proper way to answer a question.

No record of those days remains. My grandmother is dead, and those days spent there have vanished from memory, with the exception of one flash. Seated at the table, a wooden, solid, old one, with a pink cloth draped over it, pale pink with a constellation of knobbly white embroidery exploding out from one corner. Flowers on the table, of course. The crown, or halo, of my grandmother's painted black hair moving in the friendly jungle that was the kitchen, preparing food, looking over her shoulder to talk to me, using a nonsense rhyme to be playful, some combination of baby talk and loving language. A link of syllables that meant nothing but were repeated like a mantra, lodging somewhere in my brain, unaware at that moment that they would remain somewhere easily accessed, would ring out every so often, a memento of that time chosen for preservation for some purpose not yet revealed.

Summertime

In the summer one could choose between the mountains and the sea. If one was very lucky and had sufficient time and money, one could do both, spending some time in the mountains before warming up tired muscles on the beach. One of the mercies, or benefits, of living in a rather small country. In the heat of summer the seaside has a clear advantage, and you need to bring far less with you, which is helpful if you have little to begin with. The trip to the coast took less than five hours; if my father and his friends left early in the morning, they could be walking on sand by early evening, watching the rich pack up their children and beach gear before candled dinners.

They usually went to a port town which has stayed stoic throughout a number of different names. Its ancient Greek name happens to be the name my brother was called until he began university and reverted back to his given name; its current name is the feminine version of my grandfather's name, given to the town in honour of Constantine the Great's sister. Rooted in history, the town bopped and shimmered as an expensive beach resort for wealthy families wishing to escape the grime of the city.

My father and his friends play games in the water, swim out too far, take breaks on the sand where they watch the rich families and consider their lives. They observe the scraps left behind: empty bottles of mineral water, magazines, limp towels, week-old editions of *The Daily Mail* loved for their foreignness. The sun is very hot, and they brown evenly. In another city, in other cities, my mother and her sisters did the same. They poured baby oil on their skin and baked. Decades later she visits Canadian doctors who run their hand over her olive shoulder and praise her for taking such good care of her skin.

The games my father and his friends played in the sea are probably similar to the ones my father taught my brother and I in hotel pools in North America, where the electric blue water and wavering tiles represented a world removed from the hard-packed sand and deceptive glinting waves. My brother and I knew a lot of games from swim class, if you can call swimming a class, which not everyone in my family does. But there were some new ones, and some old games with new names that he taught us, from the days he played them with his friends at the seaside. They had diving competitions and swimming competitions and shouted endlessly over the pounding of the waves, surfing them on their bellies and dashing themselves onto the pebbled beach.

One day they raced to a floating dock. It was very hot that day and the water marks left by the winner of the race evaporated in seconds as he positioned himself inexpertly, toes curling around the edge of the wood, head sticking out over arms outstretched too low, not straight enough. He dove and did not surface, just blew bubbles from below. As the other boys made it to the dock and clambered on they laughed and shouted at him, and when his body floated up face-down they yelled and slipped back off the dock, leaving patches of wet that almost steamed in the heat and disappeared like a hologram. A sandbar had formed slowly and deliberately as the waves moved overnight and now it was humped like a concrete speed bump a few feet below and away from the floating dock. His neck was broken.

My father regularly mails him cassette tapes: books on tape or recorded poetry or simply a voiced letter filled with recent news. One time he sent a squat teapot with a wide spout whose lid could be taped shut so that the rough movements he has managed to acquire in one arm might allow him to swing it towards his mouth and drink unassisted. The man became a useful teaching tool; when my brother and I complained we were told of his bedsores and his withered body and then, unspoken, his lost life. Be grateful. I was in the store with my father as we picked out the teapot, discarding the plastic children's ones because they would be insulting, bypassing the elegant china ones because they would just get broken, selecting one whose lid seemed wonky anyway, so that the taping might be seen as anyone's idea, a solution for shoddy design.

Summertime II

My grandfather only cheats at solitaire when a game becomes unwinnable. He can discern this fairly easily after the tens of thousands of games he has played; sometimes he shuffles the cards and lays them out in a way that suggests he already knows the outcome but must perform the actions for some reason that cannot be disclosed. If he is not playing solitaire, he is cooking; if he is neither playing solitaire nor cooking, he must be filling in the smeary crossword puzzles in the newspapers he buys from church.

My brother invites dozens of people to our house while my father is in another city. Our friends regard my grandfather cautiously, placing their bottles in the fridge surreptitiously. Everyone communicates with him strictly through gestures and smiles. It is summer: the borders between the house and the outdoors weaken, become permeable. Voices travel through open windows, people spill out of the doorway. Grass flattens under bodies, wine soaks into flowerbeds, a snowstorm of ashes flutters down when someone knocks a saucer-ashtray off a low-hanging tree branch. My grandfather smokes; he lights cigarettes for surprised teenagers and they all puff complacently. He plays solitaire quietly, looking up and grinning whenever someone comes into the kitchen, smiles, shrugs his shoulders if asked something in the wrong language. He expresses some surprise when my friend pours herself a tumbler of vodka. When the music begins to disturb him, we turn it down.

The darkness drives more people indoors, and a backgammon tournament begins. He beats all my brother's friends roundly; they try to cheat, kiss the dice, change the rules, play in teams: nothing works. He wins seventeen games straight and drinks Turkish coffee while all the bottles in the fridge are slowly emptied.

The moon is full that night. I lie on the grass while inside people line up to play, or just watch. Two of the most ardent players roll up their sleeves and keep trying, using foreign curses when they lose, blush when my grandfather laughs and pounds them on the shoulders after a good game. These two will help my father and brother carry his coffin in a few years. Eventually, unbeaten, he goes to bed. A chorus of drunken teenaged cheering follows him up the stairs, and the party deflates a little bit when he is gone. When the police come by and ask us to wrap it up, we speak in low voices and obey, not wanting him to be disturbed.

Commerce

The capitalist drive can be very strong in a communist country. The desire to make money and sell goods – it can't be stopped, especially among the young. Especially among the young adults, the early-twenty-year-olds who bristle at the idea that it might be someone else's business how and when they make their desired millions. The secret to success normally lies in some variation of the maxim *use what you've got*. Claiming to have nothing is a lazy man's excuse, a transparent cop-out. There's a sucker born every minute, and twice a minute there's a person who can be persuaded to buy something they don't need, just because they don't yet have it. This kind of market analysis came easily to my father and his best friend, and they knew they could work it in their favour.

One of the few places they could go to was East Germany. My father and his friend brought along bags of goods to sell, and carried them up the stairs to their hostel room furtively, opening duffel bags in the secrecy of a locked cardboard-thick door, gloating on the items that would soon be transformed into cash. They were unable to get their hands on much, but they had brought bottles of cheap alcohol, more suited to stripping old paint or perhaps poisoning small animals; cheap polyester shirts that clung to your shoulderblades at room temperature, gluing themselves to naked skin and leaving behind faint red rashes; and plastic sunglasses that would snap at the hinges with the least hint of pressure. These were the ingredients. They only needed some willing participants.

The hostel was mostly empty during the day. When they came back from walking around the city, who did they spy but an entire group of German high school students; a class trip come on a visit. The students were teenagers, heady with the freedom of being away from home for the first time, giddy with the delight of exasperating their chaperones and teachers. They filled the rooms of the hostel and spilled out into the hallways and stairwells, shouting in lengthy, dense sentences, delirious with a temporary escape from the confines of home.

A more suitable opportunity could hardly have presented itself. It did not take long to strike up a conversation with two or three teenagers, who in turn spread the news. A steady stream of young Germans climbed the stairs to my father's room to spend the money their parents had pressed into their pink sweaty palms just a few days earlier on treasures from my father's and his friend's suitcases. One after another they trooped out of the room, relieved of money but carrying a shiny new shirt or a warm bottle of some undiscovered liquid.

It did not take long until the suitcases were empty. They had sold out completely. It took slightly longer for the full effect to manifest, but when it did it was magnificent. The hostel was transformed into a funhouse, a carnival, an asylum. Compound words were hysterically screamed from one floor to another. The scent of sweat and polyester hung in the air. One or two young bodies vomited, shocked at the assault on their senses that was taking place. The snapping of sunglasses was accompanied by the pounding of feet along threadbare carpets. A few fumbling gropings and wet kisses, fuelled primarily by cheap liquor and curiosity, took place among shy teenagers in stairwells.

The chaperones became furious. My father and his friend soon realized that loose lips indeed sink ships, and it was only a matter of time until they were identified as the source of the new entertainment. They withdrew into their room and turned the lights off, folding their duffel bags and counting their money. They sat in the dark, listening to the shouting and the vain efforts of the chaperones to keep the children penned up. Night fell. The teenagers passed out, or sweated themselves still, or otherwise became silent. Finally, an authoritative knock was heard at the door. My father and his friend did not move. An old pair of knees creaked, and took in the strip of darkness beneath the cardboard-thick door, heard the sound of breathing within, and nothing else. The body walked away, and the hostel slept. In the morning, the two young men woke up suddenly, their hands flying to their pockets to feel the bulge of money, taking in the deflated duffel bags as proof, and looked to the still-locked door.

The knocking had resumed, again with authority but also with restraint, and some amount of respect. It was early. It was very bad manners to disturb people early in the day. They lay still, made no movement towards the door. On the other side of the door, two Germans decided that no matter who had sold the children in their care breakable sunglasses and vile liquor, it reflected poorly on them to wake people up in the morning. And so they left, taking the children with them for a day of sightseeing, gripping skinny wrists and tugging when the children declared, pale-faced, that they had headaches and preferred to stay in bed.

As soon as the group left the building, my father and his friend shot into action, removing traces of themselves from the room. They climbed out the window and leapt awkwardly to the ground, buoyed up by adrenaline and laughter. They made it to the train station in a few minutes, running laughing through the streets, triumphant.

Oma and the Wolves

My father would urge my brother and me to eat Mars bars at swim meets, for the bursts of energy which might win us our races. He did not come to watch very often but he would always remind us to pack at least a few in with our towels and swim caps and flip-flops. My father saw Mars bars as perfectly suitable food for children, who often need bursts of energy, and bought the chocolate bars in boxes of 48 from Costco.

He possibly learned the habit from his parents, who would pack bags with fatty, sugary foods when they went walking in the mountains. When your body works hard it appreciates a Mars bar and it also appreciates thickly buttered bread and hunks of solid dark chocolate, even if it's of low quality. He and his parents and sister would vacation in the mountains, taking long walks and staying in cabins with people they were encouraged to regard as simple folk, people who served them huge bowls of hot steaming food when they came back, spoke in rough language and showed general ignorance about the state of the world around them.

The forest gets dark before anywhere else does, and it can trick you into thinking night has fallen; the trees get ahead of themselves. The four of them were walking, sometimes single file, depending on the width of the track. Eventually they came to a sudden clearing or opening; they were milling around when the wolves came into view. Somehow, in a way wolves have, one of them was chosen and it was my grandmother. My father saw his mother become somehow separated from the group, and no one shouted, not even once. My grandmother counted one, two, three, four wolves. Her husband and their two children counted one, two, three, four wolves. The wolves meandered as though they had nothing better to do; she folded her hands behind her back and kept her eyes open. My father and his sister took cues from their father, who spoke under his breath and made no sudden movements.

My grandmother walked backwards slowly, her hands still held behind her back, and the bag of food, nearly empty since they'd been hiking most of the day, still wrapped in her fingers. The wolves moved towards her casually and carefully, tightening their circle. They no longer looked at my grand-father or his children. When my grandmother backed into the tree she stayed there, pressed her back up against the bark and mashed her fingers between the tree and her body. Leaves nudged themselves in her hair and the ground near the trunk was raised slightly, from the upward pressure of the roots. She pressed down against it and stood still. Perhaps she was trying to melt into the tree itself. The wolves circled, occasionally snorting or making small clicking whines to each other. The noises were ominous, private, almost intimate. When my grandmother cleared her throat the wolves cocked their heads and listened as though she was about to address them. She told her family to meet her down at the bottom, down in the cabin where they would eat dinner together and finally get these heavy boots off. My father and his sister continued taking cues from their father and did not move, did not walk down to the cabin to take their boots off and rest.

The first wolf to smell her walked up guiltily, as if he was ashamed of himself. He pushed his snout close to her hands, against the grainy bark of the wood, and she thought she could feel grey bristles even though you cannot feel a colour and the wolf did not actually touch her. Another wolf came forward and smelled the front of her dress, the spot of coffee that had spilled from the thermos onto her knees and the smear of soft cheese that had been wiped off the knife before they used the same knife to cut fruit for dessert. The wolves were rangy, thin. They would have eaten soft cheese and maybe even fruit. They would have been happy to lick the knife clean for her. They continued talking to each other softly, from the backs of their wet pink throats. My grandmother told her husband that the children were surely getting cold and hungry and he should return to the cabin and get warm. As she said this she slowly brought the bag of food from behind her back, looking slantways into the eyes of the closest wolf so that it knew there was no disrespect or challenge in her look. They all noted the soft thud of the food landing several feet away with blinks and grunts. All four wolves padded towards the bag, for the first time leaving my grandmother completely unwatched. She moved nervously towards the rest of her family and joined them. They did not look back at the wolves as they walked down the rest of the mountain. The next morning my grandmother could not get out of bed. Her muscles had clenched so hard that they needed two days to melt back into place; during that time the four of them stayed on in the cabin with the mostly-illiterate food-makers.

Isambard

Isambard Kingdom Brunel was an engineer, which alone was more than enough reason for my father to love him. He was also British (another plus) and he appears impeccably dressed in every photo I have seen of him. It's true that black and white tends to make people look more formal, classier, but it is not Brunel's fault that he died two years before the first colour photographs emerged. He was multi-lingual and displayed a good understanding of geometry by age nine. There are surely more reasons, but it does not do to stack too much pressure on a newborn male child and so my father stopped there when recounting the reasons to name his first son Isambard.

My mother was struck dumb. To her the name sounded invented, sounded like one of my father's bizarre jokes whose purpose is not to make you laugh but to highlight a gap in your intelligence. She was unmoved by the stories of feats of engineering and couldn't care less who built the Great Western Railway, wherever that even was. My father was used to getting his own way, which in his mind is never his own way, but merely the right way, and my mother's growing stomach pressed out into open space the same way the tension between them grew slightly, pressing its way into previously empty spaces. My mother reminded my father of the friends they had who had come over and given their children bizarre, unpronounceable names. My parents never intended to do this. There was no reason to cripple the first generation's chance of fitting in, of understanding and participating in unbelievable habits like wearing blue jeans to dinner or taking off your shoes when you enter the house, by giving them a name no one could pronounce. This is what my father tried to explain. Anyone looking at the back of any of their coins could see how much England meant to these people, and Brunel was English.

In many European countries it is customary to celebrate a name day on whichever day of the year is associated with a saint bearing the same name as your own. Traditions vary but range from a preparing a special meal to celebrating it as a second birthday. In this way, St Mark saved my brother. Cognizant of signs without fully believing in them, my parents noted that on the fifteenth day of the fifth month, they were put in room 515 on the fifth floor. With a first-born child one cannot be too careful, and sometimes being cognizant of signs maybe involves believing in them slightly, or the possibility that they might be true. My father relented. His son was weighted with four names, but they were all easily translatable.

Jewish

When my brother and I were children, my father told us our mother was Jewish. He told us many things about her, many of them negative up until our formative years were safely over, but this one sticks out. I don't know why; it's just as false as most of the other claims. Maybe it's because he stead-fastly denies ever having said such a thing. There was no reason to – she's not, nor is anybody in her immediate family, and yet my brother and I are both prepared to swear on our lives that this was information he gave us.

My father is a big giver of information, though it often takes the form of a pressured insistence rather than anything as gracious as a gift or offering. It may have been a joke but, if so, it is the kind of joke that does not travel well from Europe to Canada, and is lost on Canadian children. We've reached a stalemate – my father declaring outright that this entire episode is a total fabrication, and my brother and I utterly convinced that it is not, and that it was not even a single episode, which would have raised the chances that we'd misheard (maybe he'd said she was *foolish*? *Shrewish*?) or otherwise distorted the information.

No, this happened more than once, probably fewer than ten times, somewhere in that range. It wasn't a conversation, it was just a simple fact, introduced into some discussion, for no apparent reason. There was no cause to dispute it, and it was no form of judgment – it wasn't bad to be Jewish, any more than it might be good; it simply was, like having brown hair. And perhaps this is why there was no need for follow-up questioning or clarifi-cation. I don't recall us thinking that this might connect us too to Judaism. That we were not Jewish didn't seem in any way connected to the infor-mation. The knowledge was unquestioned, which is perhaps why it rooted itself so suddenly and so strongly in the minds of my brother and I, and its senselessness is perhaps why my father has forgotten ever saying it and why he cannot imagine ever saying it in the first place.

Its senselessness might be exactly what negates its possibility of existence for him. In his life (in his mind), my father proceeds though life with brave deliberateness, living according to a strict rulebook. His confidence in the sense of his thoughts and actions has never wavered significantly, even in the face of often extreme opposition. And so, unless there was a reason, unless there was a call for it, he simply would not go around wasting words and breath telling a lie.

But he did.

My mother probably knows nothing about this entire story; she was so rarely consulted in any of our discussions pertaining to her.

World Cup

It is difficult to articulate the importance of football to citizens of countries where it plays a marginal role in the athletic environment, and no role in national identity, to say nothing of how one understands and self-identifies on a personal, individual level. The way participation in a sport, even exclusively as a spectator, can hold meaning about the way you see yourself and the world around you, was something I learned late, and still can barely understand. But children are primed to question nothing and everything, which sums up my reaction when my grandfather decided to watch his home country play in the World Cup in Berlin.

He did not welcome transatlantic travel. He found no pleasure in navigating foreign airports, he disliked the non-smoking rules on airplanes, he was ever sure his luggage would be lost, stolen, or at least rifled through, and he had become perpetually doubtful of being spoken to in a language he could understand. But for football, sacrifices are easily made, and obstacles become surmountable. Crossing the ocean to watch a football game and return less than a week later seemed, to me, both obvious and wondrous, like most things adults did.

The arrival by post of the ticket to the actual match was a cause for celebration; it was clutched more dearly than the plane ticket. It did not seem possible that the date printed on the slip of card really corresponded to a date on any calendar; this journey seemed to traverse the ordinary boundaries of weeks and months, leading into another zone where time was measured differently. Three hours was not enough to contain the importance and scope of the activity.

My father drove his father home one evening, a few days before the match, and, from his flat, took us to the grocery store to pick up some things. We came home a few hours later and, coasting up to our parking spot, saw my grandfather pacing the concrete floor of the underground parking garage, hands in his pockets, eyes on the ground. It seemed impossibly late for him to still be moving, living in the world. After we had dropped him off, he had ceased to exist until the next day, when he would assemble himself to re-enter the world I lived in.

He had lost his ticket. He discovered this as he rode the elevator up to his flat, turning his pockets inside out and feeling with yellowed fingertips in the creases where the elevator floor met the walls, in case somehow it was there but he just couldn't see it. He rode the elevator straight back down and walked back to his son's house, step by step, eyes scanning the sidewalk and trying to ignore the stiff wind blowing tissues, chip bags, receipts and newspapers across his path.

In the parking garage he circled for over an hour, layering footstep over footstep, cataloguing and reviewing every square inch. The tragedy was unspeakable, so he did not speak about it, simply kept up his tempo while my father finished parking the car. He could not be coaxed to return home and sleep, dealing with it in the morning; he preferred to keep looking, maybe it would turn up, it had to be somewhere. The misery sucked me under instantly, thrusting me back against the plush of the car seat like a shove. The anticipation, the planning, the suitcase, the stadium, the sheer vastness of the journey – all for nothing? Was there no insurance against this type of thing in the world? Could this really be allowed to happen?

The ticket did turn up. As we emptied out of the car, stumbling with sleepiness, one of us (who?) plucked the ticket out of the crevice between car door and passenger seat, where it was poking its sly cardboard side out between the walls of grey fuzzy car carpet. We had driven the ticket around all evening, unknowingly carrying it through the streets after it had fallen from his coat pocket, waiting to be picked up again.

New Year's Eve

One of first times my father really noticed my mother, she was in a rush to leave his house. It was New Year's Eve, twelve years to the day before I was born in another country, and my father was surveying the scene of his family's annual party.

They had a large house because his parents had done well. My father's mother came from a more distinguished line than his father, where enough illustrious deeds had been accomplished to sweeten or rub out some final class divides – an old suicide, a bankruptcy, my grandmother's small fat peasant hands, which I have inherited and which some have loved without understanding their significance. My grandfather married up in some ways. He was a high school principal but she was a baron's descendant who cried when he smashed crystal glasses in celebration of their wedding. He made up for having four older sisters and a dead father in other ways: by having his dead father pay with his good name for an officer's position in the army, thus giving him a life long enough to actually live it; by writing chemistry textbooks that I open carefully now, mindful of the pages that are about to turn to dust; by secreting away one of my father's school friends who for some reason wanted to stay within unfriendly borders; by crossing the ocean to raise his son's children even when they threw up their hands at his wilful misunderstanding of North American customs.

But from where I am now, my grandfather is only a father, and he stands silently observing the party, looking at the furniture that has been pushed to the sides of the rooms, the double doors that have been opened, the scraped plates lying everywhere that tell him his food was enjoyed. The music is bad, as young people's music usually is, but nothing much gets into this country anymore and as a result he knows the kids take what they can get. Does he notice my father noticing my mother? Maybe.

There are two of her, flitting around like grasshoppers. Tall and skinny, the twins play basketball better than the boys and fix their eyes on the ground whenever someone as old as my father speaks to them. The first time he spent much of the day with her, he was doing a favour for a friend. The twins' older sister was the object of one of my father's friends' affections. She was more their age but there was only one of her. She agreed to go out with him only if suitable companionship could be found for her sisters, as they could not be left alone. This re-emerges years later, when I take the bus to Montreal for spring break (this is how we do spring break, in a town where the pipes freeze and your bones freeze and the wine within your high school budget tastes like vinegar and you watch French men playing pool and wonder what it is that they want, so that you can start working on being it) and my grandfather can say only three words, over and over again: 'Alone? A girl?'

My father's friend asks him to hang out with the twins for a day, even half a day. In a country surrounded by places you are not permitted to get to, the least you can try when you are twenty-two and a man is to get somewhere with a girl. My father agrees. The two of them showed up, shadows of each other, and took the basketball court by storm. Their six year youth helped them run circles around my father and his friends, who stood flushed with age and surprise and the widening eyes of seeing someone differently.

My father hates to dance, but I know he danced at his New Year's parties because that's one of the things they were famous for. He spied my mother gathering herself up to go and slipped between the other rhythming bodies to ask her what she was doing. Shifting her body to hide her secret, she demurred and he persisted. He is a persistent man. Eventually she faced him fully, revealing the shameful tear in her stockings. Of an unbelievable cheapness, like most of the goods in the country at the time, wearing them must have been like going out for a night's dancing with spider webs on your legs, or dryer lint. But her decorum insisted she couldn't possibly continue the evening with torn stockings.

My father points out that she lives across town. It will take her an hour to get home, at least, and an hour to come back. Does he doubt she will come back? If he does, this is just an example of the wilful denial approach that I will get used to before I become an adolescent, but will not be able to characterize until years later.

My mother is determined. Staying at the party in such a state is impossible. In this moment she is alien to me. I wear stockings only under extreme duress (see above, concerning weather that bursts water pipes) and have been known to huddle in the corners of bars and nightclubs as soon as I arrive, stripping them off from under my dress in what I imagine are a few discreet movements, throwing them in the direction of my bag to be found the following morning, or not.

My mother goes home to change her stockings. It takes two trams to get home, but she goes home, changes her stockings, returns. My father is impressed. He is more than impressed. My father is a man who loves propriety, would never wear white after Labour Day, can debone a fish with elegance in any company you please, knows to keep between women and the road when on sidewalks, lays the table with a fork for each course even when eating alone, adores the old French custom of allowing anyone an audience with the King so long as they were properly dressed and observed the social rules of the day. He's done for.

Hairdresser

My grandmother's ears were pierced for her when she was an infant, thus absolving her from any involvement in this act of savagery. It also conveniently allowed her to wear beautiful earrings of finely wrought silver and gold while holding the opinion that willingly damaging your face in such a primitive way is characteristic of lower classes. She wears tiny gold crosses and occasionally discreet pearls, matching her earrings to her outfit with the same determination she brings to shining shoes and keeping handbags in perfect condition. She regards the epidemic of teenagers who drag the legs of their extra-long jeans along the pavement, stepping on them with the backs of their shoes, with pity and disgust. She sends me coded gifts that I hate translating: starched white collars made by hand and meant to be buttoned onto dresses I do not own; white handkerchiefs with initials curling in the corners, embroidered under the lamp in her flower-filled living room; small glass jars of perfume that smell cloying and threaten to break in my fat little fingers. I much prefer the bars of Swiss chocolate, the wrapped packages of cookies, the glasses of homemade jam that come in jars comfortably thicker than those of the perfume.

The gifts she brings when she comes to visit are more uncomfortable because they cannot be put into a drawer and forgotten. She comes bearing tools for re-education – hair combs that never manage to stay where they are put, shoe polish that is useless on canvas running shoes, ever more hand-embroidered handkerchiefs. She emerges fully formed from her bedroom in the mornings, never walks around in pyjamas or with hair unfixed. When she starts misapplying her lipstick because she can't see it and her hand trembles, people are too embarrassed to tell her. She brings news from her home; it becomes more and more difficult to convince her that her neighbours' noisy children are not breaking into her apartment and rearranging her things to trick her. She wants to open the window to tell them to play more quietly, but the window is heavy. When she prepares for a visit of a few weeks she touches the door of her apartment after locking it, praying that whoever is taking things and putting them back in the wrong places will not cause damage while she is gone. She is sick and tired of calling her daughter to complain that the mixing bowl, the nail scissors, the spare light bulbs, the green onions, the newspaper, the second-best pair of slippers, the magnifying glass, the box with needles and thread, her favourite picture, her address book, her yellow cardigan, her purple slip, are all not in their right places. She has walked through the apartment before leaving and looked at them all. If they are not there when she gets back, if they are moved by some evil force while she is absent, she knows she has lost.

Off the plane she is confronted by frigid cold and her grandchildren, who smell of fast food and punch each other in the backseat of her son's car. The cold weather does not lift and on the radio people are asked to stay inside if they can help it; the number of minutes skin can bear exposure is down to single digits. The house is warm and filled with food and Swiss chocolate. The streets are a sullen, dirty grey, hardened beyond negotiation with ice and frost. Touching the window to feel a hint of the outside cold gives me a delicious sense of superiority; we order piping hot pizza and tip the delivery man extra. My grandmother eats hers with a knife and fork, prompting her son to make his children do the same.

My grandmother needs her hair set. The curls are turning limp; she needs them to be reshaped. My father passes this on to me and I breathe a sigh of relief. There is no hairdresser near us open on a Sunday and anyway it's thirty below and anyway there isn't anyone in the house to get dressed up for; we've been in sweat-pants all day. My grandmother sniffs; this sloth is nothing to be proud of. I retreat behind the day of the week – the hairdresser is closed. My grandmother sniffs again and ten minutes later repeats her request. It is still Sunday. We call the salon and let her listen to the endless ringing for a few minutes. She pats her head and announces her need one final time, just before lunch. I am sent to accompany her. When we put on our coats she asks where we are going; I grit my teeth.

Outside, it's much too cold to talk, and we walk very slowly because she has trouble negotiating the frozen humps of ice that cannot be salted away. When we get to the hairdressers I stamp my feet on the pavement to get feeling back into them while she primly knocks and no one answers. When asked, I explain that it is Sunday, they are closed. After a few minutes of waiting she lets us return home, where she tells her son that she doesn't understand what happened, but his daughter brought her to a closed shop when what she clearly needed was an open shop. All afternoon she is forced to hear her grandchildren punching each other and jabbering in the wrong language and filling their faces with Swiss chocolate; even retreating behind the closed bedroom door does not provide relief. It is winning, she can tell.

THE ROAD TRIP

My father takes the saying 'go big or go home' quite literally. It's only logical: if you go anywhere, any place, you must do everything, go everywhere and see everything, or you might as well go home. This attitude has helped him see everything worth seeing in several countries, dozens of cities, hundreds of neighbourhoods. Unless he's prepared to go home, he's going to do it all.

Some people, when they travel, prefer another approach. A minimalist approach, say. They believe in the idea that vacations are for reducing the number of things one does in a day, for emphasising pleasure and eliminating stress, for focusing on one place, or activity, for rejecting the hassles of everyday life that are the reason one takes a vacation in the first place, for embracing the wander, the element of chance, the happening upon a new favourite street, or restaurant, or viewpoint. Bollocks, says my father. Lazy people have always existed and will continue to try and justify their actions until the end of time. Be unconcerned with them.

The car is a wonderful device. It is simultaneously tool, habitable space, possession and status symbol. For this, it is loved four times over by some people. As essential as a toothbrush, it permits ease of movement combined with opportunity for detour: the symbol of freedom and purchasing power. To not have a car is to be weakened, incommoded. These passions and ideals culminate in THE ROAD TRIP, a common enough type of journey but one that my father, as ever, puts his individual spin on. The Road Trip is beloved of most adults, windows down, music up, a half-empty bag of junk food spilling over the back seat. The road trip is familiar even to most children: an hour's drive to see grandparents, a few hours' journey so that one can play in provincial championships of some sport, or attend summer camp. But THE ROAD TRIP is strictly for professionals.

Most of the Eastern Seaboard became available to my father once he purchased his first car. It beckoned, inviting. Boston was obviously just a jaunt, New York was a day trip, so was Quebec City, or Washington DC. Chicago could be comfortably done, with enough time to make a few stops: a leisurely lunch, a few choice look-outs at the view, maybe popping into a mall to see what was on sale. The day allowed enough room for these distractions from the main journey, time enough to do it all before dragging one's aching limbs into the hotel bed sometime around midnight or early morning of the next day.

But why not? Life is short, the world is big. To outright reject the opportunity to see something new, have a new experience, is nothing short of ingratitude. One question, and one question only, should be asked before the outset of any journey, even a repeat journey: how much can I possibly cram into this day before dropping dead of overstimulation, general exhaustion, indigestion or a combination of the three? If this question is answered honestly, one will discover that the day leaves room for far more than initially believed. All sane people will agree. So my father hardly paused before deciding to take his mother, his wife and his infant son by car to Chicago in July. Not just any day in July, but the Fourth of July, the birthday of the nation. Fun! Joy! What a smashing start to a weekend away! People should really count their blessings.

The temperature in the car could probably have fried an egg, though this would have been unnecessary because of the enormous brunch sitting in everyone's stomach, trying vainly to digest. My father took it upon himself to act as tour guide, since none of the other passengers seemed too concerned with where they were or what they were looking at. The kilometres flew by as the heat rose and the small space of the car shrank with each passing second, pulling them all together, close-knit like the happiest of travelling companions.

Some observers may have thought that conversation was waning, but really it was just getting interesting. My father and his mother chanced upon a rich vein in the granite of the growing silences when one of them mentioned toothpaste. An underappreciated resource, when you thought about it. And, as a valuable resource, one that should be preserved, maximized. How could one ensure this? How could one make sure that they were getting all of the toothpaste, every bit of it, out of a toothpaste tube? Not just by squeezing. That was an amateur's guess. There must be better, more effective ways. Should one press it in a vise? Slit it open with a razor blade and scrape off the remnants? How would these remnants be stored? And would any toothpaste remain trapped around the opening? What was, after all, the best way to get to the bottom of this issue? It was lucky they had so much time to think about and discuss it. It is a shame you cannot rely on children being decent conversationalists: my infant brother screamed his face off during nearly all of the long hours of debate and conjecture.

The city of Chicago was hotter than the car. They tumbled out, dazed, late for the itinerary my father had prepared, nothing much, just a few highlights, one or two essential stops and then a list of other options that they could see, depending on how time went. The voiced request for rest went unheeded – it could not be taken seriously. It was barely ten o'clock. But, graciously, my father waved his hand and suggested that anyone who wanted to put on a show and complain was, of course, not forced to do anything. At this point, my mother fainted in the street, putting a huge dent in my father's plans. It was one thing for sentient adults to reject the opportunity to learn something and look around them, but there was no reason to bring others down with you. My father huffed, prescribed a glass of water for the patient and checked his watch. Happy Birthday America, indeed.

Tube Station

My grandfather was cowed by the enforcement of timekeeping when he was old. Meeting someone necessitated a window of at least forty-five minutes in case they turned up early. Catching a bus meant being at the stop with enough time to spare that he could normally walk to his destination. Getting on a plane was a source of stress so immense that he considered sleeping in the airport the night before. If someone was coming over to his house for lunch, he would resist leaving the house all morning. Better to relax, smoke a cigarette, play some solitaire, drink a coffee and wait. Why tempt fate by going for a walk with only two hours to go? When being picked up by someone in a car, he preferred standing outside for up to half an hour rather than risk the anxiety of hearing the doorbell ring without being totally ready. Rain was no deterrent, nor was nighttime or snow. Nothing could compare to the ease of mind that came from existing in perfect, complete anticipation and preparedness.

To his son, this attitude was ludicrous and unnecessary. My father adopted a much more cavalier approach to timekeeping. An invitation to dinner at half past six simply meant some time before nine. Sunday brunch, of course, meant Sunday late lunch. Anybody who turned up to a summer barbeque less than an hour after the time suggested upon invitation was identified by my father as someone who evidently did not know how things ran. Until I was thirteen, I thought 'church' was a Sunday-long, all-day, drop-in affair, because we never once arrived in time for the start of the service, and generally left while things were still going on.

Similarly, buying a flight ticket was evidence enough that my father intended to be on that flight. If he was a few minutes later than whatever time someone had decided to print on the boarding pass, it did not mean a thing to him – he would keep up his end of the bargain by being there before it was meant to take off. As to *when* exactly that was – well, that depended on what was on sale in the duty free shops. No one can be expected to predict these kinds of sales. His father, he thought, acted this way because of his personality to a great degree, but also because of his age. With old age came the increasing fear that someone, possibly the Grim Reaper, would prevent you from doing the things you wanted. Your only way to circumvent this was to pre-empt them, show up before they did. Youth and middle age – vitality, so to speak – were power.

As the years following my grandfather's death pass, his tendency to go to extremes in order to avoid being late are softened and become tender rather than comical. The chill of waiting in the winter night for a car ride warms, as if a pane of glass protects us from the weather, and now we seem to realize that actually it wasn't anyone's business how my grandfather preferred to structure his day. My father, however, seems unaffected by the passage of time, at least in terms of his approach to arbitrarily fixed deadlines. Nothing but a full-scale airport shutdown prevented him from missing a flight out of Paris. He was able to blame backseat drivers for arriving late to the airport in Lisbon (he didn't even miss his own flight that time; the backseat drivers missed theirs). He was outraged to learn that despite the fact that the plane was still sitting on the runway, he was not permitted to check in twenty minutes late to a flight out of Rome; his efforts to debate and reason his way onto the plane went nowhere.

And yet, there are glimmers. I meet him in London; he puffs his way to the station to meet me, waving and calling out to me even though he is a block away, anxious lest I start walking away for some reason, or go back into the station, or disappear entirely. In the tube station, he searches the many signs and tries to determine which direction we want to go in, even though we've already determined that before entering the station. He wants to ask the ticket seller, despite the fifteen-minute queue, despite the fact that I can explain why I know where we need to go, despite the fact that the lines are colour-coded. Because there is construction on one of the lines, he thinks we should make enquiries about our own, unrelated line. I meet him in Geneva. He is late to meet my plane and when I call him to see where he is, he hollers down the line, something about the rental car making a noise, panicked demands to sit still, as though I am the one in the wrong place, *don't* move, calm down, calm down, *calm down*, he'll be right there, everything is ok, as if sitting in a chair for half an hour is too stressful for me, as if I might get lost in the arrivals hall.

But the glimmers are not too strong. I meet him in Toronto and wait in the December wind for thirty-five minutes before he turns up, asking why I'm so early.

Venice

Venice is a sudden city, rising from the water suddenly and sinking back into it just as suddenly; suddenly showing you that what you have known until now was not complete, lacked something. Venice for the first time was almost lost amongst other cities, flat on the water in a boat filled with mostly English speakers. Multiple trips become one; I seek my hotel on a street I have been on at least five times, which has now disappeared amongst the other winding alleys. I pass the same shop selling bread and alcohol five times in my search for an address, and each time the shopkeeper looks up at me and knows I am not from here. Once I find the hotel and put my things down I think I should return to the shop and buy some alcohol but on my way back down the five flights of stairs something happens and it is another trip, where my brother and I follow our father through the streets in the dark.

We return late from sightseeing and it is dinnertime at night in Venice; I carry around a necklace I insisted on buying and will never wear. Suddenly we are in a restaurant; it was that kind of trip, where everything took seven weeks but happened suddenly. Suddenly we were in a restaurant; suddenly Germany was France; suddenly the difference between North American highways and European highways was apparent, suddenly I changed from someone who had never eaten brains to someone who had.

In the restaurant my father feeds his children things they have never tasted, periodically instructing them to smell the water of the street outside the door. Dessert was desirable, some sort of fruit in some sort of syrup. We had been out all day long, fingering delicate lace things, watching through windows as men smashed glass so hot from fire that it did not shatter but instead flowed and shouldered the smash elegantly. My father was weighted with taken photographs, my brother and I were lightened from the alcohol in the syrup. Nobody else was in the restaurant, the waiters were re-wiping clean tables and picking their fingernails and betting with each other where we were from. I tip the bowl to capture the filmy remains of the syrup and wonder why it tastes like burning.

Suddenly we were outside in the night, colder than before and yet warmer. There are few songs that my father and both his children know but we sing every one of them that night. Had the waiters thought it would be funny to give alcohol to children? Had my father thought it would be funny to give alcohol to children? The air is wet and black and we stumble and scream with laughter, propping each other up while we try to find the invisible streets, the streets that lap back and forth and shine under the moon. Suddenly we come upon it and are home. I fade and disappear as I climb the stairs and my father turns around to walk back downstairs for some reason; suddenly it is years before I am born and my father and mother walk down the stairs to the lobby of the hotel.

They nod to the proprieter; all three like each other. The hotel is named after my mother and father's new country, for no reason other than it comes early in the alphabet, ensuring his place near the top of the hotel lists that travellers peruse. As they walk through the lobby a beautiful woman walks just in front of them, gliding on air like the boats skimming just outside the front door. My father pursues her, my mother pursues my father. The woman's hair is sleek and fashionably arranged, her clothing is immaculate and the seams announce the fine firm lines of her body. She carries herself with an iron grace that my father imagines in the cold blond visions this city has seen. When she turns to offer my parents the open door the slant of her neck knifes into the crisp folds of her dress. A string of pearls drapes over her collarbone. She is a queen. This is the hotel cleaning lady, the woman who neatly arranges my mother's perfumes and matches my father's shoes together next to the bed. She carries the money they left on top of the dresser in her pocketbook of fine Italian leather. My mother thanks her for holding the door, she smiles and suddenly she is floating away off into the sunny steamy morning and suddenly again there is a cold wind and my father is walking up the stairs with two drunk children.

References

Allen, Graham. 2000. *Intertextuality*. The New Critical Idiom. Oxon: Routledge.

Anderson, Linda. 2001. *Autobiography*. The New Critical Idiom. Oxon: Routledge.

Atwood, Margaret. 2002. *Negotiating With the Dead: A Writer on Writing*. Toronto: Anchor Canada.

Augustine of Hippo. c. 392. *Confessions*, translated by E. B. Pusey. London: J. M. Dent and Sons, 1907.

Auster, Paul. 1982. *The Invention of Solitude*. London: Faber and Faber, 1988.

—2005. *The Brooklyn Follies*. London: Faber and Faber.

Bainbridge, Susan. 2005. *Writing Against Death: The Autobiographies of Simone de Beauvoir*. Amsterdam and New York: Rodopi.

Barbour, John D. 1992. *The Conscience of the Autobiographer: Ethical and Religious Dimensions of Autobiography*. London: Macmillan.

Barthes, Roland. 1975. *Roland Barthes by Roland Barthes*, translated by Richard Howard. New York: Farrar, Straus and Giroux, 1977.

—1977. *Image, Music, Text*, translated by Stephen Heath. London: Fontana Press.

—1992. *Incidents*, translated by Richard Howard. Berkeley and Los Angeles: University of California Press.

Beverley, John. 2004. *Testimonio: On the Politics of Truth*. Minneapolis: University of Minnesota Press.

Biutiful. 2010. Directed by Alejandro González Iñárritu. Los Angeles: Roadside Attractions.

Bok, Sissela. 2000. 'Autobiography as Moral Battleground.' In *Memory, Brain, and Belief*, edited by Daniel L. Schacter and Elaine Scarry, 307–24. Cambridge, MA: Harvard University Press.

Borges, Jorge Luis. 1964. *Labyrinths: Selected Stories and Other Writing*, translated by Donald A. Yates and James E. Irby. London: Penguin, 1970.

Botton, Sari. 2010. 'Conversations with Writers Braver Than I Am #1: Vivian Gornick.' *The Rumpus*. http://therumpus.net/2010/08/conversations-with-writers-braver-than-me-1-vivian-gornick/ [Accessed March 23, 2011].

Brockes, Emma. 2005. 'Interview: Joan Didion,' December 16, 2005. *The Guardian* Available at: http://www.guardian.co.uk/film/2005/dec/16/biography.features [Accessed June 30, 2011].

Brown, Laura S. 1991. 'Not Outside the Range: One Feminist Perspective on Psychic Trauma,' *American Imago*, 48(1): 119–33.

Bruccoli, Matthew Joseph and Dmitri Nabokov, (eds) 1991. *Vladimir Nabokov: Selected Letters: 1940–77*. London: Vintage.

Buford, Bill. 1990. 'Among the Thugs.' In *The New Kings of Nonfiction*, edited by Ira Glass, 160–97. New York: Riverhead, 2007.

Burgos-Debray, Elisabeth. 1984. *I, Rigoberta Menchú: An Indian Woman in Guatemala*, translated by Ann Wright. London: Verso.

Burroughs, Augusten. 2003. *Running With Scissors: A Memoir*. New York: Picador.

Coleridge, Samuel Taylor. 1817. *Biographia Literaria*, edited by James Engell and Walter Jackson Bate. Princeton: Princeton University Press, 1983.

Conway, Jill Ker. 1989. *The Road From Coorain*. London: Minerva, 1992.

—1994. *True North: A Memoir*. London: Hutchinson.

—1995. 'Points of Departure.' In *Inventing the Truth: The Art and Craft of Memoir*, edited by William Zinsser, 43–59. New York: Mariner, 1998.

—1998. *When Memory Speaks: Reflections on Autobiography*. New York: Knopf.

Didion, Joan. 1979. *The White Album*. New York: Simon and Schuster.

—2003. *Where I Was From*. New York: Knopf.

—2005. *The Year of Magical Thinking*. New York: Knopf.

—2006. *We Tell Ourselves Stories in Order to Live: Collected Nonfiction*. New York: Knopf.

Dillard, Annie. 1987. 'To Fashion a Text.' In *Inventing the Truth: The Art and Craft of Memoir*, edited by William Zinsser, 143–61. New York: Mariner, 1998.

Dunne, Dominick. 2004. 'A Death in the Family.' *Vanity Fair*, March 2004. http://www.vanityfair.com/culture/features/2004/03/dunne200403?currentPage=1 [Accessed April 20, 2011].

Eagleman, David. 2011. *Incognito: The Secret Lives of the Brain*. Edinburgh: Canongate.

Eakin, Paul John. 1985. *Fictions in Autobiography: Studies in the Art of Self-Invention*. Princeton, NJ: Princeton University Press.

—2000. 'Autobiography, Identity and the Fictions of Memory.' In *Memory, Brain, and Belief*, edited by Daniel L. Schacter and Elaine Scarry, 290–306. Cambridge, MA: Harvard University Press.

—2004. 'Introduction.' In *The Ethics of Life Writing*, edited by Paul John Eakin, 1–16. Ithaca and London: Cornell University Press, pp. 1–16.

—2008. *Living Autobiographically: How We Create Identity in Narrative*. Ithaca: Cornell University Press.

Eliot, T. S. 1922. 'The Waste Land.' In *Selected Poems*, 49–74. London: Faber and Faber, 1954.

Ellis, Bret Easton. 1991. *American Psycho*. New York: Vintage.

—2010. *Imperial Bedrooms*. London: Picador.

Felman, Shoshana. 1993. *What Does a Woman Want?: Reading and Sexual Difference*. Baltimore: The Johns Hopkins University Press.

Felman, Shoshana and Lori Daub. 1992. *Testimony: Crises of Witnessing in Literature, Psychoanalysis, and History*. New York and London: Routledge.

Foer, Jonathan Safran. 2002. *Everything is Illuminated*. New York: Penguin.

Frey, James. 2003. *A Million Little Pieces*. London: John Murray, 2004.

Galloway, Janice. 2008. *This is Not About Me*. London: Granta.

Ginzburg, Natalia. 1963a. *The Things We Used To Say*, translated by Judith Woolf. Manchester: Carcanet, 1997.

—1963b. *Family Sayings*, translated by D. M. Low. London: Hogarth Press, 1967.

Goldberg, Natalie. 1986. *Writing Down the Bones*. Boston: Shambhala Publications.

Gornick, Vivian. 1987. *Fierce Attachments*. New York: Farrar, Straus and Giroux.

—2001. *The Situation and the Story*. New York: Farrar, Straus and Giroux.

Gray, Francine du Plessix. 1994. 'The Seduction of the Text.' In *The Writing Life: Writers on How They Think and Work*, edited by Marie Arana, 3–10. New York: Public Affairs, 2003.

Harrison, Kathryn. 1997. *The Kiss*. London: Fourth Estate, 1998.

Hudson, W. H. 1918. *Far Away and Long Ago: A Childhood in Argentina*. London: Eland, 1991.

Jacobellis v. Ohio 378 US 184 [1964].

Jamison, Kay Redfield. 1995. *An Unquiet Mind: A Memoir of Moods and Madness*. London: Picador, 1997.

Johnson, James Weldon. 1912. *The Autobiography of an Ex-Coloured Man*. New York: Knopf, 1927.

Jong, Erica. 1997. 'Doing It For Love.' In *The Writing Life: Writers on How They Think and Work*, edited by Marie Arana, 64–70. New York: PublicAffairs, 2003.

Karr, Mary. 1995. *The Liars' Club*. London: Picador.

—2000. *Cherry: A Memoir*. London: Picador, 2002.

—2009. 'The Art of Memoir No. 1.' Interviewed by Amanda Fortini for *The Paris Review*. Available at: http://www.theparisreview.org/interviews/5992/the-art-of-memoir-no-1-mary-karr [Accessed: June 30, 2011].

—2010. *Lit*. New York: HarperCollins.

Kierkegaard, Søren. 1938. *The Journals of Søren Kierkegaard: A Selection*, translated and edited by Alexander Du. London: Oxford University Press, 1951.

King, Stephen. 2000. *On Writing: A Memoir of the Craft*. London: Hodder and Stoughton.

Larkin, Philip. 1986. *The North Ship*. London: Faber and Faber.

Lauritzen, Paul. 2004. 'Arguing With Life Stories: The Case of Rigoberta Menchú.' In *The Ethics of Life Writing*, edited by Paul John Eakin, 19–39. Ithaca and London: Cornell University Press.

Lejeune, Philippe. 1975. 'The Autobiographical Pact.' In *On Autobiography*, edited by Paul John Eakin, translated by Katherine Leary, 3–30. Minneapolis: University of Minnesota Press, 1989.

—1980. 'Autobiography in the Third Person.' In *On Autobiography*, edited by Paul John Eakin, translated by Katherine Leary, 31–52. Minneapolis: University of Minnesota Press, 1989.

—1986. 'The Autobiographical Pact (Bis).' In *On Autobiography*, edited by Paul John Eakin, translated by Katherine Leary, 119–37. Minneapolis: University of Minnesota Press, 1989.

Maitland, Sara. 2008. *A Book of Silence*. London: Granta.

McCourt, Frank. 1996. *Angela's Ashes*. London: Flamingo.

—1998. 'Learning to Chill Out.' In *Inventing the Truth: The Art and Craft of Memoir*, edited by William Zinsser, 63–81. New York: Mariner.

'Memory on Trial.' Narrated by Jackie Long. *File on 4*. BBC Radio 4, April 3, 2011. http://www.bbc.co.uk/programmes/b00zshnz

Miller, D. A. 1992. *Bringing Out Roland Barthes*. Berkeley and Los Angeles: University of California Press.

Miller, Karl. 1985. *Doubles: Studies in Literary History*. New York: Oxford University Press.

Minot, Susan. 2000. 'A Real-Life Education.' In *The Writing Life: Writers on How They Think and Work*, edited by Marie Arana, 47–51. New York: PublicAffairs, 2003.

Morrison, Toni. 1987. 'The Site of Memory.' In *Inventing the Truth: The Art and Craft of Memoir*, edited by William Zinsser, 183–200. New York: Mariner, 1998.

Murakami, Haruki. 1998. *The Wind-Up Bird Chronicle*. London: Vintage, 2003.

Nabokov, Vladimir. 1955. *Lolita*. New York: G. P. Putnam's Sons.

—1973. *Strong Opinions*. New York: Vintage, 1990.

—2000. *Speak, Memory: An Autobiography Revisited*. London: Penguin.

Nelson, Katherine. 2000. 'Memory and Belief in Development.' In *Memory, Brain, and Belief*, edited by Daniel L. Schacter and Elaine Scarry, 259–89. Cambridge, MA: Harvard University Press.

Oates, Joyce Carol. 2011. *A Widow's Story: A Memoir*. New York: HarperCollins.

The Oprah Winfrey Show. 2006. *James Frey and the A Million Little Pieces Controversy*. WABC, January 26.

—2011. *James Frey: Five Years Later*. WABC, May 16.

Poe, E. A. 'Annabel Lee.' In *The Harper Single Volume American Literature*, edited by Donald McQuade, Robert Atwan, Martha Banta, Justin Kaplan, David Minter, Robert Stepto, Cecelia Tichi and Helen Vendler, 783–84. New York: Longman, 1999.

Proust, Marcel. 1913. *In Search of Lost Time. Volume 1: Swann's Way*, translated by C. K. Scott Moncrieff and Terence Kilmartin. London: Vintage, 2002.

—1927. *Remembrance of Things Past. Volume 3: Time Regained*, translated by C. K. Scott Moncrieff and Terence Kilmartin. Harmondsworth: Penguin, 1985.

Rich, Adrienne. 1987. 'Delta.' In *Adrienne Rich's Poetry and Prose*, edited by Barbara Charlesworth Gelpi and Albert Gelpi, 135. New York and London: W. W. Norton and Company, 1993.

Rich, Motoko. 2006. 'James Frey and His Publishers Settle Suit Over Lies', *New York Times*, September 7, 2006. http://www.nytimes.com/2006/09/07/arts/07frey.html?adxnnl=1&adxnnlx=1309435457-VIXvub9QKn1A2iK2zbuPGg

Rosenfield, Israel. 1988. *The Invention of Memory*. New York: Basic Books.
—1995. 'Memory and Identity.' *New Literary History* 26(1): 197–203.
Ross, Michael and Anne E. Wilson. 2000. 'Constructing and Appraising Past Selves.' In *Memory, Brain, and Belief*, edited by Daniel L. Schacter and Elaine Scarry, 231–58. Cambridge, MA: Harvard University Press.
Rousseau, Jean-Jacques. 1782–89. *Confessions*, translated by Angela Scholar. New York: Oxford University Press, 2008.
Rushdie, Salman. 1981. *Midnight's Children*. London: Picador, 1982.
Shapiro, Dani. 1989. *Slow Motion*. London: Bloomsbury.
—2010. *Devotion: A Memoir*. New York: HarperCollins.
Solnit, Rebecca. 2006. *A Field Guide to Getting Lost*. Edinburgh: Canongate.
Spark, Muriel. 2001. 'Emerging From Under Your Rejection Slips.' In *The Writing Life: Writers on How They Think and Work*, edited by Marie Arana, 53–7. New York: PublicAffairs, 2003.
Stein, Gertrude. 1933. *The Autobiography of Alice B. Toklas*. London: John Lane The Bodley Head Ltd.
—1937. *Everybody's Autobiography*. Cambridge, MA: Exact Change, 1993.
Sterling, Terry Greene. 2003, 'Confessions of a memoirist.' *Salon.com*. Available at: http://dir.salon.com/story/books/feature/archives/2003/08/01/gornick/index.html [Accessed: March 23, 2011].
Stoll, David. 1999. *Rigoberta Menchú and the Story of All Poor Guatemalans*. Boulder, CO: Westview Press.
—2001. 'The Battle of Rigoberta.' In *The Rigoberta Menchú Controversy*, edited by Arturo Arias, 392–410. Minneapolis: University of Minnesota Press.
Sturrock, John. 1993. *The Language of Autobiography: Studies in the First Person Singular*. Cambridge: Cambridge University Press.
The Smoking Gun. 2006. 'A Million Little Lies: Exposing James Frey's Fiction Addition.' http://www.thesmokinggun.com/documents/celebrity/million-little-lies?page=0,0 [Accessed: June 27, 2011].
Thought for the Day. Narrated by Rhidian Brook. BBC Radio 4, May 9, 2011. http://www.bbc.co.uk/programmes/p00gtp21
Tulvig, Endel and Martin Lepage. 2000. 'Where in the Brain Is the Awareness of One's Past?' In *Memory, Brain, and Belief*, edited by Daniel L. Schacter and Elaine Scarry, 208–28. Cambridge, MA: Harvard University Press.
Whitman, W. 'Song of Myself.' In *The Harper Single Volume American Literature*, edited by Donald McQuade, Robert Atwan, Martha Banta, Justin Kaplan, David Minter, Robert Stepto, Cecelia Tichi and Helen Vendler, 1166–209, New York: Longman, 1999.
Wilson, Sarah. 2010. *Melting-Pot Modernism*. Ithaca and London: Cornell University Press.
Wimsatt Jr., W. K. and Monroe C. Beardsley. 1954. 'The Intentional Fallacy.' *The Verbal Icon: Studies in the Meaning of Poetry* [Online]. Available at: http://faculty.smu.edu/nschwart/seminar/fallacy.htm [Accessed: April 6, 2011].
Woolf, Virginia. 1928. *Orlando*. London: Penguin, 1998.

—1929. *A Room of One's Own*. In *A Room of One's Own and Three Guineas*, edited by Morag Shiach. Oxford: Oxford University Press, 1992.

—1930. *On Being Ill*. Ashfield, MA: Paris Press, 2002.

—1931. *The Waves* in *Three Great Novels*. London: Penguin, 1992.

—1976. *Moments of Being: Unpublished Autobiographical Writings*, edited by Jeanne Schulkind. Sussex: The University Press.

Wyllie, Barbara. 2010. *Vladimir Nabokov*. London: Reaktion Books.

Zinsser, William. 1998. 'Introduction.' In *Inventing the Truth: The Art and Craft of Memoir*, edited by William Zinsser, 3–22. New York: Mariner.

Index